WALTER STEPHEN could not proceed beyond Ge
due to colour blindness – the analysis of crystal
worlds for him. Degrees in Geography, Ecor
qualified him as an academic jack-of-all-trad
environmental awareness and understanding. One of his achievements was
the establishment and operation for 20 years of Castlehill Urban Studies
Centre, the first successful Urban Studies Centre in Britain.

Latterly he has taken up Interesting Victorians. A former Chairman of the
Sir Patrick Geddes Memorial Trust, he has been responsible for *Think Global,
Act Local* and *A Vigorous Institution*, collected essays on Patrick Geddes. In
his introduction to the new edition of *A Herd of Red Deer* he brought out the
importance of Frank Fraser Darling as the founder of ecology and forerunner
of David Attenborough. In *The Evolution of Evolution* Walter Stephen sets
Darwin at the centre of a circle of Interesting Victorians. All four books, plus
his biography of *Willie Park Junior: The Man who took Golf to the World*
and *Walter's Wiggles* were published by Luath Press.

Learning from the Lasses

Women of the Patrick Geddes Circle

Edited by
WALTER STEPHEN

Luath Press Limited
EDINBURGH
www.luath.co.uk

First published 2014
Reprinted 2014

ISBN: 978-1-910021-06-4

The publishers acknowledge the support of

ALBA | CHRUTHACHAIL

towards the publication of this volume.

The paper used in this book is recyclable. It is made from
low chlorine pulps produced in a low energy, low emissions manner
from renewable forests.

Printed and bound by
Bell & Bain Ltd., Glasgow

Typeset in 11 point Sabon
by 3btype.com

Contents

Acknowledgements

As Editor my first pleasure is to recognise the authority and professionalism of the team of Modern Geddesians who have contributed to *Learning from the Lasses*. Handling such a mettlesome team might have been a stressful experience. In the event, each contributor produced a readable and authoritative chapter in good time. The individual contributors have thanked those with whom they worked.

I now wish to acknowledge the support received in respect of the book as a whole. *Learning from the Lasses* has been accepted by the City of Edinburgh Council as part of its contribution to International Womens Year 2014 and the Lord Provost, The Rt Hon Donald Wilson, has contributed a Preface.

We are fortunate in being surrounded by great institutions, whose staff are not only efficient but sympathetic.

The following illustrations are reproduced by kind permission: Fig 2 (Aberdeen University Library), Fig 8 (City of Edinburgh Libraries), Fig 11 (Dundee City Archives), Fig 9 (Edinburgh City Archives), Fig 6 (National Library of Scotland), Fig 13 (Perth Museum), Fig 12 (University of Edinburgh), Fig 1 (University of Strathclyde). Figs 17–21 are reproduced by kind permission of Ernest Press and Williamina C Barker. Plate 4A is reproduced by kind permission of Artwork Brett Housego, Dundee.

The Appendix from *Who's Who 1930* is reproduced by kind permission of A&C Black Publishers Ltd.

The image of the Patrick Geddes Memorial Panel on the cover is reproduced by kind permission of Kate Henderson.

Walter Stephen

Modern Geddesians

VERONICA BURBRIDGE

Veronica Burbridge continues to do research in retirement. As Director of the Royal Town Planning Institute in Scotland she was responsible for organising the annual Sir Patrick Geddes Commemorative Lecture. She has recently been involved in helping to restore the Maclagan family graveyard, Laggan Wood, Comrie.

KATE HENDERSON

Kate Henderson is an artist based in East Lothian who specialises in stained glass and painting. She was invited to submit a proposal and then commissioned to create the Patrick Geddes stained glass panel in 2005. The panel is situated in the new headquarters of Edinburgh City Council on Market Street.

She greatly admires Geddes's forward thinking and his approach to the importance of art in society. She finds his Reference to 'Place, Work and Folk' an exciting format which has inspired her to create a new series of glass work.

SOFIA LEONARD

Sofia Leonard is a Fellow of the Sir Patrick Geddes Memorial Trust and former Director of the Patrick Geddes Centre for Planning Studies, University of Edinburgh.

As a student of the International Planning Institute of Lima, she worked in multidisciplinary teams on planning projects at a regional scale using Patrick Geddes's Valley Section as the main tool. Required reading included *Cities in Evolution* by PG in its translated version into Spanish.

She worked at the National Planning Office of Peru on the design, planning and implementation on the First New Town for 40,000 people in Peru. In Edinburgh she worked for three years for Percy Johnson Marshall & Associates in the Plan for the Porto Regional Plan, Portugal, based on the principles of Patrick Geddes. The Plan was approved and implemented by the Portuguese government. Until retirement she worked for 14 years with the unsorted papers of Sir Patrick Geddes from the Outlook Tower, to protect them for posterity.

KENNETH MACLEAN

Kenneth Maclean was formerly Principal Teacher of Geography at Perth Academy. Now retired, he still maintains an interest in the history of geographical education, a subject replete with references to the role and significance of Geddes and his 'disciples'. In common with other geography teachers, perhaps the main impact of Geddes upon his teaching was to encourage as much fieldwork as time, staffing, finance and resources permitted.

ROBERT MORRIS

R J Morris is Emeritus Professor in Economic and Social History, Edinburgh University. He was president of the European Urban History Association in 2000–2002 and is President of the Economic and Social History Society of Scotland and editor elect of the *Book of the Old Edinburgh Club*. He has written extensively on the British middle classes, on urban history in industrial England, in Scotland and in Ireland. Geddes is always a contributor to any urban history. Current research into the rebuilding in the Old Town of Edinburgh finds an active place for Geddes.

KENNY MUNRO

After graduating in Sculpture from Edinburgh College of Art and The Royal College of Art, London he attended the Oslo Summer School in 1976, established by Philip Boardman, a student of Patrick Geddes in France.

A former Chairman of Edinburgh Sculpture Workshop. Promoting his 'field-work', educational exchange arts projects and films he has followed the *Geddes Trail* to the Scots College, Montpellier, France and significantly three expeditions to India have helped raise awareness of historic Indo–Scottish connections and current work with The Green Wave Art Centre in Kolkata. He is a director of the PGMT.

SWAMI NARASIMHANANDA

Swami Narasimhananda is a monk of the worldwide twin-organisation Ramakrishna Math and Ramakrishna Mission started by Swami Vivekananda. He is the city editor of *Prabuddha Bharata*, an English journal founded by Swami Vivekananda in 1896. He writes regularly on philosophy, social sciences, religion, Indology, and Ramakrishna-Vivekananda, and Vedanta. He edits books in English, Hindi, and Sanskrit published from Advaita Ashrama, Kolkata, India, a publication house of the Ramakrishna Math. He has edited a compilation of Swami Vivekananda's teachings – *Vivekananda Reader*. He also translates old Sanskrit texts hitherto unpublished in English.

While doing research on Sister Nivedita and unearthing more unpublished letters written by her, Swami Narasimhananda came upon many letters written to Sir Patrick Geddes and Anna Geddes showing the extent of influence of Geddes's thought on Nivedita. Since Vivekananda had also met Geddes, it became an interesting subject of study.

Swami Narasimhananda is actively involved in formulating an Indian perspective on various disciplines of humanities and social sciences, especially Philosophy, Religious Studies, Comparative Religions, and Sociology of Religion. He interacts with academia and others to create an academic framework from the Indian standpoint away from a mere transplantation of external thought. In this he brings into play, various methodologies of Geddes as understood and further developed by Nivedita. This is an ongoing effort and much work is to be done.

SIÂN REYNOLDS

Siân Reynolds is Emerita Professor of French at the University of Stirling. She has explored Patrick Geddes's networks and enterprises in France, in several articles and in her book *Paris-Edinburgh: Cultural connections in the Belle Epoque* (2007). She also helped organise the exhibition 'Patrick Geddes: the French Connection' at the Scottish National Portrait Gallery in 2004.

ANNE-MICHELLE SLATER

Anne-Michelle Slater is currently the Head of the Law School at the University of Aberdeen. She is a planning law specialist with a particular interest in the development of marine spatial planning. Patrick Geddes and his ideas about town planning were first introduced to her by a visit to the Outlook Tower in Edinburgh, when she was in her late teens, and since then his ideas and activities have been a constant thread. Anne-Michelle believes in students learning by doing and in particular getting out of the classroom and looking at what is around them.

WALTER STEPHEN

Walter Stephen can be described as an independent scholar and is Publications Convener and a former Chairman of the Sir Patrick Geddes Memorial Trust. Arthur Geddes, Patrick Geddes's younger son, supervised his Geography dissertation. Influenced by Patrick Geddes, he set up and ran for 20 years Castlehill Urban Studies Centre, the first successful Urban Studies Centre in Britain, in Cannonball House, the apex of a triangle whose other corners are the Outlook Tower and Ramsay Garden.

Preface

SIR PATRICK GEDDES has many associations with the City of Edinburgh. He set up the Outlook Tower on Castlehill in 1892, was involved in the rehabilitation of older buildings as student accommodation, and was instrumental in completing the striking redevelopment of Ramsay Garden, where he himself lived for a spell. The summer schools he started at Granton in 1885 proved highly successful.

Geddes's life, ideas and accomplishments have inspired a large body of work. The present volume adds to this, but Walter Stephen, a long time admirer, has gathered together a series of essays that explore an unusual element of Geddes's life.

Many of those who fell under Geddes's spell were women. Many of those women were Edinburgh based: his wife Anna; his daughter Norah; students from the summer schools; volunteers in the Edinburgh Social Union. They took inspiration from Geddes, but gave him much in return. This volume delves into that relationship, and is a tribute to those women.

It is fitting that the City of Edinburgh Council should promote this book, which adds to our knowledge of Geddes, Edinburgh, and the role women have had in the development of modern society. Moreover, it is entirely appropriate that its publication by Luath Press should form part of the city's contribution to International Women's Day 2014.

The Rt Hon Donald Wilson,
Lord Provost of the City of Edinburgh,
City Chambers, High Street,
Edinburgh EH1 1YJ

Introduction

While Europe's eye is fixed on mighty things,
The fate of Empires and the fall of Kings:
While quacks of State must each produce his plan
And even children lisp the Rights of Man,
Amid the mighty fuss just let me mention,
THE RIGHTS OF WOMAN merit some attention.[1]

FOR THOSE WHO think that Robert Burns was a whisky-swilling fornicating lout who wrote incomprehensible doggerel it may come as a surprise to learn that in 1792 there was in Dumfries, a modest Scottish county town, a Theatre Royal where, on her Benefit Night (26 November), the exotic Miss Fontenelle delivered Burns's *The Rights of Women, an Occasional Address,* of which the six lines above form the introduction. When we realise that Tom Paine's *The Rights of Man* was published in 1792 and Mary Wollstonecraft's *The Rights of Women* in 1793 we should be amazed at how fast good news can travel.

Unfortunately, the 32 lines that follow are fairly anodyne.

Patrick Geddes was influenced by Burns. On the end of Ramsay Garden – his splendid magnet luring the middle class back to the Old Town of Edinburgh – is a handsome sundial with two quotations. One is from Aeschylus and the other from Burns – 'It's comin' yet for a' that'. Which, as every schoolboy knows, precedes the revolutionary aspiration:

That Man to Man the warld o'er
Shall brithers be for a' that.

In Edinburgh the infant Environment Society changed its name to the Edinburgh Social Union, which figures strongly later. In *To A Mouse: On Turning Up Her Nest With the Plough, November 1785* Burns expresses a tolerance for his fellow-creatures:

I doubt na whiles but thou may thieve;
What then? Poor beastie thou maun live.
A daimen icker in a thrave (one ear of corn in 24 sheaves)
'S a sma' request.

And tries to apologise on behalf of the human race:

I'm truly sorry Man's dominion
Has broken Nature's social union.

FIG.1
Ramsay Garden, Summer School, 1898.
University of Strathclyde

From August 1887 Patrick Geddes organised (with Anna Morton) and led Summer Schools or Meetings based on his Outlook Tower on Castlehill in Edinburgh. In true Geddes style, it was not enough just to run a Summer School; success had to be celebrated and recorded. So we have a series of 'team photos', one of which can be seen above.

In the place of honour in the middle is Patrick Geddes, lecturer and charismatic leader of field excursions. On his right is Anna Morton, a little stiff, organiser of the event and the social activities in Ramsay Garden. In the bottom right are the guest lecturers, one with distinctly foreign headgear. Artistically arranged as in a theatre set are the students, mature men and women, well-dressed with an interesting range of hats.

Looking at Fig 1, it is tempting to see this as a Patrick Geddes Circle, with the great man at the centre and his followers neatly arranged around him. This is too simplistic, there was never anything so neat as a circle, rather there were a multitude of circles which overlapped on occasion, touched on occasion, or did not connect in any way. Another analogy would be the kind of liquid sculpture once to be found in dentists' surgeries where, in a column of coloured liquid, bubbles rise up, break up or coalesce, or just hang around quietly. Nevertheless, the Patrick Geddes

Circle is a convenient collective noun which saves lengthy explanation and qualification, and will be used as such.

What proportion of the clientele of the Summer Meetings were women? Whatever Professor Geddes was offering must have appealed to women. To what extent was the curriculum slanted towards women? What alternatives were available to these women?

To understand Geddes, the women in Ramsay Garden and their lives it is necessary to understand the society they grew up in. The late 19th century could be said to be The Age of the Double Standard, neatly summed up by the following statistics relating to the Metropolitan Museum of Modern Art in New York:

3 per cent of the artists whose works are on display are women,
83 per cent of the nudes on display are female.

On the perceived importance of women in society, it is worth quoting from Roy Soweto's *The New Dawn* at some length.

When Jacob Bronowski, in the early 1970s, presented his celebrated and seminal television programme on the rise of mankind from primitive origins to its contemporary elevated status, he called it *The Ascent of Man*, although The Ascent of Men would have been a more appropriate title. Seven women were given a mention in the series and in the resulting book: Queen Anne because she knighted Newton; Queen Isabella I, because she, with her husband Ferdinand, backed Columbus; Marie Antoinette, because she was, well, Marie Antoinette; Queen Victoria, because in her time she ruled the world's greatest power, and Madame Curie for obvious reasons.

One of the other two women who got a mention, Ellen Sharpless, was included for the not so obvious reason that she made a pastel portrait of Joseph Priestley (an inclusion made even less worthy since Priestley discovered oxygen two years after the Swedish apothecary, Carl Wilhelm Scheele). One woman did get in on merit (apart from Madame Curie). Dame Kathleen Kenyon was from 1961 to 1966 director of the School of Archaeology in Jerusalem and was responsible for the excavation of Jericho to its Stone Age beginnings and for revealing it to be the oldest known site that has seen continuous occupation.

Bronowski could include such a mixed bag of token women in his account because it was so blindingly obvious to him that mankind had ascended almost entirely due to the efforts of men. If this was true of the 20th century, how much worse could it have been in the 19th, before women were allowed to vote, or have their own property?

What was it about Patrick Geddes and his ideas that made women relate to him? Let us look briefly at two of his more famous pronouncements.

Those American superiorities which surprise and disconcert old Europe very largely turn, indirectly and directly, upon the superior culture and status of women.

Geddes – despite the Metropolitan Museum of Modern Art in New York – is setting out a direct cause and effect relationship. He is saying that American women are superior in culture and status – to European women? Or to American men? – and as a result American society is better than that of tired old Europe where, for example, the women of France did not get the vote till 1944.

What was decided among the prehistoric Protozoa cannot be annulled by Act of Parliament

has raised quite a few hackles from those who see this as an expression of sexism. For myself, I cannot see this. It seems to me that Equal Opportunities are just that; that the opportunities must be open to all, but we must not be surprised if individuals respond to the opportunities in different ways.

Veronica Burbridge suggests that Geddes and Thomson (his running mate and co-author) emphasised the different contributions to be made by men and women. They expected that increased participation by women in social and political life would result in a redirection of social change toward a cooperative society, provided that it preserved separate sex roles appropriate to male and female temperaments. Many of the powerful women who feature in *Learning from the Lasses* would have been content with such a role, preferring to get things done by networking than by militant action.

In the 1880s Geddes, in entries for the *Encyclopaedia Britannica* and *Chambers' Encyclopaedia*, wrote on *Darwin, Darwinian Theory* and *Evolution*. In *The Evolution of Sex* he took issue with TH Huxley and his well-known assertion that:

From the point of view of the naturalist the world is on about the same level as a gladiator's show.

Geddes suggested that, as well as struggle, cruelty and selfishness in evolution, there is also cooperation; and: 'that "creation's final law" is not struggle but love.'

The ideal of Evolution is thus an Eden; and, although competition can never be wholly eliminated... it is much for our pure natural history to see no longer struggle, but love, as creation's final law.

On the death of Geddes in 1932, SA Robertson, a former student at Geddes's *Collège des Écossais*, paid *A Scottish Tribute*:

> Even a noble soul like Huxley could see in life essentially a 'gladiator's show'. Geddes... challenged the verdict in his books, in his lectures, in the flood of vivacious speech which leaped from him like a fountain. I recall the thrill which went through an audience as he traced the basal feature of all life to be the sacrifice of the mother for her offspring and closed by saying ... 'So life is not really a gladiator's show; it is rather – a vast mothers' meeting!'

Geddes's journey through life began with objective study through the microscope but, partly as a result of his illness in Mexico, his interests broadened until the objective biologist was subordinated to the subjective sociologist, the town planner, the peace-warrior. Detachment became involvement – and that appealed to many of the women of his time.

For some considerable time I have felt that an examination of the women who influenced Geddes and were, in turn, influenced by him would be a worthwhile enterprise. Unfortunately, I was unable to convince any of the busy people I approached to take on this task. Eventually I decided I could wait no longer, so I drew up a list of all the women I could trace as having been in some way connected with Geddes.

This I circulated to a number of people with some expertise in the field, with an invitation to write a chapter on one or more women on the list – or on some other appropriate women of whom I was ignorant. The response was gratifying, in that we now have coverage relating to all stages of PG's career, to all his major interests and in several countries.

There was one problem, however. Geddes had a mother, an older sister, a wife (in fact, he had two) and a daughter. Clearly there were actions and reactions with these – but nobody wished to tackle them. So these ladies became the editor's responsibility.

Which brings up the question of organisation. How should the 16 chapters be arranged? Thematically? But Geddes was too much of an intellectual will o' the wisp to be strictly subdivided. Chronologically? Which would mean the book must start with my tedious family histories. In the event I settled for a consecutive approach based on the time when Geddes and the subject of the chapter swam into each other's ken. This had the fortunate result that some chapters did group themselves thematically.

The other organisational problem related to the sheer volume and complexity of the subjects' activities. One could get lost in a forest of foot-notes, end-notes and repetitions, making a clean narrative impossible. What I have done is to provide, after the main text, an extract from the *Who's Who* of 1932 and a Geddes Chronology. These provide a framework for all the contributions. There is also a Select Bibliography, the 'basic kit' of Geddes-related references, which it can be assumed all the contributors have used.

To supplement this general information some contributors have added a bibliography and chronology pertaining to their own chapter.

What kinds of women do we Modern Geddesians consider? In the planning stages we tended to divide them into three categories – women who played an important role in PG's life, important women with a minor role in PG's life, and minor players. We have examples of each, giving a rich kaleidoscope illustrative of society roughly a century ago.

Janet Stivenson could be seen as almost the stereotype of the Scots countrywoman of the 19th century. The old Scots proverb, 'the ganging fit is aye getting',[2] fitted her perfectly. Her determination to do well for her husband and children, allied to her intense piety, made her a formidable role model – and also, perhaps, someone against whose extremes there might be reaction. Yet she had her gentler side. In the garden at Mount Tabor it was she who tended and loved the flowers while Patrick and his father measured out the plots and planted the potatoes. She had a care also for lame dogs, looking after her disgraceful father who returned from the United States to die.

With **Jessie** (the fifth successive Janet in her family) we have another Victorian stereotype. Working in the mill or in service was quite out of the question for a girl from her modestly prosperous background. Becoming a schoolmistress or a governess does not seem to have been considered, while in the Perth of that time there could be no professional opportunities for such as she. So Jessie stayed at home, helped her mother (although they always had a live-in servant) and lived a quiet social life. She did not marry, but found a kind of fulfilment as young Patrick – 13 years her junior – was growing up and she could help him along. But he soon left her behind and her support then came in the form of reassuring him that he was ready for advancement, or grumbling that he had, once again, been passed over.

Jessie did, however, have her moments. She railed occasionally at the excessive religiosity of her friends. She would walk over the hills to stay with her uncle's family at Braemar and cause great pain at home because she was missing the 'awakening' of religious life back in Perth.

In her later years, when Patrick and Anna Morton had married, and especially after Norah was born, Jessie softened a great deal and a warm relationship developed until Jessie's death at 47.

I think of the chapter I have called '*Three Little Girls with a School are we...*' as something like a piece of tapestry or a wall hanging, which is colourful and interesting but plays little part in the action in the room. The tapestry is in three colours and the weaving together of three narrative strands gives a good representation of the kind of society in which Anna Morton and Patrick Geddes were to flourish.

Three **Geddes Sisters,** Jane, Margaret and Charlotte, from the same airt as Geddes's father, but unrelated, ran a very successful finishing school in Dresden.

Agnes Tillie was the daughter of William Tillie of Tillie and Henderson, the largest shirt factory in the world (admired by Karl Marx), in Londonderry. She wrote to her cousin describing in some detail her experiences at the Geddes's school, emerging from the page as a thoroughly nice girl.

Anna Morton's father was an Ulster Scot engaged in the linen trade in Liverpool. Anna spent a year (1875) in Dresden, equipping herself for a career teaching music. She must have known of the Geddes sisters' establishment. Her life in Dresden was probably similar to Agnes Tillie's and Anna certainly shared with her a full share of moral earnestness.

At the very least, when Anna Morton was first introduced to Patrick Geddes, the 'Geddes connection' must have ensured that they got off to a good start.

Mrs Helen Nutt was the Principal of Grange House Boarding School on the south side of Edinburgh. In 1883 PG developed what he called an Order Garden for the school and read a paper on *A Type Botanic Garden* to the Royal Botanical Society of Edinburgh. The garden was a miracle of organisation in that it contrived, in a small space, to show the plant kingdom arranged systematically. More importantly, his paper was his first articulation in public of the importance of the garden as a learning tool, as a locus for practical study, as a non-controversial instrument for change – initially within the educational system, and then across the whole of society.

Anna Morton was 'the calm grey-haired lady who could bring order out of chaos.' Both she and her husband were well endowed with social responsibility, but while Patrick's enthusiasm could be electric, Anna was the one who organised, negotiated and tempered his wilder notions with good sense. Patrick taught and wrote about education, but it was Anna who managed the sometimes complex business of Home Education and somehow kept the family going while all around was falling apart.

Mention has already been made of the **Edinburgh Social Union,** often quoted as one of Patrick Geddes's most successful legacies. It aimed to raise the standard of comfort and beauty in everyday life whilst improving the general well-being of the poor. It is often seen as the key example of

Geddes's contributions to the Arts and Crafts movement, urban conservation and renewal, and social reform. Its work is seen as embracing and
implementing Geddes's triad of 'Sympathy, Synthesis and Synergy'.

Burbridge takes a considered look at the ESU and assesses the differing
contributions of Geddes, the innovator, and a powerful group of organising
ladies who ensured that the good work of the ESU continued until 1956.

The Watergate was essentially a 17th century building in the Canongate in Edinburgh. In 1896 Patrick Geddes became interested in 'a plan
of restoration and conservative reconstruction comparable to that of
Castlehill.' In **Women of the Watergate** Professor Morris offers a masterly
micro-study of this development, which survived until replaced by modern
social housing in 1970. He provides a wealth of detail on the contrast
between the women who lived in the Watergate and those who financed
and supervised the development. House plans, 'pipes and balconies', take
the description of the changes made beyond the stage of broad generali-
sation into the realm of fascinating practical information.

Veronica Burbridge reappears with **Failure in Dundee?** – a third
chapter examining the relationships between Patrick Geddes and the
Social Unions. In Dundee Mary Lily Walker started as a 'lady rent
collector' with the struggling Dundee Social Union, re-energised its flag-
ging programme and introduced new branches of philanthropy. Patrick
Geddes was 'baffled' by Dundee, but it is satisfying to note that, in 2013,
Lily Walker's double anniversary was cheerfully celebrated and the Grey
Lodge Settlement centre she founded continued to serve her community.

Patrick Geddes was a force in the movement towards university reform.
He condemned the 'cram-exam' system and wrote persuasively on home
education. **Norah Geddes** loved and admired her father but in her *Memoir*
could be quite bitter about their relationship. In A Dreamer's Daughter I
try to establish whether this was merely a matter of normal teenage angst,
or whether there was a more fundamental resentment at work.

There is not much evidence of keenness on sport and organised games
in Patrick Geddes's circle. An exception was Mabel Barker – 'a fearless
and supremely talented climber' – who displayed much of the tenacity,
endurance and – it must be said – total concentration merging into blink-
ered vision associated with top-class climbers.

Mabel Barker was Geddes's goddaughter, a responsibility he took
seriously. She trained as a teacher of Geography and became particularly
committed to Geddes's ideas on Regional Survey and on Local Study –
first-hand experience in the environment. (Local Study is, of course, the
Sympathy of Geddes's planning model – Sympathy, Synthesis, Synergy).

As a networker she was vigorous in spreading the Geddes message. As a teacher and trainer of teachers her professional life was a continual search for a place where Regional Survey and fieldwork were an integral part of the curriculum and not just a bolt-on diversion for the few. As a follower of Geddes the Peace Warrior she served in camps in the Netherlands for Belgian refugees (the Netherlands were neutral in World War 1).

PG's lifelong love affair with France and the French began with his work on the distribution of chlorophyll in animals at Roscoff in Brittany in 1878, where the sandy beaches famously turn bright green at low tide as myriads of flatworms – *Convoluta roscoffensis* – whose skin is packed with green algae living within, rise to the surface to allow these single-celled plants to photosynthesise. The love affair only ended with his death at Montpellier in 1932.

Professor Siân Reynolds (author of *Paris-Edinburgh: Cultural Connections in the Belle Epoque*) focuses on two very different Frenchwomen of the early 20th century. **Marie Bonnet** (1874–1960) and **Jeanne Weill** (1859–1925) although chalk and cheese in many ways, were part of a cohort of women in France around the turn of the century, who were reacting against restrictive French society, and chose to pursue their own projects despite legal and French bourgeois opinion.

Marie's family were close to the Geddeses. Marie was quiet and self-effacing but developed a truly Geddesian networking talent, always among women, and largely among Protestants, building a career as warden of lodgings for young women, and later still as administrator of women's organisations.

Jeanne Weill ('Dick May') was undoubtedly not a woman to be trammelled by the conventions of the day. A woman of formidable presence, she cultivated a rather bohemian appearance. The more strait-laced Marie Bonnet was unfailingly censorious of her.

Starting with journalism she became involved with the *Collège libre des sciences sociales*. This was a state-subsidised, though not state-directed 'free college', offering courses on *le social,* i.e. sociology, without being tied to any particular current of thought. Dick May described it as a 'living library'. In the aftermath of the Dreyfus affair she also launched yet another school, the *École du journalisme* – having grasped during the Dreyfus affair the power of the press. This had varying fortunes in the period up to 1914, being relatively unstructured, but offered much-valued open lectures and practical advice, both to would-be journalists and students looking for general studies.

For both women, the outbreak of war came as a bitter blow to their idealistic schemes for regenerating the youth of France through education. During the war, Weill worked on various humanitarian, war-related projects, but after the armistice she seems to have faded from the scene. Dick May died in the Alps in 1925, in what the papers described as a mountaineering accident, although some references appear to hint at suicide.

Born Ishbel Maria Marjoribanks, **Lady Aberdeen, later 1st Marchioness of Aberdeen and Temair** was the kind of woman one either loves or dislikes. She and her husband resolved to devote their lives to solid useful work, which should do something of good in the world, but her aptitude for getting things just a little wrong upset some. In an extraordinary and influential life she drove many good causes.

During two spells as Vicereine in Ireland she tackled the problems of poverty, seeing town planning as one way out of the morass. She and Geddes had a remarkable rapport and he was brought in to prepare plans and mount two major exhibitions. Unfortunately, along came World War I and the Easter Rising – and that was the end of planning!

Many years before he first set foot in India Geddes was heavily involved with Indians, in Europe, America and through correspondence.

Annie Besant is well known as a pioneering social and educational reformer in England, fighting the cause of equal rights for women in general. Yet in the prime of her life and vigour, disillusioned by the hypocrisies that she had exposed in the 'Christian values' of Britain, she went off into the mystic groves of Hindu philosophy and religion, to become a persistent fighter for Indian independence and President of the Indian National Congress. In each phase of Besant's life, her path and Geddes's crossed – to their mutual benefit.

Kenny Munro, himself a creative artist with a wealth of experience in the Indian sub-continent, moves from the straightforward consideration of a life and its achievements to a meditation on the Religion of the River, the renewal of the spirit and irrigation of the soul – a recurring theme in the poetry of Rabindranath Tagore (1861–1941), another of the Patrick Geddes circle.

We were extremely fortunate when Swami Narasimhananda agreed to contribute a chapter on **Margaret Noble ('Sister Nivedita')**. The Swami is a monk in the Advaita Ashrama, Kolkata, a branch of the Ramakrishna Math and Mission, which funded the establishment of the Sister Nivedita Girls' School in 1898.

Margaret Noble ('Sister Nivedita') was born in Dungannon, Co Tyrone. She opened a school on Froebel/Pestalozzi lines in Wimbledon and made a career in journalism. At 28, in a drawing room in London, she met

Swami Vivekananda and was swept off her feet. In 1898 she followed the Swami in order to rebuild India – which she proceeded to do for the remaining 13 years of her life. She was a revolutionary, freedom-fighter, educator, social reformer, spiritual leader, supporter of arts, womens' rights activist and so on. She became aware of Geddes and became his secretary for the Congress of the History of Religions in Paris in 1900 – with very mixed results.

Swami Vivekananda brings to *Learning from the Lasses* a very welcome Indian perspective. He is shamelessly enthusiastic about his subject and is not afraid to mention emotion – he probably uses the word 'love' more often than all the other contributors together.

'Jacky' (Mary Jane) Tyrwhitt was the link between Sir Patrick Geddes, and the Architectural and Planning professions. Geddes was an important formative influence on her career and she was instrumental in bringing his town planning theories to a wider audience after his death in 1932. She is remembered for her 'courage, determination, unquestioned integrity, efficiency and infinite capacity for hard work'.

Alternatively, Tyrwhitt is sometimes said to have been one of the last 'Moderns' who worked willingly as 'the woman behind the man'.

In the entrance hall of Waverley Court, the headquarters of the City of Edinburgh Council, is the attractive backlit Patrick Geddes Memorial Panel. Kate Henderson, its creator, is an East Lothian artist who specialises in stained glass and painting, and who created the panel in 2005. She describes how the project was realised and analyses the components and symbolism of the design plus the complexities of the actual making of the panel.

What an impressive variety of impressive women – a veritable kaleidoscope of talent!

So what of these women who influenced Patrick Geddes? What did he learn from the lasses? The kaleidoscope has many pieces, rich in colour and glittering. Clearly there was a great diversity among the women. Is there any commonality among the group, or is each woman one of a kind?

Geddes loved triads – like Work, Place, Folk, or the three doves of Sympathy, Synthesis and Synergy. Industry, Integrity and Internationalism could well be a Geddes triad and could equally well describe the subjects of this book.

Geddes's work rate was, of course, phenomenal, as teacher, planner and networker. The Index alone to the Papers of Sir Patrick Geddes in Strathclyde University Archives amounts to six volumes, totalling 1,617 pages! And this is only one of several testaments to his industry.

His disciples could not possibly keep up – some tried to live normal lives. But almost without exception, the women featured in *Learning from the Lasses* showed great commitment to their causes.

Integrity was a common characteristic. Much is made by most writers of the evangelical branch of the Free Church of Scotland which drew attention to the moral duty of the individual in society. Geddes's father joined the Free Church at the Disruption in 1843, was made an elder in 1857 and was influential in the move to the new Free Middle Church in Perth in 1887. Patrick's parents would walk down to the morning service, picnic on the North Inch, and return to the kirk for the afternoon service. In the family it is generally supposed that John McKail Geddes, Patrick's senior by 13 years, fled to New Zealand to avoid being pushed into the ministry. In the 1890s, according to Norah Geddes:

> Family prayers were said night and morning with readings from the scriptures. The maid was duly called in and when praying we knelt over the seat of our horsehair chairs.

Although Geddes was to leave behind his membership of the Free Church, Murdo Macdonald, in *Think Global, Act Local,* says that:

> Geddes's stance has rightly been described as first and foremost 'a moralist, deeply concerned with bettering man and his lot' and Geddes's Free Church background is a crucial factor in this… Geddes also makes clear his own commitment to the Free Church, asserting that it is the organisation of which he is 'proudest of all to belong to'.

But the Free Church did not have a monopoly in social responsibility and some of Patrick Geddes's followers were from the other Presbyterian churches or the Episcopal Church. Some were agnostic or atheist or turned to the East for a way of life, but all demonstrated a high moral purpose and a belief in the betterment of society which transcended points of doctrine and observance.

The Arts and Crafts movement, in which honest endeavour, fair dealing and good craftsmanship were raised to an almost spiritual plane, was another force for integrity.

Geddes was the supreme Internationalist. In a world where it took at least a week to cross the Atlantic he roamed around three continents, surveying, planning, lecturing and inspiring.

In 1917 the notepaper of Geddes and Colleagues had the following addresses:

Outlook Tower, Edinburgh
More's Garden, Chelsea, S.W.
Town Planning Office, Lucknow.

In the 1920s, his notepaper still had three addresses – the Outlook Tower in Edinburgh, the Chelsea address and the Collège des Écossais in Montpellier. His Outlook Tower provided a refuge for intellectuals unwelcome in their homelands. His exhibitions toured the world – the Cities Exhibition ending up in the depths of the Indian Ocean. Where did he get his itchy feet from?

PG's mother spent 11 years and 65 days in Corfu, Malta and Bermuda, not only supporting her husband and bringing up her family but teaching in the regimental school and accumulating enough in her own right to buy two decent properties in Ballater in 1852, jointly with her husband. Her oldest son, Robert, went to Mexico, where he became successful enough as a banker to retire at the age of 40. For John McKail Geddes New Zealand gave the opportunity to make a fortune in coffee and spice, to the extent that his widow was able to make a career out of spending and philanthropy, taking her five children on two trips to Europe, buying a grand new Daimler and staying at places like the Ritz.

Anna Morton from Liverpool spent a year in Dresden, qualifying herself to teach music and acquiring the social skills which enabled her to support and restrain her husband in so many situations at home and abroad. Mabel Barker was so committed to Geddes's ideas on Regional Survey that she moved from one post to another as each failed to come up to her high standards – and she had a spell working in the camps for Belgian refugees in the neutral Netherlands during World War I. Jacky Tyrwhitt, born in South Africa, educated in London, was another who racketed around the world as she grew in authority. After planning in England and during World War II she spent long spells in Canada, the United States and India. Involved in the Athens Centre of Ekistics, she settled permanently in Greece. Margaret Noble and Annie Besant were very different women but were similar in that each became so immersed in Indian culture and beliefs that they only returned to Europe for the next round of fund-raising.

'Industry, Integrity and Internationalism' – not a bad banner to lead a cause!

Walter Stephen

Notes

1   Robert Burns, from *The Rights of Women an Occasional Address*. Spoken
    by Miss Fontenelle on her Benefit Night, 26 November 1792, in The Theatre
    Royal, Dumfries.

2   Probably best thought of as the opposite of 'the rolling stone gathers no
    moss'.

CHAPTER I

The Mother

Janet Stivenson (Geddes) (1816–98)

THE GEDDES FAMILY correspondence is valuable in that it records the experiences of an early immigrant to New Zealand (John McKail Geddes) and the internal workings of a Victorian family unusual only in having one very bright family member who went on to earn world renown. According to John McKail Geddes's daughter 'emigration was her father's preferred method of escape to avoid becoming the minister of the family'. Further:

> It is apparent from the letters that the boys were raised in a heavily religious environment, enough to drive Jack as far away as he could possibly go.

Unfortunately, there was pressure on John McKail (as his New Zealand family call him) not only to write regularly, but to write to each member of the family at home – not the best recipe for a rich historical source, as each piece of information is trotted out several times in a mechanical fashion. Incredibly, given the state of communications at the time, John wrote home saying that he had missed two letters from Bob in Mexico and asking that the Perth copies be sent on to him, which he would return in due course! Bob's view of the correspondence became obvious when he burnt the letters with the words 'Nobody will ever want to read these'.

Within a family there are many references and allusions which are impossible for us to work out now. Wouldn't it be interesting to know what was behind John's writing to his sister:

> … hope that the Don Juan's cookery shines of the Sunday Schoolteachers flirtation with the Right Revd Sambo have made you all right?

and signing it 'Yours affectionately, A tea Pot'?

There is a deal of preaching, especially in the earlier letters, and John at first conceals the fact that he has gone to the gold diggings, and then feels the need to confess and apologise to his father. But there is also some humour, often expressed as rather ponderous semi-military banter. Patrick gave his sister the nickname 'Mousie' – which must be significant – and closed one letter 'I remain Yours, Jeremiah Diddler to Madam Snopple-

chops'. Patrick Geddes was baptised 'Peter' and through the correspondence we can trace his evolution from Peter to Patrick, taking in, on the
way, 'Pat', 'My dear Pat', 'Dear Wee Pat', and 'Patie'.

In the early 19th century Ayrshire, Lanarkshire and Fife were centres
of tambouring, highly skilled fine embroidery using a tambour or embroidery frame, done by women in their own homes and organised on the
'putting out' system. An advertisement in *The Edinburgh Evening Courant*
of 2 November 1835:

> To the Ladies
> Repository for Ayrshire and Moravian Needlework, and
> Child-Bed Warehouse

in Edinburgh's George Street, demonstrates the country-wide complexity
of the system.

The work was notoriously hard on the eyes and the embroiderers
traditionally bathed their eyes with whisky as a remedy. Janet Stivenson's
mother did not live long enough to go blind but her grandmother and her
mother were both supposed to have gone blind. Janet also lost her sight.
We do not know why, but given her life of industry and canny self-improve-
ment it would not be surprising if those had been built on the ceaseless
drag of precision work in an insalubrious setting.

The first letters centre around a tragic event which must have done
something to confirm Janet's innate seriousness. John Stevenson was a
baker in Airdrie. (Baillieston also recurs, it is five miles west of Airdrie).

Stevenson (who later changed his name to Stivenson) had a connection
with Beith in Ayrshire and Janet, aged 17, was sent there for a fortnight
with her brother John, aged 15. On Saturday 31 January 1829, during a
cold spell, Kilbirnie Loch was frozen. Young John, like many others, played
on the ice. He disappeared and after several days was found trapped in
eight feet of water under the ice.

Janet Stivenson may have felt partially responsible for her brother's
death. She was 'a favourite of the Author's' and the recipient of a senti-
mental poem of 12 four-line stanzas *On the death of John Stevenson*.

After the death of his son, John Stivenson deserted his wife and went
off to America – from where he was to emerge much later. His wife, also
Janet Stivenson, was left with three daughters and coped by making a
living by baking until she died of cholera between 1830 and 1835.

One would like to think that the effect of these three hammer blows
on young Janet was mitigated to an extent by her marriage in 1832.

Alexander Geddes was born in Grantown-on-Spey on 20 November 1810, the son of a general merchant (shopkeeper). His parents died young and he moved to the Glasgow area. On 23 December 1826, in Paisley, he enlisted, aged 15 (according to the Attestation for Regiments), in the 42nd Foot, the Royal Highlanders, also known as the Black Watch. His occupation was given as Labourer and his first three years were spent as an underage Drummer, non-pensionable. In 1829 he began pensionable service as a Drummer, being promoted to Private in 1833, to Corporal in 1834 and to Serjeant in 1836. As Acting Serjeant Major he was discharged on 25 November 1851 'having been found unfit for further service'.

The Medical Report said that:

> The Nature of the man's Disability is General Debility & Emaciation the result of long military service and climate and has neither been reduced or increased by intemperance or other vice. In a word, he is worn out and recommended for Discharge.

With regard to his Character and Conduct:

> ... his general character has been very good, having been a non-commissioned officer for upwards of 17 years – seven years of which he was Srjt Major.

Nevertheless, in 1831 he had been tried for absenting himself without leave and found Guilty, for which he was imprisoned for ten days without pay. The Army may forgive, but it never forgets! Why did Alexander go 'on the trot'?

In the 1950s, in the days of National Service, I spent an interesting couple of months. Young lads would go home on leave and just be unable to come back to base. After some time they would realise that they could not get away with it and would report to the local police, who then locked them up. I would then have to travel by train to Windsor, or Whitley Bay, or Leicester and bring the prisoner back to Aldershot and justice. Most of these lads were 'poor souls', who just could not bear to be away from home and its comforts. Others had been subjected to bullying. And others had romantic entanglements. Which of these factors lay behind Alexander's absence without leave we cannot tell, but it may be significant that he did not transgress again in his military career and the following year he was married.

With the Highland regiments went women and children. In 1822 six women per 100 men were permitted to travel, 12 per 100 in India and New South Wales, but these quotas were often exceeded. As well as supporting their men these women were paid for non-military duties as washerwomen and cleaners, their daughters under 15 could be servants or pupil schoolmistresses.

In my time there was a Royal Army Educational Corps, almost entirely made up of sergeants and officers. In initial training we had one hour of 'Education' per week. At Mons Officer Cadet School the weekly hour was devoted to the examination of political issues in which we might find ourselves involved – Korea, decolonisation and the like.

Janet was a teacher, with three areas of operation. There were the regimental children to be taught, long before the Education Acts of 1870 and 1872. Physical fitness and absence of ruptures were more important than literacy and many recruits had to be taught to read and write. Also, promotion gradually became dependent on the possession of Army Education Certificates.

The Standing Orders of the 42nd in 1833 laid down the rules:

> Non-commissioned officers are required to attend the Regimental School
> if not sufficiently well taught in reading, writing and arithmetic... Sergeants
> are expected to learn at least the first four rules of arithmetic.

By 1857 the educational requirements for promotion from Lance Corporal to Corporal were:

> Able to read, write and understand the first four rules of Arithmetic, with
> Division and Drill without arms.
>
> Understand the duties of Orderly, Fatigue and Guard Corporal.

Alexander Geddes served for ten years at home, three years in Corfu, four years in Malta and four years in Bermuda. The places of birth of the children demonstrate the instability of the military life. Robert Geddes was born in Ireland – which was not service abroad in 1839. The regiment was at Limerick that year. Jessie was born when they were in Corfu and John when they were in Malta. Another son was born in Malta on 20 July 1846 and was baptised Alexander on 1 August of that year. Of him Alexander Geddes Senior wrote:

> My beloved child Alexander died at sea on board the *Resistance* Troop
> Ship and within sight of the Bermudas on the 24th of April 1847 and was
> interred in the Graveyard at Ireland Island, Bermuda.

In 1851 the 42nd transferred from Bermuda to Halifax, Nova Scotia. Janet and the children may have watched the regiment as it marched out of the barracks for the last time to *The 79th's Farewell to Gibraltar,*

written in 1848 but already the official pipe tune for a Highland regiment
leaving its station for the last time. Janet must have wondered where it
would all end, with three young children and an ailing husband and no
prospects. In the event, the next five years were to see a complete turn-
round in the family fortunes, a new career for Alexander and the birth of
another son who was to achieve great things. Through these adventures
'something of the schoolmistress may have always remained with her'.

We do not know if the regiment sailed direct from Bermuda to Halifax,
as they had done from Malta to Bermuda, or came back to Britain and
then crossed the Atlantic again. What we do know is that Acting Serjeant
Major Alexander Geddes turned up at Aberdeen Barracks on 22 October
1851, where his discharge was recommended 'having been found unfit for
further service'. His 'Intended place of Residence' was given as Airdrie,
Lanarkshire – with Janet's sister.

In *Where was Peter Geddes born?* in *A Vigorous Institution: The Living
Legacy of Patrick Geddes* (2007) and *Where was Patrick Geddes born? The
Last Word?* (2008) I clarified, as best as I could at the time, the course of
events in the life of the Geddes family from Alexander's recommendation
for discharge on 22 October 1851. The question mark after 'Word' was a
good idea – below is my final description of the strange changes in the life
of Alexander Geddes (AG) and his family. It has to be said that some of the
details in the above works must now be said to be unsound and that both
Boardman's and Kitchen's accounts of Alexander's career – clearly based
on a common and unreliable source – are completely wrong.

For easy reference I have given each of the 'steps' a reference number.

1. On 25/11/1851 AG was given his final discharge at Chatham, with
a Service Record of 21 years and 338 days.

2. On 25/11/1851 – the same day – at an Examination of Invalid
Soldiers, Royal Hospital, Chelsea, AG was awarded a pension of two
shillings (10p) weekly on the basis of service of 24 11/12 years.

There is something fishy here; AG was being credited with three years
he had not served. Note the three years – they will recur.

3. In fact AG had been headhunted and sent for from Aberdeen to be
assessed at the Horse Guards for 'special duties'. A steady and reliable
NCO was available just as Victoria and Albert's plans for the rebuilding of
Balmoral were being finalised. Knowing them and the 'friendly footing'
on which Victoria lived with her Scottish servants, it would not be
surprising if the Royal couple had 'interviewed' AG and impressed upon
him the importance of his task – which was to be resident supervisor of
the work. This task he carried out for three years.

FIG.2 Ballater c.1890 (The two Geddes houses look over the Square to the church).
Aberdeen University Library

4. 21/8/1852. AG ('late Serjeant') and 'Mrs Janet Stivenson or Geddes, his spouse' jointly purchased a house in Ballater (eight miles from Balmoral) of eight rooms plus another of six rooms with a butcher's shop. Janet was a good housekeeper and must have managed her earnings as a teacher well.

5. On 2/10/1854 Janet's fifth child was born and baptised Peter. Over a number of years and by use and wont, Peter morphed into Patrick.

6. 20/2/1855. The Royal Perthshire Rifles (Perthshire Militia) was raised.

7. On 23/2/1855 (three days later!) AG was commissioned as Ensign in the Royal Perthshire Rifles – three years and 80 days after his discharge from the 42nd.

8. Manuscript entry on 2) above 'Letter 7.19005 from War Department 11/8/1857'. The three years service AG had had front-loaded were now deducted and his pension increased to 2/-6d (12.5p) with effect from 1/7/1857. The unusual, if not irregular arrangement was now tidied up and the 'special duties' rewarded.

9. 26/11/1857 – Ballater property sold to William Ferguson, House

Carpenter, residing at San Francisco, now at Newton of Gairn. AG had now rented Mount Tabor Cottage in Perth, which was bought at a later date.

10. 31/3/1878. Retirement of AG with the rank of Quartermaster. This man who was worn out and recommended for discharge after 21 years and 338 days in the ranks soldiered on for 23 years and 37 days as a commissioned officer! From Ensign on 23/2/1855, AG was promoted to Lieutenant on 5/11/1855, and to Quartermaster on 22/11/1856. AG was never a Captain, in fact, on his Record of Service the printed rank of 'Captain' is scored out and 'Quartermaster' inserted by hand.

11. From AG's *Particulars of Income for the year ending 31 March 1898*:

365 Days Retired Pay at 5/- per day	£91 – 5/-
365 do Pension at 2/6 do	£45 – 12/-6
Annuity for Meritorious Service	£15
Out of a total income for the year of	£295 – 18/-9

Not a bad year for one who was discharged at 41 'having been found unfit for further service'. The annuity would have been the recognition for his 'special duties'.

On 18 May 1843 the Geddeses were in Malta and it would have been several weeks before they heard of the great event in Edinburgh, the Disruption, when 470 ministers and elders walked out of the General Assembly on the issue of patronage. In so doing they were giving up 'their comfortable stipends, their pleasant manses, and present advantages of position', but down the hill at Tanfield Hall they formed themselves into The General Assembly of the Free Church of Scotland.

The Free Kirk is often seen as the epitome of 'stern Presbyterianism', embodied in a plain lifestyle, no exuberant decoration, no highly emotional music, no drama and a nit-picking Sabbatarianism – and no doubt this could be found in many of the parishes. But Murdo Macdonald, in *Anarchy and the Free Church* points out that among the lay founders of the Free Kirk were some of Scotland's most significant thinkers of the time, scientists and artists. Patrick Geddes, in later years, claimed Thomas Chalmers, the leader of the Disruption, as an 'anarchist economist', himself claiming to be an ally of anarchy. Anarchy, for Geddes was 'an-archy', without government i.e. without governmental compulsion. Geddes was to make clear the debt he owed to the Free Church, saying that it was the organisation of which he was 'proudest of all' to have belonged to.

In 1861 Mount Tabor was a villa suburb on the wooded slopes of Kinnoull Hill, across the Tay from the centre of Perth. The Geddes house was Mount Tabor Cottage (but in the legal documents it is called Gean Cottage).

For Janet Mount Tabor must have meant much more than a nice place to live. Mount Tabor (*Jebel et Tur* – mountain of mountains – as the Arabs call it) is distinguished among the mountains of Palestine for its picturesque site, its graceful outline and for the remarkable vegetation which covers its rocky, calcareous, side. There is a splendid view from its summit, which is traditionally the scene of Christ's Transfiguration.

This is where Jesus took Peter, James and John up the mountain:

> … and was transfigured before them: and his face did shine as the sun…
> and behold a voice out of the cloud, which said, 'This is my beloved Son,
> in whom I am well pleased; hear ye him.' (St Matt, XVII, 1–9)

Janet must have been constantly aware of the underlying meaning of the place she and her family lived in and been ever more committed to the good life. And it would have been very easy to see her intelligent and questioning youngest child as a 'special one'. At the same time, if one's early environment has any influence at all on adult thinking, the young Patrick would already be seeing Kinnoull Hill and the Sidlaws as more than crags and volcanic sills, fine woodland and follies aping Rhenish castles admired on the Grand Tour.

In this developing leafy suburb of Perth, ancient market and county town, major railway and textile centre, the neighbouring householders – in big houses with many servants – included:

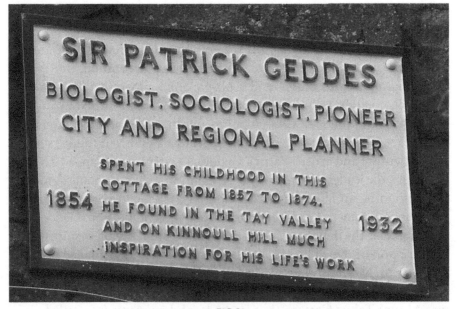

FIG.3
Plaque on Mount Tabor Cottage. *Photo by Walter Stephen*

Shipping Emigration Agent
Bank Secretary
Banker (Secretary to Central Bank of Scotland)
Editor (*Perthshire Advertiser*)
Upholsterer (employer of 27 men, 10 boys and 5 women)
Landed Proprietor
Superintendent of Lunatic Asylum
'Kept by Family'

Janet and Alexander entered enthusiastically into the life of the Free Disruption, Alexander was appointed an elder in 1857 and in 1887 played an important part in managing the move to the Free Middle Church. As a Quartermaster QM, promoted from the ranks, AG's social status was ambiguous. Locally he would have been respected for his experience and steadiness – and for having risen from the ranks. In the officers' mess the lairds' sons would have tolerated the old soldier, but he could never have been 'one of us'.

That his duties were not too onerous can be assumed from the fact that the Victoria Street Soldiers' Barracks held little more than a handful of ageing NCOs and their wives from the 42nd (Black Watch) and 92nd (Gordons). His biggest responsibility was probably being in charge of the arrangements for Queen Victoria's visit to Perth for the unveiling of a statue of Prince Albert – but this would have reinforced the family's self-confidence in their special relationship with the Queen. There would still be time to cultivate his garden and teach the young Patrick how, for example, to plant potatoes or make a box.

At the 1861 Census Alexander and Janet Geddes were living in six windowed rooms with their children Robert, Jessie, John, Peter and a domestic servant. This degree of overcrowding was to end when Robert and John left home. Robert had an unsettled start till he did very well as a banker and married a general's daughter. John emigrated to New Zealand at 17, wrote home in interesting detail, and became a successful businessman. The Geddes upbringing clearly equipped them with abundant self-confidence, enterprise and competence.

With the two elder brothers making their way in the world, things must have been easier at home. The household was now: Father, Mother, Big Sister, Servant and young Patrick. Patrick was the undivided centre of attention for his old parents (one soon to go blind) and two other caring women. The letters from Jack in New Zealand, because they describe what home was like when he was there, give us a good impression of the home presided over by Janet.

Jack was at great pains to reassure his mother: 'I attend a Free church here the Minister is not that bad and the precentor is quite as good'. His greatest pleasure was to picture home on a Sunday:

> ... to see you collected round the breakfast table and follow you to and from Church, taking your walk round the garden, getting checked for playing with Peter and hear mother reminding him if John had no sense surely he had some.

He could 'have got a situation today in a spirit store' but did not engage himself as he 'would take rather anything else than have to do with drink'.

At Christmas he could see Bob 'dissecting the duff' and Mother would say, referring to Jack: 'He will have no person to bake a duff for him'. Patrick 'would have made the wonderful discovery that you were all wrong and give a learned lecture on the rotation of the earth'.

The house at Mount Tabor was damp and at one point 'Father had a touch of the screwmatics'. When Janet was ill, Jack considered it was:

> ... an attack of the blues from thinking too much of me and fancying some evil had befallen me... you have got too good a servant and never go out to take a walk. Now that you have not my ears to box, you must take some other healthy exercise.

In 1863 there was talk of moving, which Jack vigorously opposed:

> ... Jackson's house it is not a good place for the chilblains and one of the most ugly and disagreeable places about Perth... If you have to leave the Mount I hope you will get a nice warm cottage not a Noah's Ark.

At the same time he said 'it was very little use getting a cow now when the biggest calf is away', implying that the Geddeses had kept their own cow when all the boys were at home.

Bob, the oldest son, had made one or two false starts before he settled into a successful career and happy marriage. Janet had been complaining that his salary was too small when Jack reminded Jessie that their mother:

> ... will remember how comfortable and happy she kept us when Father was earning only a pound a week.

Jack wrote: 'You are still the same kind old body putting yourself and Jessie to so much trouble'. At another time he was glad to see that:

> Your Spirits and as a natural consequence your health is good and that by your superior nursing you have got your invalids off the sick list.

When Janet was 72 she and her husband attended two health lectures given by Dr Wilson. This involved trudging down from Mount Tabor and crossing Smeaton's great bridge across the Tay to the city centre – and coming back again! Jessie's comment about the weather on the first night – not the lecture – was:

> ... last night I could not stand it was fearful nearly blew Father and Mother down and got worse after they came home.

Given Patrick Geddes's involvement with gardens throughout his life, as builder, designer and missionary on behalf of gardens, it would be surprising if Jack Geddes had been silent on the subject. In fact, when Jack wrote home to his mother it was the garden that evoked his fondest memories.

> Your attention to the briar bush brought home by me gives me great pleasure and shows that I have got some friends who my memory is dear to I often think of your flower garden and am sure there are few bushes or flowers in it but I know their whereabouts.

Another time:

> It is very kind of you to cultivate the gowans (Ox-eye Daisies) I planted. I forgot that I had left anything in the gardening line.[1]

There was remembered comedy, as when Jack wrote:

> ... knowing my motto would ever be the same as Pats when he used to go forth to slay the dockens at the Pigs sty 'Victory or death'.

> And: 'When the sow ran away and Mother and the servant had a regular Boar's hunt.'

The first sod of the Perth and Inverness Railway, linking Perth to Forres via Aviemore and Grantown-on-Spey, was cut in 1861 and the line opened in 1863. John's letter of 16 January 1864 to his father stirs things up:

> You are always talking about taking mother North to see the famous City of Grantown and now that you can go direct by the train you should 'Screw up your courage to the sticking point' and go it would be a great treat to mother. I often look back with pleasure to our tour and some of the circumstances connected with it I could point out the shop I bought the pennys worth of sweets.

The departure of her boys, the death of Jessie in 1888 and the onset of her blindness, meant that for Janet Mount Tabor must have become a dark and silent place. But she showed herself to be 'still the same kind old body' she had been when the family were at home by providing a refuge for others in some kind of need.

John Stivenson, who had disappeared to America in 1830, wrote back to Scotland from Wilmington, Delaware on 27 January 1862, addressing the letter to Mr & Mrs Geddes and starting 'My dear children'. Clearly there had been some sort of reconciliation, borne out by the chatty tone of the letter, commenting on the progress of the Civil War, the class structure of the slave states and details of family life. Later letters comment on an almost idyllic mood after the civil war despite mention of the 'martyred president'. He described the success of the northern states in the conflict and what that meant to the black population. Affluence and Yankee political propaganda seemed to coincide with bumper harvests of fruit and vegetables which he described in detail... even down to costs per bushel!

Stivenson returned to Scotland, staying with Janet till his death on 13 January 1867. He had four daughters. By his first wife there were Janet Geddes and Elizabeth Waddell of Baillieston. By his second wife in the USA were Esther and Betsy. Stivenson's property in Scotland mainly consisted of United States of America Consolidated 5.20 per cent Bonds. Alexander Geddes was the sole executor. Esther and Betty were to have 200 dollars (c£40) each and the residue of £612 14/-10 was to be divided 'share and share alike' between Janet and Elizabeth. A legacy of £306 – 7/-5 may not seem much to us today, but when we compare it with Alexander Geddes's income for the year to 31 March 1897 (£295 – 18/-9) it was not inconsiderable.

Although this will seemed a little harsh on the American connection, it is probable that there was another will in the US taking care of his American daughters. Stivenson's dying return to Scotland was clearly an attempt at final closure and his generosity in his will was a kind of apology for his heartless behaviour of 1830. For Janet the careful housewife who managed on £1 per week, this windfall would have continued the pattern of careful accumulation which characterised her life.

Census night of 1881 found the following in residence at Mount Tabor.

Alexander Geddes	72	Captain (half-pay) Royal Highlanders[2]	
Jane Geddes	64	Wife	
Jessie Geddes	42	Daughter	born Corfu
Jessie Alexander Geddes	14	Scholar	born Mexico
Walter Geddes	12	Scholar	born Mexico
Helen PE Harris	26	General Servant Domestic	born Perth

Mexico in 1881 was in a state of turmoil, where, among other hazards, the kidnapping of the children of a rich banker was more than a possibility. Robert, the eldest son, therefore sent his two children to Perth, where they lodged with his parents and were guaranteed a good education at the Academy.

Norah Geddes gives us a snapshot of Janet in old age.

> My grandmother's face had larger features and she was blind. Once, unknown to her, I was present when she changed her glass eye. She took it out of a box and I was fascinated. I was sure it was a real eye and told my nursemaid this when I went home, but she didn't believe me.

> Family prayers were said night and morning with readings from the scriptures. The maid was duly called in and when praying we knelt over the seat of our horsehair chairs.[3]

Geddes's 'The Education of Two Boys', from his Talks from My/The Outlook Tower, is probably the talk of most interest to us today and has provided a rich resource for biographers. It is almost the classic account of the beauties of home education and the education of 'Head, Heart and Hand'. Great prominence is given to the influence of 'the kind father', while Janet remains a shadowy figure notable only for her love of flowers.

Some writers have described Geddes as the archetypical 'lad o' pairts' of Scots tradition, but this is an over-simplification. He never went barefoot through the snow to school, carrying a peat he had cut himself in the summer for the schoolroom fire. While the family lived at Mount Tabor they always had a live-in maid. He clattered down the brae to Smeaton's great bridge over the Tay in good boots. He did not sit in a chaotic country classroom with 'The lave a' scrammelin' near him, like bummies roon a bike.'[4] Perth Academy was as fine a school as any in Scotland.

He left school to work in the bank, but gave that up in favour of 'home studies' before moving to London, where his early years must have been subsidised from home. He had a self-confidence which came partly from within and partly from the knowledge that he had behind him a supportive home. Janet had her own money and it may well be that she was the one who backed her clever son's initial attempts to find his true vocation.

But The Education of Two Boys was written with a didactic purpose, for which Geddes's mother was not required. Nevertheless, we can be quite certain that her influence on her youngest son was profound, demonstrating and practising the importance of hard work and integrity, inculcating the values – if not the practices – of the Free Kirk.

Walter Stephen

Notes

1   Gowans have a special place in the Scottish psyche, as in *Auld Lang Syne*:

> *We twa hae run about the braes,*
>   *And pou'd the gowans fine;*
> *But we've wander'd mony a weary fitt,*
>   *Sin auld lang syne.*

2   Once again we see the 'Captain myth' perpetuated in a supposedly reliable source. Alexander Geddes was never a Captain. The Census Enumerator wrote down what the householder told him. Who claimed a captaincy for Alexander? Alexander himself? Or Janet, his loyal wife?

Just to make matters more complicated, there **was** to be a Captain Geddes in the family. At the funeral of Alexander Geddes the principal pall-bearers were 'Professor Geddes, son of the deceased and Captain Walter Geddes, Hampshire Regiment, a grandson' – the 12-year old of 1881.

The Royal Hampshire Regiment, the 37th of Foot, although above the 42nd, The Black Watch, The Royal Highlanders in the Precedence of Infantry Regiments, was a run-of-the-mill county regiment and not a patch on the glamorous Highlanders.

3   There is more than a whiff of Burns's *The Cottar's Saturday Night* in this touching scene:

> *From Scenes like these old SCOTIA's grandeur springs,*
> *That makes her lov'd at home, rever'd abroad:*
> *Princes and lords are but the breath of kings,*
> *'An honest man's the noble work of GOD';*
> *And certes, in fair Virtue's heavenly road,*
> *The Cottage leaves the Palace far behind.*

4   'The others scrambling around, like bees round a hive.'

CHAPTER TWO

The Big Sister

Jessie Geddes (1841–88)

THE CONVENTION IS to start by defining the date of birth, the place of birth and parentage of the subject. According to the Census of Scotland 1861 Janet Geddes (hereinafter referred to as Jessie) was born in 1841 or 1842 in Forfar, Angus.

Alexander Geddes	Head	52	Quarter Master Perthshire Militia Chelsea Pensioner (born) Invernessshire, Inverallan
Jessie Geddes	Wife	44	Lanarkshire, Airdrie
Robert Geddes	Son	22	Bank Clerk, Ireland
Jessie Geddes	Daughter	19	Angus, Forfar
John Geddes	Son	17	Lawyer's Clerk Apprentice, Malta
Peter Geddes	Son	6	Scholar, Aberdeenshire, Ballater
Lenore B Fisher	Servant	25	Domestic Servant Perthshire, Scone

This immediately seems odd. In 1842 the 42nd were serving in Corfu. Not only would Alexander Geddes have been there, but his wife Janet was very much the regimental wife and would have been expected to be there also. Jessie's brothers, Robert and John, were born respectively in 1839 in Ireland and in 1844 in Malta, obviously following the flag.

At this stage it might be asked; what were the Black Watch doing in Corfu, known to us as a Greek holiday island? Alexander's service abroad was that of peacetime garrison duty. The Ionian Islands were subject to Venice from 1386 to 1797. From 1814 to 1864 they were a republic dependent on Great Britain – hence the presence of the 42nd. In 1862 the new king of Greece, a Danish prince who ruled as George I, requested that Britain give up their 'protectorate' of the Ionian Islands as a condition of his accession to the Greek throne and in 1863 the islanders voted to transfer to Greece.

In *Where was Patrick Geddes Born? The Last Word?* I tried to solve this riddle, suggesting that Janet Geddes might have been 'sent home' for the birth of the child. Most unlikely, given the conditions of service in the British army at that time. And why Forfar? As we have seen, Janet's family connections were in the west.

However, when we look at the Census for 1881 we find that Jessie's place of birth is given as Corfu, as it should have been. Someone on Census night 1861 must have been dozing or confused – not the only instance in the Geddes story where seemingly authoritative sources have slipped up.

Jessie was second in line in the family, following Robert ('Bob') and before John ('Jack') by three and two years respectively, and 11 years older than Patrick. By the time they were living in the cottage at Mount Tabor on the Kinnoull Hill they were not living in direst poverty. Behind them were the proceeds of the sale of the Ballater property, consisting of an eight-roomed house with an adjacent house and shop. Although, according to the Census, there were seven residents and only six windowed rooms – a degree of overcrowding even at that date – one of the seven was a live-in servant. So Jessie did not have to go to the mill or go blind tambouring but could live the life of the respectable Victorian spinster, helping her mother, guiding her clever younger brother, getting involved in good works and not getting married – although there was a fiancée who died.

Jessie's home life could not be described as spectacular. (In one letter her father wrote to her: 'Nothing Extraori-na-ry has taken place in Mount Tabor or the Suburbs since you left'). Mrs Patterson's cold is much improved, a cousin has a 'deranged stomach', Miss Douglas has a wedding, 'Jamesina was here and took tea with us last night'. Mother cannot find a 'receipt'(recipe) and it must be tracked down. She wrote hoping that Jessie was trying her music – 'It is diffidence that has kept you back hitherto, you ought to overcome it'. Jack thanks her for the kind presents, which are all very pretty, and for forwarding Chambers' Journal. Jessie acquired a new wisdom tooth and a sore thumb at the same time.

> The spring is a dressmaker's busy time... Mother and I will either do some of our spring cleaning or we will try and get a dressmaker to come and make my beautiful dress for summer.

Note – these were options! She did not need to make her own dresses. Jessie could be persistent. Four times she wrote to Anna ('Annie'), Patrick's wife and a new mother, about a piece of worsted. She also wanted to match ribbons.

> Tell Annie that I don't mind how broad the ribbon is if it is as broad again or nearly so as the patterns, the colour is the more particular thing about it. Though it is three times as broad as the patterns so much the better.

Then there was paraffin oil. Jessie sent full directions to Patrick for washing with paraffin oil under the heading 'Washing made Easy'.

Jessie's relationship with Patrick was big sisterly and supportive when he was young – in one letter to Jessie, John refers to 'your young pupil'. In later years she and he corresponded about lectures she attended and her worries about poor attendances at his lectures, wanting to know the exact numbers of tickets sold. She had been at readings given by Mrs Sarah Siddons (not the Mrs Siddons of the Gainsborough and Reynolds portraits). She had so little time to read:

> ... if I had more I would not be so grudging about buying books you see Ruskin I bought more than one year ago I have not read one chapter then Silas Marner last Sept just a little bit so what's the good of buying?

From her we learn that Patrick had had his portrait painted, but it was not a good likeness. She was greatly concerned that her brother should have a Chair and wrote in the third person why. 'Folks would believe in him more were he a big man than a wee man'. (This writer had never thought of PG as a wee man, but that may explain a lot). 'If he is able to write a book on Botany he is able to teach it'. And, 'I do so much wish to see him in a chair and 'getting on'. Sadly, Jessie died in 1888, the same year as her little brother was given his first Chair.

As her parents grew older Jessie had more to do with the garden. We read of strawberries and raspberries, the making of jam – and its sale. The disposal of overripe cauliflowers was a problem.

When Patrick was married and associated with the Royal Botanic Garden, Jessie sent him a plant with no leaves but:

> If Pat is a good boy and gives me some pretty thing in return I will give a plant of it when he next comes home.

In a very long letter to Patrick she wrote:

> I have got my house in order and got the gardiner (!) to sow no end of seeds as some of them are pretty old being the seeds Bob brought me. I have my doubts but am most anxious perhaps I will be able to give you something lovely and interesting but owing to this very cold weather we have only had the man one day and part of two, I do wish it would change. Jeannie and I went up the hill for mould for the seeds, when you come home you must really sort the rockeries this time there can be no excuse with all your experience so we will have several trips to the hills for earth... I suppose your garden work is stopped also... Are the Camellias still in bloom?

I hope when you come home the weather will be so fine that you will be able to bring me the life plant without endangering its life and I wish I could get some fern or something else that the gardiner will be thinning and just throwing on his wasteheap. Can you tell me this if Jack sent me home some fern leaves with seed on them could I grow them here by starting them in the frame and after that having them in the house there are some so lovely among my dried ferns that he sent home years ago and I never saw them growing in this country. You might ask the gardiner if my plan is worth it so I will share my seeds with him, We will have to get some ferns from the hill for the rockeries.

Editor's comments. The 'gardiner' would have been Alexander her father and 'the man' would have been hired to do the heavy work. At this time Bob was in Mexico and John in New Zealand. Ferns were much collected by the Victorians. Big houses, like Benmore in Argyll, had ferneries and professional plant hunters hunted several species to extinction.

Jessie had friends outside the immediate family circle. At the time of the 'awakening' – of which more below – she had a substantial correspondence with Isabella Thomson, who thought that 'God has touched the heart of your dear brother J' (John, who emigrated to New Zealand) and wrote lengthy passages advocating Jessie's conversion.

Jessie had friends in Ballater, dating from her schooldays there. In Braemar her father's brother Peter was Postmaster and General Merchant and there was great coming and going between Perth and Braemar.

On 2 September 1860 Alexander wrote to Jessie, then at Braemar with 'Uncle and Aunt'. Jessie was not to think that 'we have forgotten you we always remember at least twice a day and ask God Bless and protect you'. 'God the Holy Ghost' was working powerfully in Perth and 'many have been brought to see that they are sinners'. He regretted that Jessie was not at home at this important season and exhorted her to think of her 'State in the Sight of God' and to pray 'that God will not pass you by'. Pattie (Patrick) was in town with Alexander and 'he desires you to haste home'.

On the same day her mother thought it unfortunate that she was from home at this time –

We have had a great awakening in Perth after you left... the City hall crowded to excess every night... so many anxious souls.

She was very anxious about Jessie 'as there are so many young people you know that are anxious and some have found peace'.

She concludes on a practical note. Jessie was to bring back from Braemar 5½ yards of flannel for Papa, and ½ dozen views (postcards) nice ones. If Uncle had any good white flannel in stock she was to bring 5½ yards. Janet wanted a 'fill'd Plaid'. Uncle was to ask the commercial traveller from Glasgow to drop a note when in Perth – Janet might get it cheaper than Uncle could manage it.

A month later Jessie had moved on to Ballater and her 'Affectionate Mother J Geddes' wrote to say that she was:

> ... not a little surprised at your remaining so long after you knew our wishes on the subject. You have exceeded the time so much already and to remain another week is, to say the least of it, wrong... I would respect that young person most that would shew the most regard to her parents' wishes. I think you have long enough jaunting... I wish you home to get the benefits of the meetings in the City hall.

Then follow details of the meetings and the young men 'of your acquaintance' attending them.

Then comes a touch of blackmail.

> Tomorrow is Patie's birthday and he is not a little disappointed at your not coming home tonight, dear Jessie.

She closes with some encouraging lines.

> Seek to know what you are living for, do not be thoughtless but consider whether you are travelling hither on the Broad or Narrow way that leads to life Eternal.

At the same time her father wants to know by what train she will leave Aberdeen on Saturday – a recurrent request over the years.

> From Perth to Braemar by road via the Devil's Elbow and The Cairnwell (the highest point reached by a main road in Britain) is 60 miles. In 1866 the Deeside Railway from Aberdeen to Ballater was opened, making it possible to travel by rail between Ballater and Perth, changing at Aberdeen.

Writing from Braemar Alexander could not think of allowing Jessie to walk from Braemar to Blairgowrie, 15 miles short of Perth. It was:

> ... too great a feat for either of us. I got a conveyance for about 14 miles yesterday, were it not for that, I could not have arrived here.

Yet in 1864 John wrote to Jessie from New Zealand congratulating her on a very pleasant jaunt up to the Highlands.

> It is almost a pity that Father sold his property there, but more pleasant still would it be to meet your old school companions... You have turned a famous walker when you could climb the hills from the Spittal of Glenshee to Braemar. Was you not afraid when between the hills and no person with you?

Can we learn anything from the correspondence which tells us about Jessie's emotional life?

The Geddeses were not much given to emotion in their communications with each other but three letters from New Zealand give cause for thought.

FIG 4 shows a rather weedy young man posed against a pretty stark background. Alex Geddes wrote from New Zealand as follows.

FIG. 4
Jessie's fiancé, died aged 24.
Alex Geddes

For 140 years, in our family, this unfortunate fellow's photos have been lying in state, all but anonymous, in an envelope simply marked: 'Jessie's Fiancé, died aged 24'. From time to time I have wondered who he was and what might have been and realised it was the man's entire biography; every last detail of his life as I know it has been recorded in five words.

The situation seems absolutely clear, if unfortunate. But now note these two extracts from letters sent home by John.

You will have great jollifications at home now. I suppose Jessie will be going out to so many parties and at her lost love's marriage (Mr C-) if spite will let her. Give him my best respects.

John did not seem to be too worried about this situation, as the rest of his long letter is full of cheerful chat and is signed:

I am
Daily, Hourly, Minutely, Secondly
Presently your
Jack ass.

To his mother at the same time he wrote:

I see you have lost your friend and Jessie her lad Mr Cray. It is a wonder that he does not call on you. I would have expected him to have been the last man who would have got purse proud.

It looks as if Jessie had not one lost love – but two.

Some of the last letters were exchanged between Jessie and Anna Morton, as wife and mother with her first child. The pair seem to have hit it off together and Jessie began to play the role of kindly sister-in-law and aunt, while Anna comes through as more of a 'yummy-mummy' than the blue stocking we are familiar with. Sadly, this did not last long, as Jessie died suddenly at the age of 47.

Jessie's life was unremarkable and it might be asked whether it is worth our while spending time on it. But, as I said in the Introduction, this book is like a picture gallery and Jessie is a good example of one kind of Victorian woman. She did not have to go to the mill or work as a seamstress. Not clever enough to carve out an individual career for herself, the fairly easy family circumstances meant she was not obliged to become a teacher or a governess. Her way of life may appear banal to us, but there is some evidence to suggest that she did not totally submit to a life of devotion to others. At the time of the 'awakening' she seems to have deliberately malingered in Ballater when she should have been awakened in Perth. One of her friends wrote her long, prosy, religious letters which tried her patience. Latterly, her irritability caused anxiety in the family and may have been related to frustration at her lot.

Jessie had bad luck as her fiancé died so young (she would have been 20 at the time) and the family friend walked away. We can understand why she never married but stayed at home, perhaps finding in her care for her clever young brother and – later – for her ageing mother some of the happiness denied her by her unsatisfactory suitors.

Walter Stephen

CHAPTER THREE

'Three little girls with a school are we...'

The Geddes Sisters, Jane, Margaret and Charlotte

THIS CHAPTER SHOULD be thought of as something like a piece of tapestry or a wall hanging. Only one of the women represented had a close relationship – or even any relationship – with Geddes, but the weaving together of three narrative strands gives a good representation of the kind of society in which Anna Morton and Patrick Geddes were to flourish.

The first strand begins with John Geddes, a farmer's son in the parish of Glass in Aberdeenshire. Glass was blessed with an excellent village dominie.

> It is a fact that the Parish School of Glass at that time became famed as one of the very best seminaries of education to be found in any of our country parishes, and the number of young men from Glass, who in these days obtained bursaries at Aberdeen, was altogether without a parallel in any of our upland parishes in the north, eclipsing even many populous places where educational institutions were of a more pretentious kind.

John Geddes had aspirations and became a bookseller in Huntly. However, his father died, John returned to farming and made a success of that, without having his ambitions satisfied. His eldest son became Professor Sir William Geddes, Principal of Aberdeen University. Another son became a judge in Bengal, where he died. Alexander (later of Blairmore, the local estate he bought from the Earl of Fife) went to the United States, where he established himself as the 'Corn King' before returning to London where he set himself up as a gentleman in the West End. Two of Alexander's sons were killed in World War 1. We shall meet Captain John Geddes of the 16 Canadian Infantry and 7/9 Cameron Highlanders as Strand no 2 unravels.

John Geddes also had three daughters – Miss Jane Geddes (1835–1922), Miss Margaret Geddes (1837–73) and Miss Charlotte Geddes (1845–1919). The Geddes sisters were 'all given a really good education' by Arthur Stephen of the parish school. In a few years they:

... have been enabled to amass a fortune from their educational establishment at Dresden; and ... have left the seminary in such a condition
that their successors may soon realise a comfortable competence for life.

Margaret, the second sister, died in Dresden and was buried there.
Charlotte became the second wife of James Reid of Auchterarder House,
who predeceased her. She died in 1919 in Galashiels, bequeathing to the
parish church of Glass a set of communion plate and a fund for the relief
of the parish poor. She and Jane were buried in Montrose.

In the 1870s the German Empire had just been formed, so that Saxony
had ceased to be a separate state. The revolutionary activities of 1848
were long over yet Dresden was still the city of Weber and Wagner and
retained all the trappings of one of the richest capitals of Europe.

Dresdeners of all classes thought they lived in one of the most beautiful,
cultured and well-administered cities in... Europe... in a... seemingly
unchanging backdrop of time-honoured beauty combined with judicious
modernity.

This they were happy to share with foreign residents and tourists – and
there were 4,000 or more British and American residents.

Despite the terrible night of 13 February 1945 there are still extensive
records in various Dresden institutions. Unfortunately no trace of 'The
Misses Geddes' Dresden Establishment' or anything like it could be found.
However, a very informative entry was found in an 1870s contemporary
street directory. To be found in 21 Walpurgis Strasse were:

Geddes Margaret, Rentière

Geddes, Jane, Rentière

Maczyneta, Gräfin

What are we to make of this? Not three Miss Geddeses, but two. And
living with an exotic-sounding (Polish?) countess on three vast floors. The
sisters – one perhaps dominant and outgoing, the other quiet but hard-
working – no doubt had invested their capital in what had become their
home and had registered it accordingly. The countess was probably down
on her luck and had become, in effect, a paying guest. Her presence would
have lent some lustre to the establishment – if there was an establishment
– and she would have been an excellent mentor on the niceties of polite
behaviour.

Under 'Walpurgis Strasse', numbers 9 to 11 were still under construc-
tion, showing that the street as a whole was brand-new, between the Old
Town and the suburban *Grosser Garten* with its Zoological Garden. No
21, like all the other houses, was a big six-decker block of flats (basement,

Parterre and four more floors). What we would call the rateable value is given. From this we can tell that No 21 was the second-largest, second-best in the street – perhaps the best since No 17 was slightly bigger but had many more occupants listed.

If the Geddes sisters were to promenade in the *Grosser Garten*, whom were they likely to meet on the way? Many of the residents would have been listed in the Census of Scotland as 'Living on Private Means' or 'Annuitant'. There were some military gentlemen, a Lieutenant-General, a Major-General and several Majors. Ward was Consul-General, probably British or American. A Baron lived in No 5 and a Baroness (unrelated) in No 13. Senior officials abounded – Police Registrar, Accident Inspector, Advocates, Notaries, Bankers, Financiers and the like. There were a few doctors, a dentist, a dietitian, and an architect.

Trade was well represented, detailed entries indicating that Walpurgis Strasse was the place of residence and that the business was carried on in the Old Town. Presumably most of these tradesmen – merchants and masters – had lived 'over the shop' but had now risen to prosperity and the suburbs. A sprinkling of quite lowly occupations seemed to have located themselves on the top floors. These included a postman, a city policeman, a gardener, a lithographer, a corset-finisher, two house-painters, a seamstress and a glove-maker. This is reminiscent of the social stratification of the tenements in the Old Town of Edinburgh. In Walpurgis Strasse there lived 15 'vons', three on the ground floor, five on the first floor, six on the second, one on the third. No aristocrat lived in a basement or on the fourth floor.

What of the Dresden a finishing school would benefit from? There were teachers galore, of all sorts; a PhD in the Gymnasium, another teaching maths, language teachers, male and female. Hugo Zegler Jnr was a journalist and language teacher, his wife a pianoforte teacher. On the third floor of No 8 lived an actor. On the top floor of No 1 was an instrument maker and singer (one person). Herr Mansfeldt, music director, shared the ground floor of No 14 with a major and a merchant.

No 21 itself shows the social stratification we have just noted. In the basement was Herr Rollbed, living on private means (we can be sure his name would raise a giggle from the girls). On the ground floor were a merchant, an optician and a dealer in ribbons and fine goods. On the fourth floor were a master tailor for men, another (unrelated) master tailor and an office worker.

That leaves the first, second and third floors. Nowhere else in the street is more than one flat used by one occupant. Yet, according to the directory, three floors were occupied by three ladies. The catalogue of Patrick Geddes's Cities and Town Planning Exhibition held in Dublin in 1911 had a section called 'Great Germanic Cities', one of them being Dresden. The Town Plans of Dresden showed that the city had been in steady development for 30 years. The zones of the city were shown in different colours and reflected the controlling Building Order, e.g. factories allowed, provided the chimneys do not exceed a certain height.

There is nothing in the catalogue to suggest that Geddes had ever been in Dresden or had talked informally about the city.

It is likely that the premises in Walpurgis Strasse could not be used for a school, but would serve as a kind of hostel from which the girls would sally forth during the day.

Now for the second strand, for which the starting point is Londonderry in Northern Ireland where, just after the Second World War, there were 46 shirt factories. Arthur Hogg was the last director and manager of Hogg and Mitchell, which had been founded by his grandfather David Cleghorn Hogg, a Borderer from near Galashiels. David Hogg married Jane (Jenny) Cooke from Ramelton, Co Donegal. Arthur Hogg was kind enough to allow me to see (and copy) a letter written to his grandmother in 1872 by one Agnes Tillie.

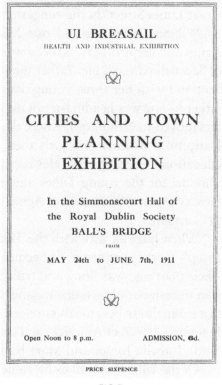

FIG.5
Cities and Town Planning Exhibition Catalogue, Dublin 1911.
Sir Patrick Geddes Memorial Trust

Agnes Tillie was the eldest child of William Tillie (1823–1904), of Tillie and Henderson, whose huge shirt factory, with a workforce of 4,500 and the largest in the world until it was demolished in 2005, dominated the Craigavon Bridge over the Foyle at Londonderry.

Tillie, born in Crookston (Midlothian), a few miles from Hogg's birthplace, was a farmer's son who learned the textile business in Glasgow before moving to Londonderry in 1851. In 1852 he was the first manufacturer to introduce the sewing machine into industrial processing, ensuring half a century of rapid growth and another half-century of edgy prosperity. He was a major figure in First Derry Presbyterian Church and had many philanthropic outlets. Of his many public offices the most notable was His Majesty's Lieutenant for the City of Londonderry. A final accolade – Karl Marx cited the good practices at the Foyle Factory in *Das Kapital*.

Agnes, his wife, also involved herself in charitable enterprises, chief of which was her interest in providing nursing for the 'working classes'. As Vice-President and founding member of the Londonderry District Nursing Society she personally financed a fully equipped District Nurses' Home in Great James Street (in the congested industrial area of the city).

William Tillie engaged one Miss Isabella Sloane as governess for Agnes and her brothers. Isabella was born in 1840, in Hobart, Tasmania, of Scottish parents. Her father died in 1848 and her mother returned to Scotland with her three young daughters, initially to Peebles where her father-in-law was headmaster of the grammar school. Mother and daughters moved to Edinburgh, where the girls attended the Edinburgh Ladies Institution. Mother and girls then went to Germany, where the girls' education was completed. Her background clearly established Isabella as a model for the young Tillies and a force for good. Her example must have convinced William and Agnes Tillie of the value of finishing school in Germany.

When Isabella was with the Tillies in Londonderry she met a young Joseph Corkey, minister of Second Glendermott Presbyterian Church. Their marriage was 'long and fruitful'. The eight sons became Presbyterian ministers in Northern Ireland, Scotland and the United States. The three daughters became missionaries, two in Egypt (for the United Presbyterian Church of America) and one in India (under the Church of Scotland). Isabella Junior and Mary both married ministers.

Of the Tillie family of eight, Agnes (the eldest) and the second daughter both married clergymen. The eldest son, William J Tillie, managed the Glasgow branch of the family firm, although often in poor health, until taking over at Londonderry from 1915 to 1928. Agnes's twin brothers, Alexander and Marshall, were educated at the Academical Institution, Londonderry (probably as day boys). This, while they were at school, became Foyle College – the Londonderry public school of which their father was a Governor. Alexander went on to the Park School, Glasgow, Glasgow University 'and abroad' before setting up a linen-manufacturing firm in Belfast. He settled permanently in London, establishing another branch there and accumulating senior positions in the City.

Marshall attended the International College in Passy, Paris for a year, before taking his place in the family firm. After his father's death he took over the management of Foyle Factory and added the Abercorn Factory with a further 1,200 workers. Like his father, he accumulated a string of public offices. At his death, he was, as his father had been, Lieutenant for the City.

So here is Agnes Tillie's letter of 3 February 1872, written from Miss Geddes, 21 Walpurgis Strasse, Dresden.

My dearest Jenny,

It is now more than a fortnight since I learned of your engagement to my cousin and yet this is the first day I have found time to write you a note of congratulation. But my good wishes are none the less hearty for being thus delayed, and I am very glad indeed that your future life will probably be in Derry so that we shall see one another much oftener than we have generally been able to do since we were at school together.

I know how happy you must be feeling just now, if your experience is like mine of this time last year, and I can fancy how the happiness will, in your case also, settle down after the first excitement has passed into a most perfect contentment and satisfaction. And I am sure it will be so with you, dear Jenny, for I remember how you used to say 'one must love a man very much before she would marry him'. But what has become of all your fine speeches about being an old maid and all that. Aha! Miss Jenny, didn't I tell you? And you used to shake your head so gravely too, and look so wise whenever I assured you that your turn would come next and very soon too.

I shall be going home in three months more, and the time has gone so quickly since I came that I can hardly believe it is five months since. Heavens. I have been very fortunate in finding such a pleasant and I hope profitable home among strangers. I can speak German now better than French but not yet read it so well, and I have very good music and singing lessons. There are a good many of us here, almost 40 including one or two day-boarders. Most of my schoolfellows are Scotch, a few English, but we are obliged to speak French and German in alternate months and English only on Sundays. Miss Geddes takes us to a great many delightful concerts, and occasionally to the opera and theatre, which I enjoy immensely.

Of course I am very busy. You know well enough what a boarding school life is, how monotonous, how full of work, how every week looks like another, and how they fly past. We had a pleasant time of rest and change for a week at Christmas, and Easter is coming soon, to bring the summer again, and then when the year is at its brightest and bonniest, in the sweet May-time, I am going home.

Mama did not mention if there was any time fixed for the consummation of your engagement but I hope it will not be long postponed. Meantime, accept my most earnest wishes for your future happiness and

Believe me as ever,

Your loving friend, Agnes M Tillie

Written three years before the residence of Anna Morton, the third strand, Agnes Tillie's letter gives at least an inkling of what nice girls there were and what Dresden had to offer as preparation for a full life. Unfortunately, since both Jenny and she had had experience of life at boarding school she didn't feel the need to give a full picture of life at the Geddes establishment. But she gave her the size of the place – almost 40 students – with one or two day-pupils but mostly boarders. Of them, most were from Scotland; the few English (and Irish) probably had Scottish connections. The curriculum was a liberal one, with specialisation in music and the modern languages of French and German. Social education was built round concerts and the theatre.

The two strands began to interweave when the niece of Agnes Tillie, the daughter of Marshall Tillie, met John Geddes, the nephew of the three Geddes sisters, in the Geddes London home, and subsequently married him.

The third strand is Anna Morton, whose background shared some similarities with Agnes Tillie's and whose experiences were also likely to match hers. We think of the prosperous Victorian as a stern paterfamilias, ruling his dull conformist household with a rod of iron. Yet both sets of parents sought improvement, social and intellectual, for their children and were happy to release them – in suitably controlled circumstances.

It would have been satisfying to be able to establish a connection between the future Mrs Patrick Geddes and Miss Geddes of Walpurgis Strasse, but 'Geddes' is a common enough name in Scotland – for example, the Edinburgh telephone directory has about 100 Geddeses – and many Scottish women in the 19th century managed schools, hospitals, lunatic asylums and the like – in many countries.

It would have been even more satisfying to establish that Anna had attended Miss Geddes's establishment and to have discovered more detail about the life and curriculum there.

However, although Anna Morton was in Dresden three years after Agnes Tillie, the finishing schools were limited in number and would have shared the same kinds of activity, perhaps even the same teachers – of music, for example. So Anna would have known of the Geddes establishment by repute and might even have met some of the girls from there. Her prosperous father's Ulster Scots textile background certainly matched Agnes Tillie's. Anna had her full share of moral earnestness, which Agnes also had. She emerges from the page as a thoroughly nice girl. It comes as no surprise to learn that she later married the minister of First Derry Presbyterian Church, as hinted at in her letter.

Anna emerged from her 'gap year' capable of supporting herself as a teacher of music and with a social conscience. It is hardly possible for us to say to what extent Dresden was to feature in the home life of the Geddes family. Certainly the home was filled with music. Anna led and all the children played. Did Anna ever reminisce about her student days in 'Florence on the Elbe?'

As we shall see in Chapter VI Anna became involved in the Oliphants' 'Secular Positivist' debating group meetings on social problems, where she met Geddes. They became engaged and then married in her parents' home in Egremont, Liverpool.

With the intertwining of the Geddes sisters, the Londonderry connection and Anna Morton emerges a generalised picture of the nature of the society with which Patrick Geddes was to engage. Here were no frivolous 'huntin', shootin' and fishin' 'aristocrats in their great estates but serious and successful entrepreneurs accustomed to coming and going in the wider world, yet with a social conscience and the means to do something about it.

One fact sticks out from this background. When Anna Geddes first heard the name 'Patrick Geddes', or was first introduced to him, perhaps at her sister's home, it would not have been a name completely out of the blue. It would have had resonances associated with the Misses Geddes of Dresden, with their establishment, with the city itself and with the kind of girl who went there – 'one of our sort', but in the nicest possible way.

Patrick and Anna were off to a good start.

Walter Stephen

CHAPTER FOUR

PG'S First Garden

Mrs Helen Nutt

THE GRANGE IN EDINBURGH is a rather special district of broad streets, large Victorian villas with big gardens and fairly recent infill of enclosed quality residential blocks. A grange was a kind of out-station of a religious house, with a farm and granaries subject to an easier discipline than in the mother house. Edinburgh's Grange was the grange of St Giles. After the Reformation the Grange was acquired by William Dick, who built a tower house on the land in 1618. In the 19th century Sir Thomas Dick Lauder, an interesting, if minor, character of his time, transformed the old Grange House and began the process of feuing out the estate as a high-status suburb, which began in earnest in 1864. In terms of urban development it is worth noting that, without actually looking for them, one could pick out at least four private schools within a few yards of Grange House while, in a fully built up area measuring 3km by 2, it was not found necessary to build a Board school.

Sir Thomas Dick Lauder, 7th Baronet of Fountainhall (1784–1848) was a good all-rounder who

> could make his way in the world as a player, or a ballad singer, or a street fiddler, or a geologist. Or a civil engineer, or a surveyor, as easily and eminently as an artist or a layer out of ground.

After military service he became Secretary to three important national bodies, the Board of Manufactures and Fisheries in Scotland, the Board of British White Fishery and the Royal Institution for the Encouragement of the Fine Arts. He was active in organising public support for the 1832 Reform Bill. He wrote novels and travel books and was asked by Queen Victoria to write the official history of her 1843 Royal Progress in Scotland. If he is remembered today it is subliminally in one of Edinburgh's finer Victorian suburbs. Thus we have Grange Road, Court, Loan and Terrace, Fountainhall Road, Relugas Road, Dalrymple Crescent, Dick Place, Lauder Road, Cumin Place, Seton Place, Findhorn Place, commemorating family members or properties.

Dick Lauder's *An Account of the Great Floods in Morayshire in 1829 in the Province of Moray and adjoining Districts* was published in 1830, a truly remarkable achievement. Torrential rain and the fact that so much farmland had been 'improved', resulting in a swift run-off, combined to give rise to spectacular flooding in North-east Scotland. Dick Lauder showed great enterprise and energy in following up the flood, interviewing witnesses and inspecting damage.

It is not surprising that such an inquisitive soul should be the first to investigate the origin of the famous Parallel Roads of Glen Roy, which he did in 1818, in a paper to the Royal Society of Edinburgh (*The Parallel Roads of Glenroy*). His main qualification for investigating the Parallel Roads was a love of country and a quick, lively mind.

By the 1880s the Dick Lauders found that the 40 windowed rooms of Grange House were more than they could cope with and the house was rented out as Grange House Boarding School. The Principal was Mrs Helen Nutt (37), who had a daughter, Emma (7), a scholar. Whaley B Nutt (45), Helen's husband, was a Teacher of Vocal Physiology and Elocution who would probably have had a hand in the girls' correct upbringing.

Resident on Census night 1881 were three teachers, two of English and Music and one of French and German, 11 servants and a visitor. This infrastructure of 18 persons supported 32 boarders. Fifty persons in 40 windowed rooms represent a degree of overcrowding unacceptable even at that time – but on the other hand many of the rooms would have been quite large. But again, the biggest rooms would be class – and other public rooms unsuitable for living or teaching in. A woodcut in Grant's *Old and New Edinburgh* shows the Drawing-Room in Grange House, 1882 with a lofty decorated ceiling, walls smothered in paintings and floor space cluttered with an archipelago of tables, chairs, pouffes and pot plants.

Into this worthy institution came, in 1883, Patrick Geddes, who proceeded to construct 'a small Type Botanic Garden' and then give a paper on it to the Botanical Society of Edinburgh on 14 June 1883.

There are various kinds of garden – formal, informal, vegetable, of one colour like the white garden at Sissinghurst. Geddes's first garden was uncompromisingly systematic, an order garden – known thus because the plants are arranged according to their Orders in the Plant Kingdom.

He took an existing rose garden measuring 100 by 40 feet, cleared it, leaving the gravel and turf walks and planted it up systematically. Starting with the Ranunculaceae in the bottom right and using the 11th edition of the *London Catalogue of British Plants* it is possible to trace a 'trail' which follows the printed order on the ground, more or less directly, through the Malvaceae, via Geraniaceae, Compositae, Primulaceae and many others to the top right corner. There the Dicotyledons are left and

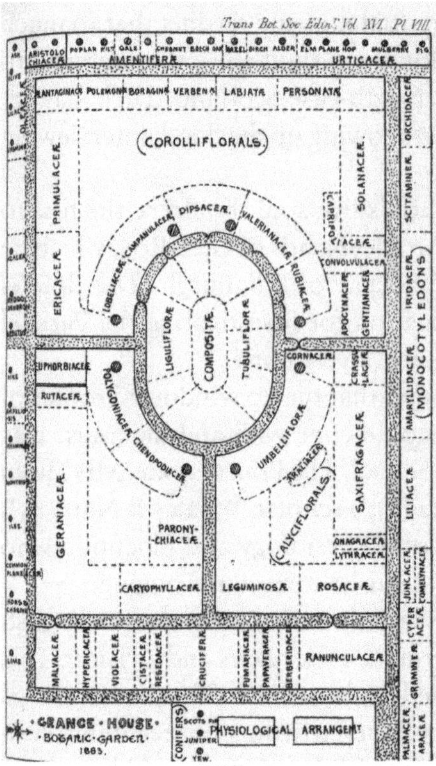

Trans. Bot. Soc. Edin." Vol. XVI. Pl. VIII

FIG.6
Grange House Botanic Garden, 1883.
National Library of Scotland

the trail follows the Monocotyledons (Irises, Lilies etc) to end with the Juncaceae, close to where it started.

Geddes then goes on to enumerate the advantages of such a small type garden of this kind. It 'exhibits at the glance the general relationships and divisions of the vegetable kingdom'. Its compactness means 'that even any village school may have its garden'. In towns 'dreary wastes of evergreens or blank spaces' could become useful, beautiful and scientific gardens. 'The expense of laying out such a garden is only a few pounds'.

Educationally, through a garden 'an intelligent interest in nature' may be aroused, the powers of observation be awakened and disciplined, as well as the 'reasoning faculties'.

Drawing, painting, and designing become delightful by its aid… manipulative dexterity… is thus rapidly and easily acquired… the other sciences… become more interesting and intelligible… neither Wordsworth nor Virgil would ever lose a reader who had learned to know asphodels and celandine, and watch the bees come and go in the school botanic garden.

In 1885 HM Inspectors of Schools would not report a Board school as first-rate without a museum and Geddes suggested how '… easy and reasonable it would be also to recommend the possession of a garden'.

Finally, Geddes assures us that careful experiments with university students and school children show that the latter '… studied with most ease, most enjoyment, and best educational result'.

These arguments were to be used in many forms and many contexts for the rest of Geddes's life.

Geddes's paper raises many questions. How did Geddes meet the Nutts and win them over to his proposal? His garden plan is a miracle of design, putting together dozens of plots in varying sizes in a precise order.

Did he sit down with a large sheet of paper, a pencil and a ruler and work it all out? Did he evolve his own classification or borrow an existing one? (He thanked 'very particularly... Mr Lindsay, curator of the Royal Botanic Garden, for his kind counsel and material aid'). Did he copy the layout of existing gardens and, if so, which? How was the garden used? Were its aims fulfilled?

Here we are on very shaky ground. Grange House, as a school, was still in business in 1891, when the *Edinburgh and Leith Post Office Directory* lists the school as under the direction of Mrs Whaley B Knut (spelling!). In 1892 Whaley B Nutt, teacher of vocal physiology and elocutionist, and Mrs Whaley B Nutt were still in business but by 1895 Mrs Whaley B Nutt was running a Boarding School for Young Ladies under her own name at Currielea, Colinton Road. Grange House went into decay and was demolished. The grounds were built over in two phases. In the first years of the 20th century respectable terrace blocks were built along Grange Loan. Behind these, post-World War II, a new street was laid out – Grange Crescent – and the land filled in with bungalows and modest villas.

Nutt is not a common surname – in Scotland, at any rate. But in the Strathclyde Geddes papers the name bobs up three times. Under 'Sociology and Health' there is correspondence with Alfred Nutt relating to the Medical Pathological Club, medical education and National Health Society Lectures. An undated pamphlet on *Embryology and Hygiene* appealed for support for a proposal to train woman lecturers in that subject. It was probably produced under the auspices of the Women's International Congress and had three signatories: Mrs Alfred Nutt, Professor Patrick Geddes and Professor AC Haddon. Geddes corresponded with one W Nutt anent the Paris Exposition of 1900.

Everyone must start somewhere. In 1883 Geddes was a Demonstrator in Botany at the University of Edinburgh, teaching, researching, writing papers, eager to get on. But at Grange House he showed that his interests were more than narrowly academic. He wanted to get students away from the microscope and into the open air. For Geddes a garden was initially a place for systematic learning, but it was to develop into something aesthetic, to be planned into every urban development, and be a non-controversial instrument for social change.

Walter Stephen

Chronology

1864   Development of Grange estate
1881   Census returns for Grange House Boarding School
1883   PG developed Order Garden for Grange House Boarding School and reads paper to Royal Botanical Society of Edinburgh
1892   Mr and Mrs Nutt still in business at Grange House
1895   Mrs Whaley B Nutt now running Boarding School for Young Ladies at Currielea, Colinton Road.

Bibliography

Census of Scotland 1881, Edinburgh and Leith Post Office Directory

Patrick Geddes, FRSE, *A Type Botanic Garden* (in *Transactions of the Botanical Society of Edinburgh*, Vol XVI, 1883)

James Grant, *Cassell's Old and New Edinburgh, vol 3* (London, Paris and New York, no date)

Sir Thomas Dick Lauder, *An Account of the Great Floods in Morayshire in 1829 in the Province of Moray and adjoining Districts* (Edinburgh, 1830)

CHAPTER FIVE

Wife and Pillar of Strength

Anna Morton (Geddes) (1857–1917)

AS THE WIFE of Patrick Geddes, Anna Geddes has rightly received a great deal of attention and admiration. Anna Morton (1857–1917) became Patrick Geddes's wife in 1886 and was to become the mother of their three children. She shared many of his ventures and some of his enthusiasms. Through his long absences and frequent changes of residence she kept the family together and its father on course. Geddes was frequently on the edge of bankruptcy and Anna was the rock on which he was able to build his creative life.

We know, not least from PG himself, what were the early influences on Geddes's life and thought. A main source for Anna Morton's background was Philip Mairet, who made it clear in his introduction that Arthur and Norah Geddes, Anna and Patrick's surviving children, had complete confidence in Mairet as a biographer and had freely placed in his hands personal papers and family letters, giving him real freedom of selection and final judgment.

Arthur Geddes, 40 years after his mother's death, wrote:

Patrick and Anna, man and wife, achieved and maintained success through all their adventures together and apart. Without Anna, without the intimate relationship they made together, Patrick's flashes of discovery might have lacked the fire which sustained thought and civic action. Without her he could not have dwelt so continuously nor with such understanding in the sick core of the Old Town. A great-hearted man with many faults, he could not have attained his moral stature without her ardour of love, faith, and clear-eyed critique. She too felt herself fortunate, in spite of the difficulties of sharing so nomadic a life, so many anxieties and risks. Anxious friends frequently condemned the risks; but the decisions were shared. And Anna, as musician, kept ready to resume teaching if need be, as her valued friend Marjory Kennedy-Fraser had done when left a widow. She knew that, should the worst befall, she could face the future. Her children knew only that she played and sang for her own sake and theirs and because she loved it.

Amelia Defries, while Geddes was still alive, wrote of the *Exposition Internationale* at Ghent in 1913. PG arrived late, but fortunately:

His wife came with him, the calm grey-haired lady who could bring order out of chaos. Even more valuable… was her power of intercession, her ability to tone down Pat's cerebral high-voltage when some bewildered soul was in danger of electrocution.

As Miss Defries said:

> Mrs Geddes found time, while sorting books and jotting down notes, to enquire as to my health and living arrangements; and a few days later she had me in much better rooms, working shorter hours and living more normally than during the last three months.

Clearly this was a marriage of true minds and they continued to write each other love letters for all of their married lives. Yet there is a suggestion that they were so close and so busy that the efficient organisation of the children left little space for 'over-flowing mother-love', as Arthur phrased it, or, as Paddy Kitchen suggests, the constant need for discipline quelled spontaneity and the expression of personal instincts. Anna had 'her full share of moral earnestness'.

> Both were moved by the new spirit of social service and both had a streak of puritan severity in their idealism. Their rejection of the religious ideas of their parents did not incline them to laxity in self-discipline; it made them rather less tolerant of self-indulgence, sometimes in others as well as in themselves.

Thus says Philip Mairet.

Even Alasdair, loyal, courageous, trustworthy Alasdair. could say: 'no human being could live as well as work with PG and survive'. Yet Anna survived for over 30 years of marriage and, at the end, Geddes felt he had to use subterfuge to conceal Alasdair's death from her, to spare her one last blow. When PG's own parents died, it was Anna who was with them and carried out the formalities of registration.

When she married, Anna was 28, rather old for a Victorian bride, and quite a blue-stocking. How did she get to this point? Frazer Morton, an Ulster Scot, was a prosperous textile merchant in Liverpool and a strict Presbyterian. He had strong opinions, not least on the conduct of young ladies. Even jumping or climbing were taboo and only the mother's relatively easy attitude softened the home atmosphere. Yet Morton had a hidden weakness: he learned – in secret – how to play the violin, so that music became the one indulgence permitted in his family. We are told that Anna was a highly educated young lady of great intelligence, not beautiful but with great personal charm. Her school was known for its polite learning, with its 'Italian and the use of the globes'.

At 18 she studied music for a year at Dresden, where, heavily fathered but liberally educated, she became the first of her family to go through the painful experience of having to break away from the church of her parents. We can see the Misses Geddes's Dresden establishment as a 'finishing school' concerned with appearances only, but Anna emerged from her 'gap year' capable of supporting herself as a teacher of music.

After Dresden she took up music teaching and set up her own girls' club near the family home in Liverpool. The desire to render social service led her into contact with Octavia Hill, Josephine Butler and others, although no opportunity arose for her to work with them in London. She was involved in the incipient movement for the emancipation of women. In 1882 she spent the summer with her brother in Odessa and on her return home began paying visits in winter to her sister in Edinburgh.

Anna's younger sister, Edith, had married a James Oliphant, headmaster of the Charlotte Square (Edinburgh) Institution for the Education of Girls and a friend of Geddes. Another sister, Rebecca, married Peter Dott, an art dealer, and settled in Colinton, then a picturesque village outside the town. On a visit from Liverpool Anna attended some of the Oliphants' 'Secular Positivist' debating group meetings on social problems and later wrote to Geddes. PG, Oliphant and the Morton sisters were founder members of the 'Environmental Society' in 1884. A correspondence developed in 1885 until, on a Sunday early in 1886, Geddes proposed to Anna in the Royal Botanic Garden.

With typically planned spontaneity Geddes, although the garden was closed to the public – it being the Sabbath – had access. Anna was invited to meet him there. The setting was calm and peaceful. Geddes happened to have with him a piece of opal he had brought back from Mexico. He must have had in another pocket a geologist's hammer, with which he split the opal. Just as the Highland soldier and his lass split a silver bawbee as a token of their love, so half the opal was given to Anna and half kept by Patrick (PLATE 1B). (The two parts of the opal have been reunited and are to be found on the mantelpiece of Claire Geddes, the couple's granddaughter.)

Anna and Patrick were married in her parents' home in Egremont, Liverpool on 17 April 1886. Their first six married months were spent in Geddes's Princes Street flat, then they moved to James Court, off the Lawnmarket in the Old Town of Edinburgh. This was the first of many moves, almost beyond the wit of man to chart, of which some account is given in the chapter on Norah Geddes. In respect of James Court Geddes said:

It is good to renew sympathy with one's fellows in their poverty once more; we have been too long away from the Lawnmarket and tend to forget; at least I do.

For Anna, however, there were few opportunities for escape from the demoralising grind of living amongst the poor.

In brief, after five years the first part of Ramsay Garden was finished and a fine flat was available for the growing family there. But the family could not afford to keep it up, so it was rented out to a senior officer from the adjacent Castle. The Geddes family only lived there in August during the Summer Meetings, when the Outlook Tower was the administrative centre and the Geddes flat the social centre and Anna's music came into its own. In the summer term Geddes was committed to Dundee and a house across the Tay at Newport was usually taken. Latterly, part of the

FIG.7
Anna Morton (Mrs Patrick Geddes) with Norah and Alasdair.
Philip Mairet, The Life and Letters of Patrick Geddes

winter would be spent in London (Hyde Park Mansions) and, from 1910, Crosby Hall (a 1470 house, the home of Sir Thomas More, which had been dismantled and which Geddes determined should be rebuilt by him.)

As well as his teaching, examining and writing, Geddes was an extremely active (if occasionally obscure) lecturer, partly to advance his career, partly to enhance his income and partly to finance his projects. For example, in connection with Crosby Hall, Geddes 'gave fund-raising lectures all over the country on the necessity of respecting the past in order to prepare for the future.'

1900 was a stimulating year, with eight removals in ten months. In April the family moved to Paris to prepare for the great Paris Exhibition at the Grand Palais and Petit Palais. Anna was in the thick of it, organising and networking while *enceinte*. Norah and Alasdair, aged respectively 13 and nine, had a French governess but seem to have been allowed a great deal of freedom as well as being given responsibilities. They were 'privileged to help with the clerical organisation' of their father's International Assembly, preparing folders and distributing them by post 'or otherwise'. They also delivered notes, letters and invitations in a hurry.

One day they were sent out by their father to find a *fiacre* and find a nurse to attend to Anna and, later, were sent out for the day while Anna suffered a miscarriage.

Amelia Defries paints a picture of Anna as the calm centre of the storm. Around her was the turmoil of frequent change of residence, of keeping up with the frequent enthusiasms of her husband, of fulfilling the various roles expected of her – wife, mother, moral arbiter, home teacher, secretary, hostess, housekeeper. To these must be added anxiety about money – and for good reason.

The Geddes family life was by no means extravagant. Simplicity, even frugality, was the order of the day for food, drink and clothing. We have

FIG.8
Patrick Geddes c.1898.
Philip Mairet, The Life and Letters of Patrick Geddes

seen how Jeannie Geddes and Anna struck up a friendship. Anna, Patrick and Norah occasionally visited Mount Tabor, where Alexander and Anna became quite close. It was Anna who cared for Alexander in his last days and it was Anna who was responsible for registering his death and feeding the local press with material for the obituaries – and for perpetrating the myth of 'Captain Geddes'. In *Who's Who* of 1930 Captain Geddes pops up again – but it would have been Patrick Geddes who provided the material for the entry. Hopefully for the last time I repeat that Alexander was never a Captain. In the Army records the printed word 'Captain' is scored out and 'Quartermaster' substituted. A household bill addressed to 'Captain Geddes' has the Captain scored out and 'Lieutenant' substituted – by Alexander himself.

One wonders why the Geddes family chose to represent Alexander as being what he was not. Could it have been simple ignorance of the niceties of the military world? Could it have been snobbery? Yet Alexander had had the distinction of having been headhunted for special duties for the sovereign – and been rewarded for them.

Geddes famously said 'I can't and won't keep accounts' and the impression we often get is of financial chaos, permanent cash-flow problems and the ceaseless pursuit of sponsors and good managers. But he worked to the manager's satisfaction in the bank in Perth and must have been perfectly able to balance the books on paper. Rather he just could not be bothered with, or did not have time for, the trivia of bookkeeping. His later life saw him wheeling and dealing with consummate ease while Paddy Kitchen suggests that he had that kind of facility with money which comes from a low regard for its importance and reminds us that economics was one of the subjects he wrote about.

In Alexander Geddes's *Particulars of Income for the year ending 31st March 1898* there is an item: 'Bonds, Patrick Geddes, Edinburgh – £28', indicating a loan from PG's father of, perhaps, £500. When Alexander died Mount Tabor Cottage was left to his sons, Robert, John and Patrick. The brothers gave the cottage to Anna, 'in recognition of her affection and care of our late father in his old age'. In the *Notes for Executors* relating to PG's Will of 1 April 1916 Mount Tabor Cottage is still subject to a bond for £450.

PG was in serious difficulties with Ramsay Garden around 1893–4. He was saved by a legacy of £2,000 from Anna's father's death. (Boardman says £1,500). Geddes persuaded the first occupiers to buy their properties in advance. The Oliphants rallied round the Geddeses. In 1895 James, husband of Anna's sister Edith, was living in 11 Ramsay Garden, while John C, his younger brother and a teacher in his school, was at 14 Ramsay Garden.

> One overly cautious lady, however, refused to pay until she saw her quarters actually completed and this annoyed Geddes so much that he bought what was to have been her flat himself. He could then make her pay rent as a penalty for lack of confidence, but only by tying up capital he did not have. Later, he would confess to Norah that this was the beginning of the money troubles which periodically beset him and his family. Indeed, the building of Ramsay Garden inadvertently caused Anna much emotional stress even before the financial worries came along.

Anna was not so foolish as to gift the legacy to PG. There was a loan which, one presumes, was cleared off when the Town and Gown Association bought Geddes out.

For Professor Morris the real disaster for Geddes was his 'garden village' at Roseburn, which rated several pages of self-justification in his *Notes for Executors*. The Outlook Tower – 'the world's first sociological laboratory' and Geddes's pride and joy – cost £400 annually to run and drew in £122.

'Don't thee marry for brass, but marry where brass is' was the old

Yorkshireman's advice. Anna's background was comfortable, based on the successful Liverpool family business. But on Frazer Morton's death Anna's brother 'gambled and endangered' the family business. Another brother, Frazer:

> ... though interested in study not in business, took it up when it was ruined, and learnt his trade so well that he could e.g. tell the quality of pork by smelling the point of his penknife after sticking it in. He was perceptive and of delicate senses.[1]

More emotional stress for Anna.

Anyone who knows anything about Geddes becomes conscious early on of his constant need for cash. Not for outward show or the classic road to ruin – 'fast women and slow horses'. There was always a good cause or 'another of my as yet disastrous yet not ill-conceived endeavours' to be supported. One sometimes feels embarrassed at reading what looks very like a begging letter to this one or that.

In the *Notes for Executors* PG acknowledges that he owes Victor Branford ('old and peculiarly esteemed and valued friend and colleague'):

> ... certain sums viz several advances, at crises of difficulty, each of £50.
> Of this something has been repaid; but the bulk remains.

Martin White of Balruddery was PG's longest and biggest patron (and creditor) and Geddes takes more than a page to thank him for his generosity and tolerance. He seems to recognise that he will never be able to clear his debt and asks his executors to meet the sums due 'as fully as funds allow' and to 'place themselves unreservedly in his hands'.

Clearly Geddes was walking a financial tightrope, but he was not indulging in any behaviour unusual at that time. His intentions were honest, but he lacked the strength of character needed to cut out the interesting developments and to concentrate on tight management. Yet in all this one of his most attractive characteristics was his optimism, his rueful acceptance that things had gone wrong, but that things would still turn out right.

Looking ahead, Geddes grew no more cautious as he grew older. In 1926 the governmental war damage agency awarded Geddes £2,054 as compensation for the loss of the Cities Exhibition at sea in 1914. As Boardman says:

> The kindly disposed reader will immediately wonder into which of his deficit undertakings this money was placed: the struggling Tower in

Edinburgh, the cataloguing of its precious contents, or the repayment of overdrafts; or perhaps another college to be founded on more acres of dry heath, with the blasting out of more rocks to create more deficit vegetable gardens. But PG did none of these things with this windfall.

The windfall was swallowed up in the *Collège des Écossais*!

For Anna, however, with her respectable commercial background, it must all have been a living nightmare. There is much to suggest that the first decade of the 20th century was a period of growing tension and disharmony between Anna and Patrick.

1914 proved to be an eventful year for Geddes. In the summer his successful Cities Exhibition in Dublin had to close early as the Linen Hall was requisitioned for warlike purposes. He and Alasdair went off to India at the invitation of Lord Pentland, Governor of Madras. The Cities Exhibition was lost at sea as a result of enemy action. At the Outlook Tower a replacement Cities and Town Planning Exhibition was quickly rustled up which was shipped out to India in time to open in Madras on 17 January 1915, after Alasdair had worked frantically on its display. Meanwhile, PG had busied himself in a string of Indian cities. They returned to Britain but Patrick returned to India in the autumn of 1915, where the Cities Exhibition had arrived at Calcutta. This time Anna was his companion.

Back in Europe in 1916, Geddes contributed to an *Exposition de la Ville Reconstituée*. While he was back, teaching, in Dundee, Anna was left in Paris to struggle with the exhibits and to organise 'distant and uncertain lecturers by correspondence.' Very loyally she remonstrated with her husband about putting too much into his programme. Mildly she wrote on 10 June – the day before the opening – that she 'was supposed to cover the 180 sq metres in the one day!' Two days later she wrote:

> I don't see how I am to prepare any programme with so little to go up as you give me – No fixed dates; save that you arrive sometime before 9 July... No word either from or of Mr Fleure.[2]

Late in 1916, Patrick and Anna returned to India and for the first half of 1917 things went very well for PG, with plenty of work and receptive audiences – '... a very distinct phase of intensified lucidity & vision'. Anna, however, had dysentery and fever and PG wrote to Alasdair of the need for her protection from anxiety. Return to Europe was impossible because of the U-boat menace, so the couple began to plan for a summer meeting in Darjeeling. But in April Geddes received a cable informing him of Alasdair's death in action. Fearful of the effect of this news on Anna's health, Geddes did not inform Anna. As Alasdair's weekly letters continued to arrive by mail steamer, Geddes would read them out to his ailing wife.

From the hospital in Lucknow Geddes took Anna to stay just outside Calcutta with an Indian doctor known to them from his student days in Edinburgh. (In 1876, the first Indian graduated from the University of Edinburgh). Anna was far from well – it is suggested that she was carrying enteric (typhoid) fever contracted in the hospital in Lucknow[3] PG was in a dilemma but Anna insisted that he carry out his Darjeeling commitment.

Partly thanks to Anna's organisation the Darjeeling meeting was a great success. Geddes was kept furiously busy, although he found time for a daily letter to Anna.

> He planned to visit her the first weekend in June. But the doctors discouraged the trip at this time for fear the news of Alasdair's death might have to be told, since his letters had ceased arriving. A week later a wire summoned Geddes to Calcutta in all haste. The journey took 22 hours, and in the meantime Anna succumbed to the fever despite all efforts to prolong her life.

Some weeks later, Geddes wrote to Amelia Defries:

> I spent the day beside her – and then in evening the old Indian students she had mothered, as they said, when in Edinburgh… came at short notice, all in Indian costume and barefoot and carried her, six by six, on an open funeral bier all the three miles to the Crematorium, I following… Then on the steps all sang Rabindranath Tagore's 'Farewell' – a strangely penetrating funeral hymn, and they sprinkled incense over her and flowers… and so now have but her ashes to bring home.

Poor Anna! Even at the end unwilling to hold back her mercurial husband. Dying in a land so far and so different from her several homes. And yet, at the end, supported by a liberal comradeship.

Walter Stephen

Notes

1   Paul Laxton found two relevant press cuttings in the Liverpool Mercury.
    At the displenishing sale of the contents of Frazer Morton's house there were:

    ... a valuable walnut semi-grand pianoforte of full trichord compass by
    Bluthner (a selected instrument): duet music stool, American organ, five
    octaves, with four stops and knee swell, in oak case.

    It would be nice to think that these instruments had been played by the young
    Anna.

    The Morton business had clearly diversified beyond linen. The newspaper
    recorded an alleged theft of 12 shoulders of American bacon, belonging to
    Frazer Morton, from a warehouse.

2   HJ Fleure (1877–1969), zoologist and geographer, best remembered today
    for such as: *Human Geography in Western Europe, The Peoples of Europe,
    Races of England and Wales, A Natural History of Man in Britain.*

3   Typhoid has an incubation period of 7–14 days and lasts for about a month.
    It is most likely that Anna picked up the infection in the good doctor's house,
    however unacceptable the idea may be.

CHAPTER SIX

Sympathy, Synthesis and Synergy

Patrick Geddes and the Edinburgh Social Union

Introduction

THE EDINBURGH SOCIAL UNION (ESU) is often quoted as one of Patrick Geddes's most successful legacies. Aiming to raise the standard of comfort and beauty in everyday life whilst improving the general well-being of the poor, the ESU is presented as the key example of Geddes's contributions to the Arts and Crafts movement, urban conservation and renewal, and social reform. Its work is seen as embracing and implementing Geddes's triad of 'sympathy, synthesis and synergy'.

However, whilst the establishment of the ESU owed much to Patrick Geddes, he played only a minor role in its development and administration. The ESU's success and longevity (1885–1956) was due to the dedication and commitment of a group of talented and powerful Edinburgh ladies. Their focus and working methods were often at odds with what we know of Patrick Geddes and his approach to life; but were welcomed by many of their housing tenants who, it was reported, expressed a preference for living in accommodation 'under the ladies'.

This chapter explores the background and experience of the women who were responsible for the operation and success of the ESU. It considers their relations with Patrick Geddes; their contribution to the development and operation of the Social Union; and the impacts of this work on their own lives at a time of immense social change.

Three individual women stand out amongst those involved in the management of the ESU: Mary Louisa Maclagan, who played an important role along with Patrick Geddes in establishing the organisation; Elizabeth Haldane, who provided an important link with the work of Octavia Hill in London; and Helen Kerr, who was the longest serving member of the ESU's Executive Committee.

Following these leaders was an army of volunteer, mostly female, rent collectors, for whom the ESU provided new management experience and involvement in social issues; and a number of female artists who contributed to the decoration of public spaces and the provision of craft education classes.

In her memoirs, Elizabeth Haldane commented on her work with the ESU and the changing opportunities for women at the turn of the century.

> It was as though one had got away from the dullness of the drab life which was the lot of so many unoccupied women into something that was not only real but full of excitement.

> Without this voluntary action, little would have been achieved.

Background

By 1877, under the influence of Octavia Hill in London, the first Kyrle Society had been formed to improve surroundings and to decorate public meeting rooms. By 1883 this movement had spread as far as Glasgow. By this time the divided nature of Edinburgh as a 'tale of two cities' was also very evident: the fine architecture of the New Town and its well-to-do residents contrasting sharply with the poverty and sordid slums of the Old Town. It was only a matter of time before something similar to the Kyrle Society would be established in Edinburgh.

Patrick Geddes returned to Edinburgh in 1884 and provided the necessary catalyst for action. With a lectureship at the University, he soon immersed himself in the life of the city. He contemplated the deep social divide from his lodgings at 81a Princes Street, looking upward to the Old Town, to James Court and to the future Ramsay Garden. He won the Ellis Physiology Prize at the Edinburgh University and enjoyed the success of his biological research. He was in great demand for public lectures and extra-mural courses across Edinburgh, many of which were attended by or specifically for women; and for his frequent lectures to the British Association for the Advancement of Science and the Royal Society of Edinburgh.

Central to Geddes's thinking at this time was his view that evolution was about co-operation; not just, as suggested by Darwin, about competition. This work culminated in 1889 in the publication of *The Evolution of Sex* co-authored with Arthur Thomson. This challenge to Darwinian theory proved controversial and may have cost Geddes further success in his career as a biologist. However, at this time, Geddes began to explore the implications of his theory for sociology and town planning. His views on this and on the differences between male and female sex roles in working towards a more co-operative society would have been the subjects of intense debate amongst the intellectuals of his day.

James Oliphant was headmaster of the Charlotte Square Institution for the Education of Girls (and was to become Geddes's brother-in-law). The 'Secular Positivist' debating group met regularly at the Oliphants' providing ample opportunity for philosophical discussions. A favourite topic was the need for action to improve the quality of life for the poor in Edinburgh, where the mismanagement of cheaply rented tenements was seen as a disgrace. Co-operation, sympathy and synergy were seen as central to this work with 'how to achieve a more co-operative, egalitarian and cultured society' a major issue for debate.

Oliphant delivered a public lecture on *The Education of Girls* in 1889 in which he strenuously opposed the opinion that girls should be educated as if they were boys. He discouraged undue competition and advocated forms of education for girls

> which combine the highest degree of natural interest with the smallest amount of nervous strain.

Similarly, Geddes and Thomson emphasised the different contributions to be made by men and women. They expected that increased participation by women in social and political life would result in a redirection of social change toward a cooperative society, provided that it preserved separate sex roles appropriate to male and female temperaments.

Educational opportunities for women were increasing and Oliphant's school in Charlotte Square was central to this movement in Edinburgh. Women were beginning to take a more active role in public life, local politics and social service through their involvement in local organisations such as School Boards and, by 1895, in local government. In its operation, the ESU provided a nurturing ground for the talents of its female volunteers. Patrick Geddes was clearly supportive of this contribution but could not have predicted the massive change in women's role in society which was just beginning.

Around 1884 Patrick Geddes suggested that the Secular Positivists should form an 'Environmental Society' but this proposal seems to have been dropped in favour of the title 'Social Union' which better reflected the totality of their artistic and social concerns and interests and mirrored developments in other urban areas across the country – and resonated with the plight of Burns's mouse.

Aims of the ESU

Established in 1885, the ESU aimed to improve the well-being of the poor in Edinburgh. Its work on housing, social services, education and amenity was to be carried out in such a manner as to encourage 'sympathy and fellowship between different classes', and to ensure that benefits were accrued by both recipients of services and their benefactors. The ESU typified a new approach to dealing with poverty and social issues as private and voluntary organisations took over from the churches in the delivery of assistance to the poor in an age opposed to State intervention. ESU members were greatly influenced by the philosophy of Carlyle and Ruskin and by the evangelical branch of the Free Church of Scotland which drew attention to the moral duty of the individual in society. Influence also came from the Arts and Crafts movement in identifying the need to restore beauty to everyday life and from actions in other parts of the country to address urban poverty and living conditions.

When it was initially proposed in 1884, the ESU saw the campaign against poverty and miserable housing conditions as being about improving the standard of comfort of the poor mainly by laying stress on the value of beauty and order in the surroundings of life. The initial aim was to begin by decorating public halls and other places where the poorer classes met, to advocate window gardening and to offer entertainments using the example of other bodies such as the Nottingham Social Guild.

These aims were closely connected to concerns about the impact of the City of Edinburgh's slum clearance schemes on the physical and social integrity of the Old Town, and to issues of improving the quality of life for the city's inhabitants through the renovation and management of slum property. It was quickly realised that this would offer good returns for owners and tenants alike.

The latter objective quickly began to dominate the work of the ESU and within its first few years the organisation evolved into a professional philanthropic body, with a carefully managed and successful housing department. It adopted principles first tried out by Octavia Hill in London where philanthropic persons were encouraged to buy older houses, carry out reconstruction and hand over these properties to be managed on behalf of the owner whilst encouraging order and cleanliness. This became known as 'five per cent philanthropy' as potential philanthropists were guaranteed a modest return on their investment. A prospectus for the Glasgow Social Union published in 1898 emphasised the financial opportunities for investors in such properties.

Founding of the ESU

A meeting to formalise the establishment of the ESU was held at Patrick Geddes's lodgings, on Tuesday 6 January 1885. At that meeting, it was agreed that Geddes would represent the group at the Industrial Congress to be held in London on 28 January. The ESU provided Geddes with a useful platform from which to voice his opinions. Never slow to speak out, Geddes was openly critical of the other papers at the Congress, describing them as 'deficient in not discussing the immediate practical questions which lay to their hand'. He announced that:

> The society that he was representing proposed to consider such questions as the housing of the working classes, and the promotion of art education and recreation. They proposed to limit their political action until they had made a fair experiment of existing surroundings. After they had discussed such improvements as these they would consider the question of the actual distribution of wealth.

(It is doubtful that the ESU's financier and business benefactors, who supported free market principles, would have approved of this latter objective but their reactions are not recorded.)

The group that gathered at Geddes's lodgings on 6 January 1885 was described as 'friends of Patrick Geddes'. It included James Oliphant and his wife, Edith; Mr H Bellyse Baildon, lecturer, and secretary of the Edinburgh Philosophical Institute and of the University Extension scheme; Dr George Alexander Gibson, Resident Physician at the Edinburgh Royal Infirmary; Mrs Jeannie Craigie Cunningham, wife of William Cunningham, a wealthy Edinburgh manufacturer; Mrs Jane Whyte, wife of the Rev Alexander Whyte, the inspirational Free Church minister of St George's Church in Shandwick Place, and sister of Dr Alexander Freeland Barbour, later responsible for the restoration of White Horse Close; Mr Frank Dias, an architect and close friend of Robert and John Henry Lorimer; and Geddes's colleague, Mr Arthur Thomson. Also present were John Oliphant, James's brother; a Miss Wheeler; and a Miss Craigie (possibly Alice Craigie, sister of Jean Craigie Cunningham). The latter three attendees were artists who contributed to the ESU's early work on the decoration of public meeting places.

The group had been invited by Patrick Geddes and Mrs D Douglas Maclagan. The early relations between these two founding members are not well documented but Mrs Maclagan was a wise choice for a partner in such a venture. Artistic and philanthropic interests, and family connections in the Royal Society of Edinburgh and local financial institutions, were likely factors in bringing her into Geddes's circle of contacts. Later that year, she and her husband, a stockbroker, purchased property at 6 James Court, Edinburgh for management by the ESU. This was an indication of their commitment to the cause; recognition of the potential investment returns; and recognition of the immediate effort needed to save the physical and social fabric of the Old Town of Edinburgh.

Mrs Mary Louisa Maclagan

Mrs Maclagan was born Mary Louisa Kerr, on 7 May 1853 in Hamilton, Ontario, Canada. Her father, Archibald Kerr, born in Paisley, Renfrewshire, had made his fortune as a merchant in Canada. Her mother, Catherine Maclaren was the sister of William Paterson Maclaren, a member of the business elite of Upper Canada. By 1861 the Kerr family had retired to Edinburgh and was resident at Ravelston House, Corstorphine (PLATE 2A). By 1871 Catherine Kerr had been widowed and was living in Bowdon, Cheshire. It was there that in 1876 Mary married David Douglas Maclagan. In doing so she became a member of a very well respected and well-to-do Edinburgh family, famous in the city for its contributions to the worlds of medicine and finance, and for its philanthropic activities. In his biographical note on the medical members of the family, Derek Doyle notes:

> People who knew the Maclagans well characterised them by their energy, vision, graciousness, humour and commitment to serving others and their Christian faith.

By 1885 Mary and David Douglas Maclagan were living at 5 Eton Terrace, Edinburgh; they had been married for nine years and had four children. Mary's father-in-law, David Maclagan (1824–1883) had been the Manager of the Edinburgh Life Assurance Company and was well known for his philanthropic activities. More significantly, her uncle-in-law, Sir Andrew Douglas Maclagan (1812–1900), was the Professor of Public Health at Edinburgh University and by 1885 had become President of the Social and Sanitary Society of Edinburgh, which was later to merge with the ESU.

Initial Development of the ESU

Mrs Maclagan's contribution was pivotal to the establishment and operation of the ESU. Besides acting as the first secretary of the ESU's Art Guild, she was a member of the Executive Committee from 1885–1920, and Treasurer to the Housing Committee from 1889.

At the first meeting of the ESU on 6 January 1885 three guilds dealing with art, music and nature were established. The Art Guild, for which Mrs Maclagan would act as secretary, was to be chaired by Patrick Geddes. However, a few days later, when the Executive Committee met on 8 January, these three Guilds had been changed to Art, Recreation, and Education; with an additional Housing Guild. It was agreed that the housing of the poor should be added as a major project and that the approach should be based on that of Miss Octavia Hill, with whom Patrick Geddes had recently had a meeting. A few days later it was Mrs Maclagan who suggested that the houses for the poor could be bought by a limited company with the management left to the Housing Guild of the ESU.

By February 1885, discussions were taking place with other similar organisations; a letter had been received from Miss Mary Kerr, concerning joint work with the Guild for Help. At a meeting at Mrs Maclagan's home on 13 March it was resolved that the two organisations would remain separate but would work closely together and would prepare a Directory to the Charitable Agencies in Edinburgh.

The Housing Guild

In 1887 it was Mrs Maclagan who drafted the rules that the ESU was to adopt in connection with the management of property; and in 1889, after the death of Mrs Eleanor McBride, she became the treasurer of the housing department.

The ESU imposed strict rules on tenants; regular payment of rent, cleanliness, and good behaviour were required; drunken and disruptive tenants were quickly evicted. A great deal of emphasis was placed on the influence of the rent collectors who trod a difficult path between collecting rents and imposing standards and acting as a friend and counsellor.

Mrs Maclagan was given the responsibility for negotiating with owners of property throughout the Old Town and beyond and was responsible for discussions with the burgh surveyor about the possible future of property such as that at Whitehouse Close. Her attention to detail is clear from the minutes of the ESU.

For example, it was reported on 13 February 1901 that she was responsible for negotiating the detailed management conditions with Mr Findlay, the proprietor of the *Scotsman*, for his property near the Water of Leith. He had wished to impose certain restrictions which Mrs Maclagan had 'considered untenable', however, she had suggested that the ESU might offer to manage the property for seven years as an experiment. She proposed detailed and strict arrangements for supervision and control of management, rent collection, caretaking, repair and maintenance. By 27 February she was able to report that Mr Findlay had agreed to these arrangements with reference to properties in the Dean village and that the ESU had declined to take on further properties due to the pressure of work. This suggests that the Executive Committee had clear lines of command. Its members worked decisively, had a rational view of their own capabilities, and knew when to say 'no'.

As Treasurer of the Housing Department, Mary Maclagan played a key role in ensuring that the work of the ESU was efficiently managed and that a reasonable return was guaranteed to landlords. She was keen to ensure that any actions 'paid their own way' and in 1890 proposed the establishment of a second hand clothes shop in the East Arthur Street property – an enterprise which she was sure would soon become self-supporting.

Johnson and Rosenburg noted that there is no evidence to suggest that either Patrick Geddes or his wife played any significant role in the work of the ESU Housing Committee or in its management services. In her biography of Geddes, Helen Meller notes that Geddes had no interest whatsoever in the:

> ... tedious and time-consuming process of housing management which was very much the role of volunteer lady philanthropists.

Their enforcement of strict rules and procedures appear alien to what we know of Patrick Geddes's own working style.

Patrick Geddes had more experimental work in view and worked alongside the ESU to bring about his own ambitions. By April 1887 he had taken up residence in 6 James Court, a move which was frowned upon by some. Arthur Thomson wrote to him in 1886:

> I am afraid you are making a martyr of yourself for the sake of the Social Union. You are too intense ... I wonder how you can get on with so much to think about.

The accommodation inhabited by Patrick Geddes and his wife at 6 James Court was owned by Dr Peter McBride, whose wife Eleanor, had acted as the Treasurer for the Housing Department until her death in 1889. In 1888–89, Geddes paid rent of £35 to the ESU and occupied one of Peter and Eleanor McBride's 17 properties which they had bought in October 1886.

The group of Edinburgh philanthropists who managed the ESU believed in the free market and did not believe that housing subsidies would solve the housing problem. Rather they believed that if houses could be built to pay there would be plenty of people ready and anxious to build them. They therefore saw a reasonable return on investment as a key component of their work and investment in housing as widening their investment portfolios. In her report of 1901, Elizabeth Haldane reported that the ESU had paid proprietors sums varying from three and a half per cent to six per cent for the properties entrusted to their care.

Decorative Arts

Geddes's own interests emerged more fully in relation to the Decorative Arts Committee of which he was Chairman. Here again he worked with the ESU and on his own accord. The ESU embraced both the decoration and ornamentation of public spaces and the development of craft skills education. As Secretary of the Arts Guild, it was Mrs Maclagan who took the lead in organising craft classes across the city and in seeking artists for the decoration of public halls.

As early as March 1885 lessons in woodcarving were being taught by Miss Florence Sellar at two studios, one within Alexandra Buildings in Shandwick Place, an education and studio complex run by and for women artists. In 1887 the ESU was involved in the development of recreational evening classes across the city and later in 1890 a range of craft education classes was developed in the new studios in Lynedoch Place.

Both the classes and decorative work involved a number of female artists notably Phoebe Anna Traquair and her students. A lesser known contributor to this work was Miss Florence Sellar (1857–1939), the daughter of Professor William Young Sellar, Professor of Humanity at Edinburgh University. Florence served on the ESU's Executive Committee in 1886–7; however, her connection with the ESU was short-lived as in September 1887 she married John McCunn (1881–1910), the first Professor of Philosophy at the University of Liverpool. Florence was described by one of her husband's colleagues as his 'brilliant wife who taught many of us what good talk could be'. She appears to have been a dynamic, talented, intellectual woman. Later she was the author of biographical works on *John Knox* (1895), *Mary Stuart* (1907), and *Sir Walter Scott's Friends* (1909).

Something of Florence's direct and confident style is seen in her correspondence with Patrick Geddes regarding a proposed carving of his *Arbor Scientiae* and *Arbor Vitae*. Her letter of 10 July (1886?) criticised Geddes's proposed design for carvings for a lintel and mantel over a fireplace stating that the design was too complicated to be carved. Florence expressed her frustration and general dislike of the design:

> ... the skull and mortar board are neither grotesque nor solemn, simply vulgar... the telescope is bad, the plough (with the bit of field beneath) worse; the beetle succeeded but the butterfly looks like an illustration of natural history... I think another generation might look upon the mantelpiece with indulgent amusement as a measurement of hasty arrogance.

Florence considered that she did not have the capacity to put the design into a simpler and more practical shape and excused herself; 'the society might vote me too independent and recalcitrant a person to be a member' but as 'an obedient servant to the Union' she would do her best to satisfy them but 'should not care to have it associated with my name'. To emphasise her point she declared that 'decorative art should be a delight to the worker' and in proposing a simpler design suggested that he should either use her design or find someone else.[1]

Other projects by the Decorative Arts Committee appear to have gone more smoothly. Early in 1885 Mrs Maclagan took the lead in organising a number of projects: the decoration of the dispensary at Fountainbridge was entrusted to John Oliphant to supervise; the Misses Wheeler and Craigie were entrusted to complete the decoration of the Courant Shelter in the High Street. The decoration of the Robertson Memorial Mission Hall in the Grassmarket; the decoration of the Tron Church Hall, and Niddrie Street by a pupil of Mrs Phoebe Traquair's; and Phoebe Traquair's own work on the mortuary at the Sick Children's Hospital all date from this time.

Other artistic and craft training ventures were started. Mrs Maclagan was an active member of the ESU's Guild of Women Bookbinders, which met regularly at the Dean Studio and which contributed to the second Guild of Women's Binders exhibition in London in 1898; she was an accomplished woodcarver and embroiderer and by 1907 her artistic skills had turned to supervising the design and building of a mansion house for the family's summer residence in Comrie, Perthshire.

Elizabeth Cumming noted that Geddes had:

> divorced himself from the ESU by the early 1890s when in the aftermath of the Edinburgh Congress, held at the National Portrait Gallery 28 October–1 November 1889, he considered that the Decorative Arts Committee was travelling down what he thought of as a traditionalist Arts and Crafts road to create a guild of handicraft concerned with British and specifically London design practice and standards.

These tensions may have been partly due to his differences of opinion with William Morris but also with the emphasis given to education and training within the ESU programme. Differences of opinion may have begun as early as November 1888 when Mrs Maclagan proposed that the Decorative Department should be discontinued and merged with the Art Class Department. She considered that it was desirable that the training of decorative workers be undertaken by the Society; she suggested that the relation of the decorative department and the art classes be reconsidered.

In November 1888, Mrs Maclagan suggested that Dr Andrew Douglas Maclagan should be invited to preside at the AGM of the organisation. He did so and took the opportunity to add his support for the emphasis on the housing work and crafts training of the ESU. Over the next five years classes were to continue in wood carving, metal work, and book binding with recreative evening classes for girls and gardening projects for children in many parts of the city. By 25 January 1889 Geddes was organising a meeting of the Decorative Committee to be held at his own home to which a lengthy list of 'supporters' was invited and it would seem that much of his own work in this field, particularly relating to Ramsay Gardens and student housing, springs from this time.

Differences of opinion regarding financial and organisational matters were also beginning to emerge. By 1888 there were signs of tensions and disagreements between Geddes and the Committee members. In January 1888 the Executive Committee declined to take over the kindergarten and girls' club which had been started at James Court. It was considered 'inadvisable to have anything to do with schemes over which the ESU had no direct control'. The matter was left for another meeting and by December 1889 the grant for Geddes's kindergarten had been discontinued.

Tight management of finance was central to the ethos of the ESU Executive Committee. In November 1888 it was carefully minuted that:

> Mr Geddes was given permission to undertake decoration of James Court Hall *on condition of presenting estimates of expenses.*

Finance was always an issue and in February 1889 it was noted that the decorative handiwork exhibition had incurred a loss and it had been necessary to make a call on the guarantors to the extent of two-thirds of the sum guaranteed. In the case of the ESU this amounted to £6.13.4.

Later in October 1889 the members of the Executive Committee were presented with accounts relating to the purchase of curtains for James Court which had been purchased by Mr Geddes without the permission of the Social Union Executive. The Secretary was instructed to send Mr Geddes the special subscription of £5.5s given to him for decorative purposes and at the same time to disown all liability for such unauthorised expenditure.

Elizabeth Cumming described Geddes as 'an enabler who also wanted to steer his own ship'. It seems that Geddes liked to go his own way and paid little attention to the niceties of finance and committee requirements. However, the importance of his early efforts in establishing the ESU cannot be denied. He had given publicity to the organisation at the Industrial Remuneration Conference, his move to James Court had brought local leadership and practical example, and he had led an initial deputation to discuss housing reform with Octavia Hill in London. This meeting had established the principles upon which the work of the ESU would be based and had introduced Patrick Geddes to Elizabeth Haldane, someone who would become a key player in the ESU and in wider social reforms.

Elizabeth Haldane (1862–1937)

In her memoirs, Elizabeth Haldane recalls the chance meeting with Patrick Geddes that led to her involvement with the Edinburgh Social Union.

> A deputation headed by Professor Patrick Geddes was sent in 1884 to discuss the matter with Octavia Hill and it happened that the day on which they called I also had gone to see Miss Hill, on receiving an introduction from a younger sister of my mother's, who knew that I found life unsatisfying and wished to help me. Miss Hill told the deputation that she would have to train the lady who might start work in Edinburgh. They were nonplussed until Miss Hill turned to me and asked if I would help, I was rather taken aback, as I was young, about 21, and had no experience. But at last I consented and this ended in a good deal of work in this direction and a successful start being made in Scotland.

Elizabeth Haldane was born on 27 May 1862, the fifth child and only daughter of Robert Haldane (1805–1877), Writer to the Signet, and his second wife, Mary Elizabeth Burdon-Sanderson (1825–1925). Three of her brothers had outstanding careers: Richard Burdon Haldane, politician and Lord Chancellor, John Scott Haldane, physiologist, and William Stowell Haldane, a lawyer.

Elizabeth was a member of the ESU's Special Executive Committee for Housing from 1897 and by 1903 was also serving as a member of the Industrial Law Committee of the ESU which had been established to look at breaches of the Factory and Workshops Act, in particular commenting on and lobbying for the conditions of laundry workers in the city and taking a wider interest of conditions affecting women in the workplace. By this time she was playing a more important role in supporting the political career of her brother, Richard Burdon Haldane, and was in London more frequently. However, Elizabeth Haldane continued to be involved with the ESU, serving on the Executive Committee from 1926 and was appointed as an Honorary President in 1930.

Elizabeth Haldane's graphic description of the living conditions of the ESU's tenants whom she visited and of the difficulty she felt in taking even small amounts of rents from people illustrates the wide social and economic gap between ESU housing managers and their tenants. Her writings also shed light on the differences in ideologies in relation to public versus private provision of housing for the poor:

> One saw the immensity of the problem and the means taken seemed to me (who had imbibed a good many radical ideas) inadequate without State help, and to this Miss Hill demurred. She thought it would introduce a deleterious political influence.

The ESU rent collectors, trained by Miss Haldane, were instructed not to impose their own social values but to 'help others to help themselves'. Much of the success of the ESU depended on their work which was to: visit homes weekly, collect rents and saving book money, see to repairs, and complaints, and befriend residents and give kindly help and assistance as needed. A splendid portrait of this work was given by the late Anne Mathams in 2007, who commented:

> What does it tell us about civic order in Edinburgh that, on the same day of every week for years, along the same routes through some of the worst housing in Western Europe, several unaccompanied women carried bags of cash without any untoward incident whatever?

By 1896 there were more than 20 ladies working as rent collectors and receiving regular training every year. The list of rent collectors in the annual report for 1896 indicates that most of these ladies resided in the

New Town, the West End or the suburbs on the south side of the city including Morningside/Merchiston/Warrender Park and the Blackets.

The difference in the experience of life between rent collectors and residents was considerable and there appears to have been an ongoing debate and soul searching about moral responsibility and the fine line between interfering and influence. One rent collector in the Pleasance area of St Leonards reflected:

> Sometimes life moves on with amazing rapidity among your flock. One couple gained possession of their home on Friday, were married on Saturday, their baby was born on Monday, christened on Tuesday, died on Friday and the funeral was held on Saturday. This I think is the most breathless succession of life's great events I have ever come across.

Later Years

By 1897, demand for occupancy of ESU tenanted property was running high. The annual report for that year reported 15 applicants for one house with dozens turned away every week. The organisation was at full stretch and cautious about starting new social and educational work because of the time taken in collecting rents. Reports were favourable with much upgrading of properties and tenants reported as preferring to move to another property managed by the Social Union.

By 1896–7, the Executive Committee members consisted of Miss FE Balfour, Mrs Helen Kerr, Mrs Mary Maclagan, Mr James Oliphant, Miss Mary Kerr, and Mrs Cunningham. Mrs Helen Kerr became Superintendent of Housing in 1889 and was to become the longest serving member of the Executive. She was an Honorary President from 1930 until her death in February 1940.

Helen Kerr (1859–1940)

Mrs Helen Kerr was born Helen L Howden, the daughter of James Howden, a Chartered Accountant and Mary Elizabeth Shaw Stewart. In 1888 when Helen married George Kerr MD, her family was living at Gogar House, Midlothian and by 1891 she and her husband were living at 6 St Colme Street Edinburgh. Her sister-in-law, Miss Mary Kerr who lived at 9 Great Stuart Street, was also an active member of the ESU and a member of the Executive. The Kerr family fortune, like that of Mary Maclagan and Peter McBride, was based on Canadian business links.

George and Mary Kerr's parents had been partners with John McBride in the Greenock based firm of McBride, Ehlers and Kerr linked to the Newfoundland fishing industry. There were therefore strong family business links and Canadian connections among some of the chief ESU benefactors.

Dr and Mrs Kerr and Miss Mary Kerr played important roles as owners of properties at Brown's Court managed by the ESU. In 1896 22 flats at Campbell's Close, which had been compulsory purchased by the city, were also sold to Dr George Kerr. The ESU volunteers then organised the physical improvements to be carried out and became responsible for management and rent collection.

Under the leadership of Helen Kerr, the ESU became an important and respected force within the city. By 1897 the Corporation of Edinburgh showed its confidence in the ESU's working methods by handing over for management the first three blocks built under its improvement scheme of 1893. The Social Union agreed to manage the new development at High School Yards, and their work gradually extended to cover developments at Tynecastle, Tron Square (PLATE 2B), Portsburgh Square and Potterrow. The decision to take on this work must have involved a degree of compromise on the part of the ESU as in line with Octavia Hill's policy, they continued to oppose state provision of housing for the poor.

By 1901 the ESU's Annual Report stated that it managed 24 properties, eight of which belonged to the Council. The properties contained 650 families in total. Soon after Octavia Hill's visit to Edinburgh in 1902, the ESU withdrew from its work in managing houses owned by the Corporation. In its Annual Report for 1904, the Housing Committee provided a variety of explanations for this decision: the ESU's approach was based on the small-scale reconstruction of existing houses which differed from the Council's own larger mass building schemes; and the ESU was against subsidy and public provision and wholesale demolition and in this it disagreed with the municipal approach. It may also have been that members were keen to placate Octavia Hill, who Elizabeth Haldane describes as 'sensitive and easily upset when the little things of life went wrong'.

Later in 1925 the Edinburgh City Council proposed to employ the ESU once more in managing some of its property, as it was noted that conditions had become less satisfactory under the new system of house agents when compared with the ESU. However, this proposal was strongly opposed by a representation from the Edinburgh District Trades Council who were adamant that charity should not be mixed with business and that 'no busybodies were wanted as rent collectors'. This attack on the ESU was continued in the local press which asserted that the management of a household was up to the individual housewife who should be able to 'keep coal in the bath if she wishes'. The ESU was immediately defended by Sir William Haldane (Elizabeth's brother) in a letter to the *Scotsman* praising the ESU for its business-like approach. The lady members of the Executive Committee made no formal comment; it was their male relatives who fought the public battle on their behalf.

Management and Leadership

Mary Maclagan, Helen Kerr and Elizabeth Haldane were typical of the philanthropic middle-classes who engaged in philosophical discussion and sought practical means of achieving their goals. Personal responsibility and influence came higher up the agenda than political power, and legislative and state provision. They were the daughters of commerce, of finance and of enterprise and had their own investments and inheritance. At the same time close contacts with the Free Church, the medical profession and the university provided a sympathetic and guiding culture based on individual and social responsibility.

At the time of the establishment of the ESU, they were not used to wielding political power directly through the voting system or as major figures in public life. However, through family connections, they exercised positions of considerable influence. Individually, they were used to managing complex households, to training staff, to making the household books balance, and to making things work. They did not have the vote but this seemed less of an issue than finding practical solutions to practical problems. By the 1920s Helen Kerr and Elizabeth Haldane were both playing important roles in relation to issues of social reform at Scottish and UK levels.

Mary Maclagan played little role in the work of the ESU from 1912 onwards and finally resigned from the Executive in 1920. A letter read at the AGM on 30 November that year records her regrets at being unable to play any further role in the ESU and particularly the housing committee.

> It is a wrench to feel that I have no part even in name in the ESU which was so near my heart.

An accident (understood to be a tram accident which required her to undergo a leg amputation), the burning down of her house in Comrie by militant suffragettes in 1914, and the death of her daughter, Mary, in 1915 must all have taken their toll.

> At first after my accident I hoped that in time I would be able to get about
> more easily and feel the burden of myself less heavy but I see now that it
> is not to be...

She and her husband remained members of the ESU but by 1923 retired
to what had been their summer residence at House of Ross, Comrie. Mrs
Maclagan died on 29 September 1943 and was buried in the family's private
graveyard at 'Happy Valley' above the Milton, Comrie, Perthshire.

In contrast, Helen Kerr's role in Scottish social services continued to
grow in strength. She submitted evidence to the Royal Commission on the
Poor Laws and Relief of Distress in 1907. This evidence was drawn from
the results of a survey of 1,400 Edinburgh schoolchildren and their homes
in 1904. In 1912 she was appointed to be a member of the Royal Commission on the Housing of the Working Classes in Scotland and she chaired
the Women's House Planning Committee for Scotland (appointed 1918).
Helen Kerr served as a member of the Board of Management of Edinburgh Royal Infirmary where she was a member of the House Committee
and also acted as the convener of the Nursing Committee. She worked for
the establishment of the Scottish Board of the College of Nursing and in
1921 she was appointed to the Astley Ainslie Trust which was setting up
new provision for convalescents in Edinburgh. Helen Kerr did much
towards the establishment of the nursing profession and the collaboration
between the Edinburgh Infirmary and the University Settlement's School
of Social Service. Her many contributions included acting as an adviser
for the development of Rosyth; and later she became a JP. In 1920 she was
awarded an Honorary LLD from Edinburgh University for her work in the
social services.

Helen Kerr's philosophy and work are set out in two publications
published in 1912. The first, a chapter on Edinburgh in *Social Conditions
of Provincial Towns* edited by Mrs Bernard Bosanquet, emphasised the
importance of management and of incremental action based on philanthropy and co-operation as solutions to poverty and housing provision.
The second, written as 'Mrs George Kerr' was titled *The Path of Social
Progress. A discussion of Old and New Ideas in Social Reform* and here
she pleaded for:

> More understanding of the issues and a greater thoughtfulness in the
> application of the various remedies which in quick succession the State
> is bringing to bear on the Nation.

Both these publications drew on the experience and techniques adopted
by the ESU Housing Committee.

Elizabeth Haldane's career also developed in the fields of social policy and action. She continued her connections with the ESU until 1930. After 1900 she played a prominent role in both voluntary associations and public bodies and became the first woman to be appointed a JP in Scotland. Elizabeth Haldane was a lifelong believer in women's suffrage and supported the constitutional campaigning of the National Union of Women's Suffrage Societies. However, she considered that the 'greatest advance' dated from the early 1870s, when local bodies such as school boards were instituted on which women could not only vote but serve as members. She regarded this as possibly more important than the eventual concession of the parliamentary franchise. In her personal life, support for family seems to have come before all else. One of her friends, Violet Markham, considered that she had sacrificed her own ambitions to the claims of family obligations during her mother's long widowhood:

> I often wished that her life had been less wholly devoted to the service of others and had belonged more to herself.

She died in Auchterarder, on 24 December 1937 and was cremated at Warriston crematorium, Edinburgh, on 28 December 1937.

Conclusions

Patrick Geddes likened himself to 'the boy who rings the doorbell and then runs away'. He acted as a social conscience and an inspiration to others to whom he often left the practicalities of implementation. The establishment and operation of the ESU provides a clear example of this approach.

Some biographers have suggested that ESU members felt abandoned and let down by Geddes when he moved on to work on other projects. However, a detailed review of the minutes of the ESU shows that the success and longevity of the ESU was due to the hard work of some very talented women with extra-ordinary commitment and management expertise. Mary Maclagan, Helen Kerr and Elizabeth Haldane were three key contributors. Personal responsibility and influence came higher up the agenda than political power, and legislative and state provision. It was these qualities which drove forward their philanthropic work. The success of the Edinburgh Social Union was dependent on a group of middle-class philanthropists and their followers, most of them women, who had the connections, management ability, attention to detail, time, financial resources and commitment to exercise profound social influence in an age when their political influence was largely denied.

Patrick Geddes made important connections in principle, and amongst influential people, often by working across boundaries and in innovative and experimental ways. Whilst his writings with Arthur Thomson emphasise the contribution to be made by women, this was a conservative view of their roles and responsibilities. It is doubtful that he could have envisaged the long term changes to the status and role of women particularly in political and economic spheres which were about to take place or to predict the contributions to be made to social policy and practice by some of the key members of the Edinburgh Social Union with whom he worked.

Veronica Burbridge

Editor's Note

1   This is perhaps the best point at which to make an apology and correct an error.

Clearly Geddes had an interest in woodcarving – note the difficulties with Florence Sellar – and it will come as no surprise that young Arthur attended woodcarving classes in 1910 as part of his education in 'head, heart and hand'. Plate 7b of *Think Global, Act Local* shows 'The Dragons of Wardrop's Court' and on page 34 I commented on these in rather patronising terms.

I have since been rapped over the knuckles for my obtuseness and have had the opportunity to examine Arthur's work for myself.

Wardrop's Court – in the heart of 'Geddesland' – is accessed from the Lawnmarket by a wide close, at either end of which are two dragons, commissioned by Patrick Geddes. The pair of dragons at the Lawnmarket end was carved by JS Gibson, a professional; the inner pair by Arthur.

The dragons have recently been renovated and restored by Edinburgh World Heritage and the City of Edinburgh Council and replaced in their original location. I took the opportunity to inspect Arthur's Dragons closely and report that they are not copies of Gibson's, and therefore not poor copies. The carving is highly effective and appropriate to the Scots pine used.

Another Arthur's Dragon. On a suggestion from his father, Arthur carved a beautiful shrine of Saint Theodore in memory of his brother Alasdair. Saint Theodore is senior to Saint George in Eastern Europe. The shrine shows a serene soldier impaling a fearsome dragon and is now in the home of Anne Geddes Shalit, Arthur's daughter, in Sweden.

Arthur and I had one or two misunderstandings. I hope I have now cleared up this one and would like to apologise to his memory. Arthur was clearly a skilled craftsman, but above all, for me, he was a stimulating and inspiring figure, who still influences me.

Chronology

1880	PG demonstrator in Botany, Edinburgh University
1884	PG proposed Environment Society
	PG visited Octavia Hill and met Elizabeth Haldane
1885	ESU established on 6 January
1885	PG address to the Industrial Congress in London on 29 January
1885	Woodcarving classes started at Alexandra Buildings, Shandwick Place
1885	Arrangements begun for the decoration of public spaces such as the Dispensary at Fountainbridge; and the mortuary at the Sick Children's Hospital
1885/6	Property purchased at James Court by Peter and Eleanor McBride and David Douglas Mary Louisa and Maclagans
1886	PG's Marriage to Anna Morton
1886	Gerard Baldwin Brown invited to give lecture series for ESU
1887	PG resident at James Court
1889	Publication of *The Evolution of Sex* by PG and JA Thomson
1889	PG took part in The Edinburgh Congress held at the National Portrait Gallery 28 October–1 November
1890	Mrs Maclagan proposes second hand clothes shop in East Arthur Place
1890	Lynedoch Studio opened
1896	Property at Campbell's Close bought by George and Helen Kerr
1897	ESU invited to manage property for Edinburgh City Council
1902	Octavia Hill visited Edinburgh
1902	ESU withdrew from management of Council property
1906	Merger of the ESU and the Social and Sanitary Society
1907	Mrs Helen Kerr submitted evidence to Royal Commission on the Poor Laws and Relief of Distress
1918	Mrs Helen Kerr appointed to membership of the Royal Commission on the Housing of the Working Classes in Scotland
1920	Helen Kerr was awarded an Honorary LLD from Edinburgh University for her work in the social services
1920	Elizabeth Haldane and Helen Kerr appointed JPs in Scotland
1956	ESU ceased work after 71 years; properties were handed over to the City of Edinburgh

Bibliography

Bremner R, 'An Iron sceptre twined with roses; the Octavia Hill system of housing management' (*Social Service Review* 1965 the University of Chicago Press, 1965)

Conway J, 'Stereotypes of femininity in a theory of sexual evolution' (*Victorian Studies*, Indiana University Press, Vol 14, No 1, pp. 47–62, 1970)

Cumming E, 'Patrick Geddes: Cultivating the Garden of Life' (in F Fowle and B Thompson (eds.), *Patrick Geddes: The French Connection*, Oxford, 2004)

Cumming Elizabeth, *Hand, Heart and Soul, the Arts and Crafts Movement in Scotland* (Birlinn Ltd, Edinburgh, 2006)

Ferguson Megan C, *Patrick Geddes and the Celtic Renascence of the 1890s* (2011, visited 25 April 2012)

Geddes, P and Thomson, JA, *The Evolution of Sex* (Walter Scott, London 1889)

Haldane E, *Mary Elizabeth Haldane: A record of a hundred years, 1825–1925*

Moore Lindy, 'Young ladies institutions: the development of secondary schools for girls in Scotland 1833–c.1870' (in *History of Education, Journal of the History of Education Society*, Vol 32, Issue 3, pp. 249–272, 2003)

Oliphant J, *The Education of Girls, a public lecture delivered at the Charlotte Square Institute,* 30 January 1889 (Macniven and Wallace, Edinburgh, 1899)

Renwick C, 'The Practice of Spencerian Science: Patrick Geddes's Biosocial program 1876–1889' (in *Isis*, History of Science Society and University of Chicago Press, Vol 100, pp. 36–57, 2009)

CHAPTER SEVEN

Women of The Watergate

DURING HIS EDINBURGH YEARS Patrick Geddes became a major property developer. By 1896 he had amassed over £40,000 in real estate. In terms of late 20th century values this was equivalent to around £4 million in relation to prices or £16 million in relation to average wages.

This was impressive for an academic who had hardly reached mid career. The spectaculars of Ramsay Garden, Riddles Court and James Court are well known but when he launched his property company, the Town and Gown Association Limited in 1896, mention was made of plans to balance the clearances and gentrification of the upper Lawnmarket with development in the Lower Canongate, known by its location at the Watergate.

> Here only two or three acquisitions remain to be made to complete a plan of restoration and conservative reconstruction comparable to that of Castlehill; and again large areas of dilapidated slum are giving place to courts in which sanitary and picturesque conditions are combined... a 'Holyrood Hall' may ere long balance University Hall.

The outcome of this ambition was a distinctive complex of buildings. One tenement, 13 Canongate, involved the reconstruction of an essentially 17th century building and hence survived the demolitions of the mid 20th century. The main building was destroyed as late 19th century improved working class housing was little valued in the 1960s and 1970s. These buildings involved two groups of women and tell us much of the way in which Geddes related to the working class population of Edinburgh and attempted to create environments for them.

The Census manuscript of 1901 was the most complete account of the women who came to live in the Watergate. All but one of the households claimed two rooms with windows. Six of the 34 'heads' were women. Most male-headed households had one adult female listed second in the schedule. Most were given as 'wife', although Andrew Stevens, widower aged 72, formerly an engine fitter lived with Elizabeth Nicol, servant, widow and housekeeper aged 71. Only John Brannigan, platelayer, widower had no female, unless we take Ellen McCalman, lodger and wife of a second lodger, as housekeeper. The men needed women.

This was an astonishingly crowded environment. The 166 people recorded in 1901 lived in 69 rooms, nearly 2.5 people per room. The distribution within the Watergate was very uneven. In households of four or fewer, 48 people lived 1.5 to a room. In the households of six or more, 113 people lived 3.3 people per room. Even so they were better accommodated that many of the poor and working class in Edinburgh. Seventeen percent of the Edinburgh population lived in 'single-ends' whilst nearly a third had 'room and kitchen'.

This was a population living on the edge of poverty and a 'reading' of the Census manuscripts showed the variety of strategies they used to keep on the right side of the line. The most comfortable were the seven households headed by skilled male wage earners. Alexander Dow was born in Glasgow. His wife, Catherine came from Paisley. He had recently moved to Edinburgh. All his four children, including a one year old son, were born in Glasgow. The motive for his move was almost certainly a job in Ford's Holyrood Flint Glass Works, a few minutes walk away on South Back Canongate. He was a glass beveller, a skilled man whose wage would support his family. Patrick Murphy and his wife Mary were born in Ireland. He came to Edinburgh in the early 1890s where his six children were born but he was a Corporation Scavenger. He would have an unskilled wage although the Corporation job would have provided more regular and reliable work than the casual labour of many of the other labourers.

Like ten others, the Murphy family balanced the family budget by taking a lodger, Michael McDermot, a railway surface man, who was also born in Ireland. There was only one instance where the wife of a skilled worker saw the integrity of family space invaded by a lodger. This was Alexander Beaumont's wife, but he was an iron moulder and his lodger an apprentice iron worker. The link of trade was crucial. Of the ten households taking lodgers, there was evidence in four of them that the lodger was a relative. In others, there was some form of community link.

The other major escape from poverty was evident in the nine cases where more than one income came into the house. John Daniels was a house painter, an irregular and at best semi-skilled wage but he had two teenage sons, one, aged 16, an apprentice house painter and another, aged 15, a station messenger. There was enough to sustain a household of seven, including three younger children, without a lodger. There were five households small enough to avoid the pressures on welfare of growing numbers of children. Three others had no obvious defence against rent arrears, malnutrition and inadequate clothing.

The six female-headed households deserve careful attention. Two of the women were widows and four were 'wives', implying men who were absent. In these households, three gave no occupation, two clearly stated they were 'housekeepers' and Margaret Laurie was a 'hawker in china'. 'Housekeeper' was a title appropriate to them all. Three took in boarders and four had additional income brought into the house by their teenage and adult children. In many of these households there was a complexity of action and resource. Anne Murtagh, widow, housekeeper, aged 44, was born in County Cavan, in Ireland but her daughter, born in County Down was an apprentice envelope maker and Anne's housekeeping involved taking three railway labourers as boarders. Two of them were born in Cootehill in Cavan. There were hints of family and community resource and connection embedded in these migrant networks. These links were strengthened by the neighbouring household of Peter Mullan, cable car driver. He, his wife, brother and boarder were all born in Cootehill.

Margaret Laurie employed another strategy, common to male- and female-headed households. She was a 'hawker in china' working on her 'own account'. This supplemented the income from her teenage sons who worked in the local breweries. She was one of several 'penny capitalists'. John Bolland was a licensed broker whilst David Bowie grandly announced that he was a 'fencing and gymnastic instructor', although the valuation roll called him a 'fireman'. Nicola Arpino combined the resources of migrant network, family and petty trading. Aged 37, an Italian subject like the rest of his household, he was a 'confectioner's shopkeeper'. The valuation rolls recorded him an 'ice cream dealer'. His father, aged 69, 'blind and paralytic', 'formerly farm servant', was also in the household as were two lodgers, one of them a nephew, who were 'confectioner's assistants'.

The women of the Watergate were engaged in a multi-dimensional battle with poverty, a struggle to clothe, to feed and to pay the rent which maintained them as a 'room and kitchen' family and not 'single enders'. Those who engaged in petty trading engaged in another contest, this time with the authority of the local state and the moral anxieties which dominated Scottish society. It was not that what they were doing was illegal, but it was seen as being on the edge of legality and a threat to the moral and environmental order which authority was trying to impose on the town. The Edinburgh Municipal Police Act of 1879 devoted 18 clauses to the activities of brokers like John Boland and Margaret Laurie.

They were required to obtain a licence from the magistrates and to keep careful records of the goods they purchased, and not to dispose of such goods for seven days but make them available for police inspection.

Brokers were feared as a means of disposing of stolen or fraudulently obtained goods. Margaret Lawrie, hawker of china, was subjected to a web of clauses designed to prevent obstructions of street and pavement.

There was a small but key group of women who were crucial to the building of Watergate, as they were to many other properties in Edinburgh and beyond. As with many properties, they supplied the finance, directly or through lawyers and trustees. Despite modest improvements in such matters such as the reforms of married women's property rights in 1881, Scottish women were still excluded by law, custom and practice from many aspects of the cash economy. One response to this was to invest property rights for women directly or indirectly in real estate. In many cases this was done through trustees who were used to protect daughters and widows.

Women's finance was crucial to the building of the Watergate for Geddes and his partner Lord John McLaren. In May 1893, McLaren raised £1,200 from the widow and daughters of John Newton Burns, formerly a coalmaster based in south Edinburgh. The Bond, operating through trustees, involved Mary Douglas Straton or Burns, 14 Jordan Lane, widow of John Newton Burns, Marion Burns or Heggie, with the consent of her husband John Heggie, bank accountant, Edinburgh, Janet Dalrymple Burns or Cowie, with the consent of her husband Archibald Cowie, shipbroker, residing in Cardross and Sarah Janet Burns, residing at 14 Jordan Lane, Edinburgh.

In 1895, McLaren raised £1,700 from Christina Ballingall or Patterson, 3 St Mary Place Portobello, widow, whilst Geddes raised £1,450 from trustees of the late Mary Stewart or More, Craigmore House, 23 Craigmillar Park, Edinburgh. A mixture of demography and Scottish inheritance practices meant that many property rights were divided in a way that included many women, together with the additional barrier of 'husband's consent'.

When McLaren and Geddes purchased the property rights of the Watergate, they had to deal with a variety of issues created by inheritance practices and gender. The property rights were shared between the following:

Annie Jackson or Watson wife of John Watson, commercial traveller, Hull;

Janet Baxter Wilson Jackson or Armstrong sometime named Janet Jackson or Armstrong, wife of Henry Alexander Armstrong residing sometime in Coventry, thereafter in Derby and now 26 Quay St Manchester;

Christina Robertson Mitchelhill, widow, Melbourne, Australia or elsewhere furth of Scotland;

Margaret Mitchelhill or Sinclair, wife of Donald Sinclair farmer, now or lately near Melbourne, or elsewhere furth of Scotland;

Jessie Mitchelhill or Macpherson, 207 St Andrews Road, Pollockshields, Glasgow, wife of Archibald Macpherson, fishmonger, 33 Dalry Rd;

Rachel Mitchelhill or Broome, wife of Broome, lately residing in Melbourne, Australia or elsewhere furth of Scotland;

Elizabeth Mitchelhill, Louise Mitchell and John Mitchell, all residing at the Grange, Eucha, Melbourne, Australia or elsewhere furth of Scotland;

Agnes Ireland or Smith, 15 Newington Rd, Edinburgh, widow of George Hay residing at Frederick St, Bridgeton, Glasgow;

Peter Hay, sometime dyer, Leith Walk, now residing at Inglis Green, Slateford husband of the late Jessie Ireland or Hay.

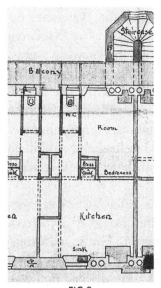

FIG.9
House Plan from Dean of Guild Petition, 31 May 1894.
Edinburgh City Archives

The fortunes and needs of the Watergate linked the tenement to the income and property of a variety of women. Many were in the suburbs of Edinburgh but, given the migration propensity of the Scots, others were scattered across the globe.

Geddes was a great reader of Ruskin. He was deeply influenced by Darwin. He was a field biologist and follower of Herbert Spencer. Thus he was concerned with the influences of environment on the 'evolution' of urban populations. The Dean of Guild plans show something of the environment he was creating for the women of Watergate.

With minor variations, the house plans had standard features.

Each household had its own front door and its own internal sanitation, offering some privacy. The two rooms and the bed recess offered a minimal level of privacy within the family and household. Externally other features were in evidence. A complex of rain water and soil pipes ensured waste was carried from the building. The open balconies meant that the winds of Edinburgh dispersed the smells linked with disease and degradation.

Central to the Geddes principles of social 'evolution' was the importance of aesthetic stimulus and this was evident, albeit at a minimal level, in the Watergate. Geddes's architect Frank Simon provided a series of half-timbered gables and a light coloured harling for the upper floors. There were hints of crow steps by the chimneys and, in a last minute addition to the plans, a turret straight from the text books of Scots baronial architecture, was added to the south-west corner. Photographs taken just before demolition show a shabby but still distinctive building with gables that would not have been out of place in an English suburb, and crow steps and a turret to give a visual reminder that this was Scotland.

Further details of the environment created for the women of the Watergate were contained in the feu charter of 7 September 1894 agreed between John McLaren as feudal superior and Patrick Geddes. In terms of the hierarchies of authority which were enabled by the Scottish feudal system, Geddes was clearly the subordinate. Geddes was required, within the year, to erect a tenement of dwelling houses and shops with four storeys to the Canongate. They were to have an annual value of at least four times the feu duty, which was to be £50 a year on the whole tenement. The materials and appearance were specified in some detail. The street level storey was to have pink coloured Hailes stone for the rubble work and, for the dressings, polished red stone from Moat Quarry in 'Northumberland'. The upper floors were to be rubble work from Hailes, which was to be plastered with cement and rough cast of yellow or other approved colour. The importance of aesthetic stimulus was evident in this

FIG.10
The Watergate c.1964 – artist's impression.
Olrig Stephen

detailed specification. The Watergate was intended to stand out from the greys and browns surrounding it. It was the artisan answer to Ramsay Garden.

The feu charter placed further limits on the use of the buildings and the courtyard behind. The ground at the back of the said tenement was to be 'an open space for bleaching or drying clothes and no buildings of any kind shall be erected thereon in all time coming'. The buildings were 'to be used as dwelling houses and shops only and no trade or manufacture or operation shall be carried on upon the ground ... which may be deemed a nuisance... injurious or prejudicial.' In other words, the development was to be reserved for residential and retail in an area where industrial establishments were increasingly crowding out residential space.

Next to the Watergate was White Horse Close. This was Edinburgh Social Union territory. Geddes had split from ESU and a comparison of the management styles showed why. White Horse Close was managed by the lady visitors of the ESU. The Monday morning visits were supportive but strict discipline was imposed. There were clear rules against lodgers. The Watergate was managed by George Brotherston, an experienced house factor who knew the Canongate well. His offices were in St John Street. He was chairman of the St Cuthbert Parish Board and active in the Canongate Ward Advanced Liberal Committee. The radical liberal network was probably the link with Geddes and McLaren.

Geddes did not look to detailed supervision of his tenants. He offered them an environment with possibilities of household privacy and integrity, of health and air circulation and positive forms of aesthetic stimulus. After that evolution were left to the processes of the market and the relationships of the household. It was an equivalent if very different form of self-regulation from that of the student halls.

Boardman and others have promoted the version of Geddes as an innovative intellectual who left the practical details to others, of the visionary battling along in the uncaring world of Edinburgh. Property dealings like that of the Watergate showed this was not the case. His commitment as manager was one of the selling points for the Town and Gown shares. He was surrounded by competing visions for the improvement of the poor and working classes. He was sought after as a partner by men like Lord John McLaren. Watergate was part of the learning process which, for Geddes, was Edinburgh.

Professor Robert Morris

CHAPTER EIGHT

Failure in Dundee?

Mary Lily Walker, Patrick Geddes and the Dundee Social Union

IN APRIL 1888 Patrick Geddes was offered a part-time post as Professor of Botany at University College Dundee. He was to teach in the summer terms; an appointment which lasted until 1919. In practice, this arrangement was not totally successful for Geddes or for the University. However, the opportunity to continue his academic career would have tempered his disappointment in failing to secure the Chair of Botany in Edinburgh. During his time in Dundee, Geddes was to inspire further work on social reform and was free to follow his wider interests in civics and town planning, to maintain his base in Edinburgh, and to continue the work for which he is now best known.

In Dundee, Geddes joined a young, talented, and enthusiastic group of academics headed by Principal William Peterson (1856–1921), D'Arcy Wentworth Thompson (1860–1948), Professor of Biology, James Alfred Ewing (1855–1935), Professor of Engineering; and John Edward Aloysius Steggall (1855–1935), Professor of Maths and Natural Philosophy. These academics shared Geddes's concerns about poverty, health, and squalid living conditions in Scottish cities. James Ewing, inspired by the work of the Sanitary Association in Edinburgh, had instituted the Dundee Sanitary Association, which originally dispensed advice on remedying defects in houses and this provided the basis for the development of a social union to address wider issues.

The inaugural meeting to establish the Dundee Social Union (DSU) was held on 24 May 1888, a few weeks after Patrick Geddes arrived in the city. D'Arcy Thompson ascribed the foundation of the DSU to James Ewing and John Steggall and this is likely as the two major areas of the DSU's early work were housing and sanitation. However, Thompson noted that by 1889 concerns had spread to other areas.

> While Ewing was thinking of housing and sanitation, Geddes was thinking of the dullness of men's lives and the need for something more than bread alone.

Patrick Geddes's influence in the early days of the DSU is clearly visible. The organisation adopted similar objectives and working practices to the Edinburgh Social Union (ESU), and gained inspiration from the work of Octavia Hill. Initially, four small slum properties were purchased to be managed by the DSU, with restricted rent paid to the proprietors. Gradually the work extended into programmes of work on education, health and well being. The initial work included a Sanitary Committee appointed to look into the poor condition of housing in Dundee. This committee undertook a questionnaire of inhabitants, produced a very critical report and met the Dundee Police Commission to pass on concerns.

Patrick Geddes joined James Ewing and John Steggall on the DSU's first General Committee, which had 27 members. These included professors, clergymen, professional and business men, Dundee's Provost, and several women, including Mary Lily Walker, a gifted student and close friend of D'Arcy Wentworth Thompson.

It was Mary Lily Walker who was to become the driving force and inspiration for the work of the DSU and for the development of social work in Dundee. Her name lives on in the 'Lily Walker Centre' at 105 Ann Street, Dundee, the City's main reception point for the homeless. She is also one of the 25 women celebrated in the Dundee Women's Trail.

Only a few records of the DSU's work remain. However, a detailed account of Mary Lily Walker's life and work is given in Myra Baillie's thesis *Mary Lily Walker of Dundee: Social Worker and Reformer* whilst early appreciations of her work were written by her close friends, D'Arcy Thompson and Meta Peterson.

Mary Lily Walker was born on 3 July 1863, the first child of Thomas Walker, a Dundee solicitor, and his wife, Mary Allen. She attended Tayside House, a private school for girls, and in 1883 was one of the first students to register when University College, Dundee took the unusual step of opening its classes to women as well as men. She was a close life-long friend of Margaret Grace (Meta) Peterson, the sister of UCD's young Principal and was drawn closely into the intellectual life of the University. She had a brilliant University career and was soon working on academic papers with D'Arcy Wentworth Thompson. She attended lectures given by Patrick Geddes, whose work she found 'infinitely suggestive' and she became a close friend of his wife, Anna.

The only known photograph of Mary Lily Walker (FIG.11) suggests a serious, thoughtful young woman.

Mary Lily Walker and the DSU

In 1888, Mary Lily Walker began her social work career as a volunteer unpaid DSU 'lady rent collector'. During the 1890s, she spent time at two women's settlement houses in London (the Women's University Settlement in Southwark, and the Grey Ladies on Blackheath Hill). She came into contact with Octavia Hill and on her return to Dundee in 1899, founded her own settlement house, Grey Lodge, which served as a centre of social work connected to the DSU and which continues to serve as a community centre.

FIG.11
Mary Lily Walker.
Dundee City Archives

Between 1900 and her death in 1913 Mary Lily Walker rescued the DSU from decline and redirected and re-energised its programme by arranging conferences, bringing in guest speakers, and introducing new branches of philanthropy. She was a part owner of a DSU property, and of one of Patrick Geddes's Town and Gown Association properties in Edinburgh. However, she began to see that voluntary initiative alone would not improve the condition of the poor, and in 1901 she became one of the first female members of the Dundee Parish Council.

In 1905, Mary Lily Walker co-authored an important sociological survey of Dundee. Together with Emily Thompson and Alice Moorhead (Dundee's first female doctors) she was instrumental in establishing the first women's hospital in Dundee together with associated children's clinics. She introduced the first restaurant for nursing mothers ever established in Britain and kept in touch with new approaches to social work at home and abroad. She served as a member of the Dundee's Distress Committee and Insurance Committee and in 1907 presented oral evidence to the Royal Commission on the Poor Laws.

In her early contribution to the work of the DSU Mary Lily Walker had much in common with the ladies of the Edinburgh Social Union. However, although she is recorded as having spoken at the same event as Elizabeth Haldane, there seems to have been little communication between the two organisations which evolved differently in the two very different cities. Mary Lily Walker's personal journey was to take a very different route from that of her Edinburgh counterparts.

The evolution of Lily Walker's approach was described by her close friend, Mary Peterson:

> As her knowledge grew and her sympathies deepened, she abandoned, often with regret, opinions and methods to which tradition and education had led her, and adopted others which she felt more nearly satisfied her ideals of Christian citizenship. Hints of the nature of the shift may be found in her Housing Commission report. She no longer made fervent exhortations to the middle class to get involved in the wellbeing of the community. She now believed that 'the most clamant need is to make our workers discontented with their present surroundings, and in some way to fire their imagination with a concrete ambition towards a higher standard in their condition of life'.

She came to the clear recognition that philanthropy could not solve the rising tide of urban social issues and that more radical means would be required.

Common Roots of the ESU and DSU

Strong similarities may be seen in the origins of the Social Unions in Edinburgh and Dundee with Patrick Geddes playing an important stimulating role in each case. The teaching of Carlyle and Ruskin, the Arts and Crafts movement, concerns for the operation of the poor laws, religious teachings on the individual's moral responsibility, and the sheer visibility of the appalling conditions in which many people lived stirred the better off citizens to action.

Lily Walker was a committed Episcopalian and her religious commitment was strengthened through her time with the Grey Ladies, Blackheath Hill, London but according to her biographer, Myra Baillie,

> ... she saw clearly the differences between nominal Christians and the half-believers and agnostics of the UCD intellectual milieu; she wrote to her friend, Anna Geddes 'I know the follies and with sorrow I say it the dishonesty of many who call themselves Christians and how much better you are who don't.'

The middle class activists whose work was central to the development of both the ESU and the DSU came from similar backgrounds with strong representation from academics, medical practitioners, the churches, business, and arts and crafts. Lily Walker's background and early education was similar to that of Anna Geddes, her sister Edith Oliphant, and Elizabeth Haldane. She shared an interest with Anna Geddes in the establishment of girls' clubs and between 1891 and 1894 superintended the DSU Girls' Club, which had 30 to 50 members, until it was discontinued due to a 'want of workers'.

Like Mary Maclagan and Helen Kerr in Edinburgh, Lily Walker served as the Superintendent of the DSU Housing Committee and did much to raise the awareness of Dundee residents to the plight of the poor and to encourage them to engage in voluntary work. However, this task appears to have been more difficult in Dundee. The DSU's work was hampered by a rapid turnover in volunteer rent collectors. The initial high expectations in 1888 of anticipating no difficulty in procuring the services of other ladies quickly faded and almost every annual report in the 1890s lamented the lack of ladies willing to do the work, especially during the summer months when the Union had to employ a professional house factor.

Dundee was a very different city from Edinburgh. Lily Walker noted that Dundee's distinctive situation militated against the successful operation of a scheme based on Octavia Hill's approach. The large number of married women working in the jute mills and factories meant that rent collecting had to take place on Saturdays, which was inconvenient for both collector and tenant. Lily Walker recognised the inconvenience to the middle class ladies, but nevertheless appealed to their sense of social duty.

Both the ESU and the DSU were conscious of the difficult road to tread between providing help to improve living conditions and being criticised as middle class interfering busy bodies trying to control other people's lives. In Edinburgh, the ESU appears to have been more successful in their programme of work to decorate public spaces, and to provide craft skills training and recreation. In 1890 the DSU's Committee for Art and Recreation was founded and began to organise simple entertainments in the Drawing Room of the Young Women's Christian Association in Tay Street. It also built a small hall in Carnegie Street where various clubs met for sewing, singing, musical classes and other activities. However, Myra Baillie noted:

> By 1896, the DSU had disbanded its Recreation Committee, having failed to cross class lines by means of recreational pursuits. Dundee's class

barriers remained rock solid, requiring rather more than an appreciation of drawing room entertainments to surmount them.

Like Elizabeth Haldane, Lily Walker came to see the advantages of state intervention; this was not a view shared by Helen Kerr who continued to call for increased voluntary commitment and private provision of housing for the poor. Like Elizabeth Haldane and Helen Kerr, Lily Walker was to become more politically active albeit at a different level of government; taking a more personal and vocal form in an inhospitable local government; and focusing on more radical practical projects.

Both Elizabeth Haldane and Lily Walker were dedicated to the care of elderly sick parents and did not marry. Elizabeth Haldane worked closely in support of her brother. Once Lily Walker's invalid mother had died, her work and friends became increasingly more important. Friendships with the artists Margaret (Madge) Valentine and Janet Mary Oliphant, nieces of the Scottish author, Margaret Oliphant, were particularly supportive as was the friendship with Alice Moorhead, one of Dundee's first women doctors, with whom Mary Lily Walker did much to provide medical and social services for the women of Dundee and to lobby the Parish Council on the conditions of poorhouses. Both Madge and Alice suffered early deaths (both associated with childbirth) and grief and the loss of her friends appears to have been a driving force in Mary Lily Walker's commitment and dedication to working for the poor.

Conclusions

Patrick Geddes retired from Dundee in 1919 and went on to take up the chair of Sociology and Civics at the University of Bombay. In his farewell lecture he told his audience that he had been 'baffled' by the problems of Dundee, saying 'Beyond this little garden I have practically failed to make any real impression upon this great industrial city'.

Lily Walker had died on 1 July 1913 at the age of 49. Her experience in local government in Dundee had been one of 'frustration and disillusionment'. However, her legacy included the Women's Hospital; the Grey Lodge Settlement centre; the results of ground breaking research on the health and well-being of the poor in Dundee; the early training of women in the social work profession; and numerous services for children and women in the poor areas of Dundee. She was one of an important group of Scottish women, of whom little is known, who were inspired by Patrick

Geddes and who played a valuable role in addressing issues of social reform in Scotland.

Geddes may have felt he had failed in Dundee, but Lily Walker had not.

2013 was a double anniversary for Lily Walker. It was 150 years from her birth and the centenary of her death. Despite the rubric for the celebrations ('Dundee's Forgotten Heroine') she was not forgotten and the poster for the Mary Lily Walker Celebration promised a cheerful and engaging programme (PLATE 4A).

Veronica Burbridge

Chronology

1888   PG appointed Professor of Botany at University College Dundee
        Inaugural meeting of the Dundee Social union held on 24 May
        Mary Lily Walker became rent collector for DSU
1891   MLW became superintendent of the DSU Girls' Club
1893   MLW visited the Women's University Settlement, Southwark, London
1898/9 MLW joined the Grey Ladies, Blackheath Hill, London
1899   MLW returned to Dundee
1901   MLW became one of the first female members of the Dundee Parish Council
1903   MLW established Grey Lodge, Dundee
1905   Publication of the Dundee Social Union Report on 'Housing and Industrial Conditions and Medical Inspection of Children' by MLW and Mona Wilson
1906   MLW appointed to the Dundee Distress Committee
1913   Death of MLW aged 49 on 1 July
1919   PG's retirement and farewell lecture (Dundee)
1930s   Work of Dundee Social Union and Grey Lodge Settlement amalgamated to form the Grey Lodge Settlement Association
2013   MLW Celebration, 27–30 June in Dundee
Today   The work goes on. Grey Lodge, 21 South George Street, Dundee is a community centre, providing resources and accommodation for self-help groups, working with vulnerable groups and assisting community initiatives
        The Mary Lily Walker Centre at 105 Ann Street, Dundee is the main reception point in Dundee for all homeless or potentially homeless people

Bibliography

Baillie, Myra, *Mary Lily Walker of Dundee: Social Worker and Reformer*
    (Open Access Dissertations and Theses. Paper 6019, McMaster University,
    Canada, 1996)
Peterson, Mary M, ed., *Mary Lily Walker of Dundee: Some Memories*
    (Dundee, 1935)
Thompson, D'Arcy Wentworth, *1938 – Fifty Years ago and now: A presidential
    address: on the occasion of the fiftieth AGM of the Grey Lodge Associa-
    tion.* (Dundee 1938.)

CHAPTER NINE

A Dreamer's Daughter

Norah Geddes (Mears) (1887–1967)

SHORTLY AFTER THEIR marriage in 1886, Patrick Geddes and Anna Morton left their flat in Princes Street, in the New Town of Edinburgh, for 6 James Court, a near-slum off the Lawnmarket, in the Old Town, where they began – by precept and example – to improve the lot and self-image of the urban poor. The Geddeses had a whole flat – complete with Anna's piano – so that the locus of Norah's birth was unusual.

> On the lower floors lived the cobbler, the plumber's mate and the Corporation's street sweeper whose wives kept a clean house and presentable children. On the top floor were the tinker families it was impossible for the others to associate with, such was the dirt and vermin of their houses.

Norah's brother Alasdair was born in 1891 and Arthur in 1895. In 1894 the family moved to 14 Ramsay Garden, to the biggest of PG's co-operative flats ('13 rooms and two balconies'). It was so big, in fact, that the family could not afford to live there and it had to be rented out for most of the year to the family of a senior officer based at Edinburgh Castle. In the summer term, when Geddes was carrying out his duties at Dundee, they usually stayed in Newport. The family never had conventional summer holidays as they returned to Ramsay Garden for the 'Summer Meetings'.

The Education of Two Boys has been a rich source for biographers. Written and published in 1925 it is clearly reminiscence recollected in tranquillity – and for a purpose. It might be supposed that the two boys would be Alasdair and Arthur, but they are, in fact, Geddes himself and Alasdair, Arthur not being a suitable model.

Geddes pitches right in – 'Let me begin with mis-education' – with an attack on gambling and whether it should be repressed by law or checked by bettered education and conditions. The present system comes in for violent attack:

> Consider this biological view of such parents – who by abandoning their young to supposed (or even really gifted) super-parents provided with artificial orphanages called boarding-schools (or more accurately, standardising shops) – lapse necessarily, and to a serious extent, from the

mammalian level, and its intelligence accordingly, since thus acquired in nature and needing to be developed in civilisation.

Yet Alasdair had decided he needed a year at Edinburgh Academy to make sure he was not disadvantaged by his lack of conventional schooling. Home education, working on farms and at Millport Research Station, and an Arctic expedition, were not enough.

Geddes then proceeded to his own childhood and upbringing. His home and early adventures there and in the neighbouring Sidlaws are described – and behind it all is the benign presence of 'the wise father', ensuring stability and an education of 'Head, Heart and Hand'.

Where does Norah, the eldest, fit into this? Was a girl's education not important enough to be worth an article in an American sociological periodical? Let us consider first the question of stability and continuity. One hears so much today of parents who feel unable to move 'because of the child's education'; what was Norah's experience?

As we have seen, there were two fixed periods in the year. In late spring and early summer PG was teaching at Dundee and his family were based in Newport, south of the Tay but very accessible by ferry or by train over the Tay Bridge. In August the Geddes flat in Ramsay Garden was the social centre for the Summer Meetings. A full catalogue and itinerary of where and when the family rested for the remainder of each year would be tedious in the extreme, but a roughly chronological list will be found instructive.

Craufurd, in Broomieknowe, an attractive suburb above Lasswade, was a country house club:

> … to be shared out amongst friends, each member undertaking to spend so many weeks in residence there with their family if any. There was a resident housekeeper and the terms were most moderate.

Norah's principal memory of Craufurd was of Sunday morning talks at which her father, by folding a piece of paper, would expound his 'thinking machines'.

Nearby, at Hawthornden, Mrs Hill Burton had a house, aided by Jeanie Currie. Norah, aged five, made up the numbers in an Infant class of 50 or so 'ranged in ascending rows'. Norah was not impressed.

> When not otherwise engaged we had to sit with arms behind us and that seemed to me an indignity hard to swallow. Miss Currie reigned from the centre of the room and I presume she taught us something but now I do not know what it was all about, but I disliked the atmosphere of rigid discipline.

A winter in London, at Hyde Park Mansions, left two abiding memories, of pea soup fog and of her mother's pocket being picked while she sat on the top of an uncovered bus at night.

Mrs Hill Burton was the widow of the Historiographer Royal of Scotland and had her main residence at Boleskine, on Loch Ness. In 1897 Patrick and Anna went off to Cyprus for three months. Norah, Alasdair and the infant Arthur were left in Mrs Hill Burton's care – and on subsequent occasions. Jeanie Currie taught children from the estate and nearby farms and Norah and Alasdair joined in 'with some profit'. Norah remembered learning a whole page of spelling – 'A thing I never did before or since' – and how to use the dictionary. The local children taught them some Gaelic while the Geddes children tried to teach them French. Mrs Hill Burton read to them (in French) the Fables of La Fontaine.

But the most educative experience was the freedom to roam the estate, to meet the estate and farm workers and to learn from them something of their skills and traditions.

Mrs Hill Burton died suddenly in 1900 and when the Geddes family returned from the Universal Paris Exhibition it was to Valleyfield, near Dunfermline, to Innesforth. Mrs Hill Burton had intended to leave Innesforth to Jeanie Currie but had died before the necessary provision had been made. However, she had made the three Geddes children her residuary legatees. Paddy Kitchen says that Geddes contrived that the legacies be devoted to Innesforth and Jeanie Currie be established as tenant there.

Norah, however, wrote:

> This was a crying injustice. So when able, at the age of 18, I had a deed
> drawn up, making over the possession of the house to our Auntie Jeanie.
> I had no difficulty in getting my brothers to agree to this.

Both accounts may be true. The result was that the Geddes family had a cheap alternative home and Jeanie Currie was able to run Innesforth as a little home school for the Geddes children and Miss Currie's niece – an arrangement that lasted for at least four years.

The 'curriculum' was Geddesian. Book-learning till lunch. Afternoon was more creative – music/dancing, sketching, expeditions, play-acting, assisting the gardener (Professor Geddes). Alasdair would do some carpentry.

The regime was quite puritanical. 'We always had cold baths'. 'We learned to endure cold, hunger and fatigue'. No pocket-money. No machine-made toys. Plain food and plenty of milk.

At Innesforth we learn of the first stirrings of adolescence. Norah admired a few of the boys she met and male visitors like her Oliphant uncle. When visiting the Beveridges of Pitreavie she and the two Beveridge boys were puzzled by the behaviour of toads in a pond and disentangled the pairs – not realising that they were interfering with 'the essential processes of their nature, the fertilisation of the spawn'.

'At the age of 16 I was a child in all appearance', wrote Norah. Mr Marshall Bruce Williams was a man she 'admired and very much liked'. Norah's mother agreed that Norah and he should go to Pond Cottage for an additional one of his discourses. In the summerhouse she was surprised – 'but flattered and attracted' – when he proposed marriage 'but to delay consummation (he put it some other way) for some years ahead'. Norah did not encourage him. There followed a muddle of secrecy, misunderstanding and revelation. Norah's mother was furious but also concerned that she had somehow pushed Norah into an ambiguous situation by scolding her on the day of the proposal. Mr Williams had a difficult half hour with Anna, no more presents were given, a pendant was returned and Mr Williams faded away to London.

Again at 16, Norah enjoyed reading *The Cloister and the Hearth* but was puzzled

> … when Margaret and the hero spent a night in an armchair and the
> next thing was she was expecting a baby.

A couple of days later, when Anna and she were gardening, she asked – 'How do babies begin, Mother? What starts it?' There was a long pause, then, before Anna could speak, Norah said 'No, I don't think I want to know just now.' And the moment passed.

Musical education was never a problem. Anna had taught piano and theory of music before she was married and wherever the family went there was music. (In Dresden she had been rebuked by her landlady for singing 'Gretchen at the spinning-wheel' with too much passion!) In the Ramsay Garden flat there was a pipe organ and every house they stayed in had a piano or an organ. Anna taught Norah and Alasdair sight reading, singing by ear and had them compose tunes of their own.

Norah had years of piano tuition and practised regularly, but gave up at 15 because she had no facility,

> … even after having profited by some excellent and very helpful lessons
> by Mrs Kennedy-Fraser when I played some of the easier Chopin preludes
> and got pleasure doing so.

The day opened with a Latin hymn with Anna at the piano. Two books of French moral action songs, Chorales by Bach and Beethoven, a tragic tale of the Crusades, a roistering preparation for battle, 'The Heavens declare the Glory of God' from Haydn's *Creation* – kept them going for years.

French was spoken at the breakfast table and 'with our French friends and governesses we covered quite a lot of ground'. For several summers:

> We had the advantage of the presence of my parents' great friend Marie Bonnet. She gave us lessons in French, I suppose, but all I remember is reading *Les Trois Mousquetaires*.

(Marie Bonnet is the subject of Chapter 11 by Siân Reynolds.)

As we have seen, 1900 was a stimulating year, with eight removals in ten months. In April the family moved to Paris to prepare for the great Paris Exhibition at the Grand Palais and Petit Palais. Norah and Alasdair were 'privileged to help with the clerical organisation' of their father's International Assembly, preparing folders and distributing them by post 'or otherwise'. They also delivered notes, letters and invitations in a hurry.

> This we did with pleasure, but unfortunately Mother was not very discerning about social distinctions in a foreign country. We often went dressed in overalls of grey-blue check material worn only by the school children of the People. *'Enfants du peuple'*. The result was that when we asked the concierge for directions as was often necessary, they directed us up the back stair. But we had our dignity and the dignity of our mission to maintain, so we insisted on going up the stair proper or also outwitted the concierge – a dragon in human form. I remember one day we were proud because in the same afternoon we had a letter for Monsieur le Comte un Tel, Monsieur le Duc de Quelquepart and as climax one for Monsieur le Prince Bonaparte.

Anna would take them to afternoon concerts, after one of which they were given a lift home by Albert Kahn ('... a millionaire philanthropic Jew who endowed scholarships for students') via the Bois de Boulogne and his Paris home and garden.[1]

Newport was the place for biology, formal and informal. At thirteen Norah attended her father's class in Botany.

> I found the lectures interesting and the garden demonstrations too that my father conducted. He used to say to the students 'You've got a hinge to your back, let me see you use it'... This was held for two hours in the afternoon and I found it something of a strain working for so long in so minute a way... cutting sections or making drawings from the microscope or dissecting flowers or making floral diagrams.

Her father's lecturing she found 'vivid and arresting'. Unlike the French, he did not announce beforehand what he was going to say and then say it.

> Nobody could foretell what would come next, perhaps not even he himself. Many other subjects cropped up which had a bearing on what he had to say, though the relation might not jump to the eye. He explained what a feat of engineering a cornstalk was, showed it as a tubular girder of extraordinary strength.

> There was a Botany excursion every Saturday afternoon to the Carse of Gowrie or the Sidlaws and I enjoyed these... my father was at his best on these excursions. Coming home we all sang students' songs to help us along the way, there being no buses. The best excursions, perhaps, were the Sunday ones, when Gerald and I and Alasdair went alone, or with Rudmose Brown.[2]

Norah did the Botany course two years running, at 14 being given a first class certificate by her father's assistant, since she was not a regular student. At 15 she took the Zoology class of D'Arcy Thompson and 'enjoyed the marvellous clarity of his explanations and his blackboard drawings'.

She was sent on the Zoology class as a way of enlightening her in 'sex matters'.

> I don't think that penetrated, and yet I was quite clear about the anatomy of the creatures. We dissected the usual frog, rabbit, pigeon, snail, skate, dog-fish, mussel and the cockroach I thought the neatest of all. I was quite uncurious about sex as I suppose why it did not penetrate.

Each of these courses comprised 50 lectures and 100 hours of practical work. At the end of the Zoology course she sat an exam, at which she did not do as well as she thought she might have done. She blamed her parents for not providing her with a textbook till nearly the middle of the course. Nor could she write fast enough – 'for lack of school practice'.

One incident may be relevant – it certainly seemed important to Norah. One afternoon at Newport Norah came into the house with a spot of blood on her dress. She and Rudmose Brown had been engaged in a tussle, he had cut his finger and a little blood had gone on to the dress. Anna was furious – 'These games must stop!' They were not seemly at Norah's age (14). Norah was amazed and ashamed that she could not trust her own judgment as to what was right and what was not and took it very hard.

One of my responsibilities at one time was to inspect, on behalf of the local authority, the quality of the education being provided by those who

had chosen to educate their children at home. In most cases the academic
core was satisfactorily covered, the most common deficiencies being in
respect of socialisation and physical activities – games and physical education. For Norah there were always two maids and occasionally a governess
at home, with a constant stream of interesting adults and short-term
superficial contact with other children but no real indication of close
companionship with anyone but Alasdair. But with the Botany and
Zoology classes at Dundee she was in a group in the lecture room, in the
lab and on field trips.

At the age of eight she joined a gymnastics class in the Charlotte
Square School run by her uncle James Oliphant. In later life all she could
remember was the apparatus in a large hall lit from above, and performing
on the parallel bars 'in a kind of gloomy twilight'. Marshall Bruce
Williams, at Innesforth, taught the use of Indian clubs 'which we learned
to flourish with some dexterity'. In the converted coach-house – which
doubled as the school-room – they had a trapeze. 'He taught us various
stunts and that was an excellent thing'. At one stage he taught her how to
box. 'I got as far as learning how to parry blows, a useful art'. Anna got
wind of this and put her foot down – firmly. Single stick took its place.

At first they used long rose shoots with the thorns removed and at first
they had neither hand guards nor helmets. Presently Mr Williams
procured two helmets and the regulation ash-plants with guards.

> We set to nor did I come off altogether worst. Every now and then I
> disarmed my opponent by a turn of the wrist I could neither control nor
> avoid. Nor could I avoid catching him by mistake on the inside of the
> right knee where it hurt. He was not above aiming in revenge at my
> vulnerable parts in particular where I was unprotected by a jacket and its
> pockets, but I never let him know when it hurt me nor did I betray any
> satisfaction when he had to lift his weapon off the ground. I kept my eyes
> on his, and could tell by their glint when a stroke was impending and was
> not a mere feint. Sometimes we called out *Touché!* at every successful cut
> of the opponent and sometimes we went at it ding dong.

At 'the little private school' (see below) there was an ex-army gymnasium
teacher who said she should have been a boy. (A teacher chaperoned the
class).

Patrick Geddes was anxious to keep his children out of the tedium of
school, taking for granted that they would swim through his home education plan to pass the Scottish Universities' Entrance Examination in their
stride. But there was a clear need for systemisation and specialisation.

Anna gave the children lessons in the earlier stages because 'my parents held the theory that parents should be the educators and in my case no continuity was possible'. Norah's dedication might be judged by the fact that, when she was supposed to keep a diary, she 'used to wander round the house asking the maids what I had done the day before'.

At various stages the specialists were called in to balance the curriculum. Latin was taught by the headmaster of the Valleyfield village school. At nearby Culross Norah had water-colour lessons from a local artist. In Newport Mr James Douglas – 'a consummate water-colour painter' – also gave her lessons. Back in Edinburgh a Miss Alice Gray – 'a talented exponent of the art' – took her on for water colour lessons. They did not quite hit it off:

> She made me spend successive lessons on one still life, putting on washes, washing them down till they acquired a rich patina and a certain quality I was not in search of.

Miss Aimeé Hochstetter was a friend of Anna's. She had an atelier which employed a number of girls in her business of artistic dressmaking.

Once a week Norah was sent there to learn how to sew. Norah liked this:

> … when Miss Hochstetter read to me the while, but I liked less being relegated to the workroom with the girls. Their lack of refinement grated on me and I felt it a sort of indignity to be compulsorily associated with them: snob if you like but I think the feeling has another aspect. I don't think this experiment lasted long.

It was probably when they were at Innesforth that: 'To serve as a guide to our studies we took St George's correspondence course', which had 'periodic exams'.

In her 16th year Norah was sent to 'a little private school' in Newport, run by the Misses Wayman, in the first summer passing Higher English, French and German. Lower Latin and Higher Maths were more of a struggle and Norah completed her 'formal' education without the entry qualification for an MA course in arts and science.

At every stage and at every house Norah had been gardening and now she had decided that she wanted to be 'a garden designer, or landscape architect as it is sometimes called'. There was no suitable course in Edinburgh so she was sent to the School of Art to copy diagrams of the orders of classical architecture, to paint (more) water-colours and to sketch casts of ancient statues.

Norah was happy enough doing these things, but they did not help much towards becoming a landscape architect. When she approached the heads of departments she was told: 'If you can draw the human figure you can draw anything'. When she said she needed to be able to make perspective drawings of imaginary gardens she was given perfunctory lessons in perspective.

Her father was in London and could not help, but on his return found her a place with an old architect friend. His technique for rendering trees was deplorable and his whole style was wrong for Norah's purpose. But PG had his finger in so many pies that it was possible for Norah to enter the world of work as her father's assistant, after spells in Corsica and Montpellier. She spent much of three years in Dublin trying to organise gardens in corners of its old town, as she and her friends had done in Edinburgh, her scheme being incorporated in the national health policy for Ireland which Lord and Lady Aberdeen were promoting. Then there was the management of the Outlook Tower and Geddes's other Edinburgh projects, including Edinburgh Zoo.

Geddes's view of the beauty of physical labour was not always appreciated by lesser mortals. Norah wrote on 19 October 1910:

> This afternoon Miss Le Maistre and I and two helpers were working in the Open Spaces. While I was alone in the King Wall, hordes of boys

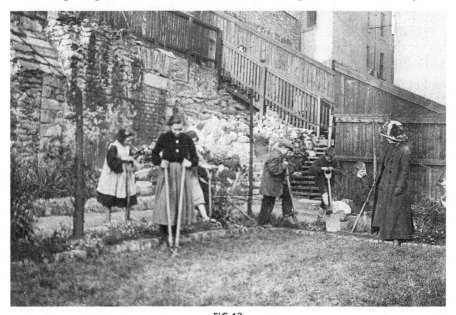

FIG.12
Young gardeners in the King's Wall Garden.
Patrick Geddes Archive, University of Edinburgh

came in and made a regular bear garden, watering the soaking ground, tying the hose in knots, scraping up the ash, threatening each other with the dangerous ends of the hoes, and swinging on the posts. They declared at intervals that they were all on strike. I took it more or less as a joke and got them off in a little while to the West Port carrying some tools. Of course the problem is a difficult one. Where enough to give so many to do in a small garden?

And again on 30 November:

I am very tired of grubbing in the Open Spaces and count on this week being the last – 1,000 small bulbs, at 50 for 1/-, have just been landed on us and I wonder how many of the miserable things will flower... Mr Mears seems very active just now and sends me strange diagrams, and discourses on art and symbolism.

Mr Mears was, of course, Frank Mears, Secretary of the Open Spaces Committee, Geddes's second-in-command and collaborator in, for example, the Photographic Survey of Edinburgh of 1905, for which he drew an excellent series of sketches showing the growth of Edinburgh. Mears went on to have 'a good war'. As Captain Mears he served under Alasdair (Major Geddes) in the Army Balloon Corps as a forward observation officer for the artillery. After the war he ceased to work in Geddes's shadow and went into practice on his own.[3]

On the Home Front World War I saw a shortage of labour on farms and in gardens as the men went off to war. Lady gardeners were in demand for servicing the heating systems of estate greenhouses as well as planting and cultivation and Norah busied herself in related organisations at home and in Belgium. For example, in October 1916 Amy McGregor wrote to Norah asking her to find a lady gardener to plan a garden at the new house on Loch Striven of her sister, Lady Anderson.

Norah and Mears were married in 1916 and Norah's life became that of the conventional wife and mother, her three sons Kenneth, Alasdair and John being born, respectively, in 1917, 1918 and 1921. Geddes tried to tie her in to the family by making over to her the furnishings and contents of 14 Ramsay Garden. These had belonged to Anna but the flat had had to be sold to the Town and Gown Association. Nevertheless the Mears family continued to live at 14 Ramsay Garden and Norah, in effect, managed the Outlook Tower. In 1931 she set up an 'Outlook Tower class' for pupils of low attainment in conventional education. Run on Geddesian lines it attracted a clientele for whom – for example – special arrangements were made with the Central Library.

Up to the time of her father's death Norah kept some distance between her and her father. There were spells of disagreement – as when Norah thought PG's marriage to Lilian Brown inappropriate – alternating with reconciliations.

From the start of her memoir Norah takes pride in listing her father's achievements and her affection for him is clear. Her poem 'The Tower of Patrick Geddes' sums him up very neatly.

I know an old house, a tall house, a stone house,
That stands upon a narrow street,
Yet looks from hills to sea.
If up its stair you clamber,
From chamber to chamber,
It may be you will find your feet
Can never more be free.

For if you meet the Enchanter there,
With searching eye, unruly hair,
He'll put a spell upon you,
A strange compulsion on you,
And if you do come down again
'Tis by another stair.

A stair that leads to no fair meads
Of Indolence and Ease,
But through the maze
Of Thought for days,
Till new ideas hum like bees,
And the time is come for Deeds!

In her memoir he is usually 'Daddy' and reads to her. She and Alasdair set up a 'Society for keeping Daddy young'. And he signed his letters 'Your affectionate Daddy' or (at age 77) 'Love to all, Daddy P'. But his expectations may have been too high and he may have found it difficult to unbend with his children.

On Sunday walks at Scotscraig, near Newport, there were fine displays of rhododendrons. Knowing her interest in flowers, Geddes would bombard his tired daughter with questions, looking for 'intelligent answers which were not forthcoming'.

Anxious for approval, Norah 'formulated some interesting thoughts' which she showed to her father. Father said she was quite right to put down these buds of thought – 'Without buds there would be no shoots and flowers'. Norah was disappointed with this dictum as she thought her thoughts were already flowers. And Anna was miffed that she had been bypassed. (This incident must really have rankled as Norah relates it twice).

Another disappointment was when, before she had 'done' fractions PG asked Norah to find out what a third of a quarter of a fifth would be.

> I drew a circle, quartered it and so on. When I told him what I had found out and showed him, he did not take any interest and had forgotten all about it.

There were periods of 'half estrangement' and times when Geddes thought he had lost Norah. Norah disapproved strongly of her father's remarriage and there seems to have been a long silence between them after this event – although the long list of pros and cons for his knighthood, written three months before his death, is genial enough.

When teaching in one of our famous Edinburgh schools I became conscious of a kind of middle-class deprivation. In our small boarding-house were boys dumped as a result of broken marriages or the vigorous pursuit of careers overseas. Among the day boys were many who were given every material possession but lacked attention from parents aspiring socially or working extremely hard.

Where was the author of *The Evolution of Sex* (1889) when Norah was groping with the problems of changing from childhood to woman-hood? Was he unapproachable by an anxious child? Was he unable to communicate in a **real** situation? Or was he simply setting the world to rights elsewhere?

The relationship with Anna was an edgy one. In the memoir she is always 'Mother' despite – or perhaps because of – her much greater 'time on task'. Although there were maids and governesses she had the burden of the child-rearing and I suggest that the strain of coping with her erratic husband, the finances and the family were not conducive to an open display of affection – as Arthur Geddes reported to Philip Mairet.

In Perth Museum is a copy of *The Philosophy of Arithmetic* by TD Miller, Rector (of Perth Academy). This is a substantial volume containing all that was necessary to cover the Higher Mathematics course, with line illustrations. No doubt the good Rector sold this book to his Higher candidates. The title page (FIG.13) calls it a Fair Book and written on it, in a fine Gothic hand, is the owner's name – 'P Geddes. Perth Academy.MDCCCXXX'.

Before examining it I had hoped to find it a very personal document. Perhaps I would find scribbled annotations or admonitions to self. There

PLATE 1A
Mount Tabor Cottage, Perth. Home of Janet, Jessie and Patrick Geddes.
Kenneth MacLean

PLATE 1B
The Betrothal Opal, in the hands of Claire Geddes, grand-daughter of Anna Morton
and Patrick Geddes. *WMS*

PLATE 2A
Ravelston House, childhood home of Mrs MacLagan.
WMS

PLATE 2B
Tron Square, Edinburgh Corporation 1899, managed by ESU.
WMS

PLATE 3A
Wardrop's Court. Arthur Geddes's dragons restored.
WMS

PLATE 3B
Pipes and Balconies. Courtyard of the north block of
the Watergate. Dean of Guild Petition, 1 May 1894.
Edinburgh City Archives

PLATE 4A
Mary Lily Walker Centenary – poster
Artwork Brett Housego

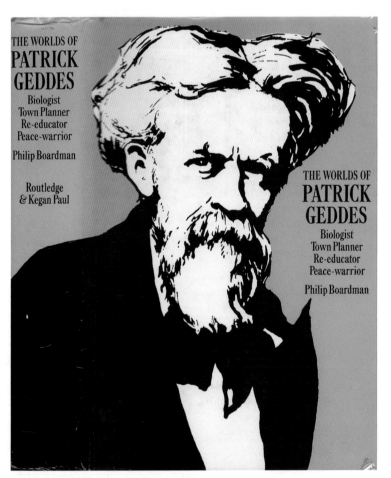

PLATE 4B
Patrick Geddes, Polymath. *Routledge and Kegan Paul*

PLATE 5A
Friar Row, Caldbeck. *Kenneth MacLean*

PLATE 5B
Annie Besant in Australia, 1922
Kenny Munro

PLATE 6A
The *Golden Boat* in Kolkata. Note photographs of Geddes and Tagore. *Kenny Munro*

PLATE 6B
The *Golden Boat* in Ballater. *Kenny Munro*

PLATE 7A
Sister Nivedita's Girls' High School, Kolkata (opened 1898). *Advaita Ashram*

PLATE 7B
Nivedita – Vajra/Thunderbolt. *Advaita Ashrama*

PLATE 8A
Roy Villa, Darjeeling. Here Sister Nivedita breathed her last. *Advaita Ashrama*

PLATE 8B
Painting the Geddes Panel. *Kate Henderson*

might be little sketches and comments on the good Rector's teaching, or some reference to Geddes's mother's supervision of his homework. Unfortunately, apart from the page illustrated, the rest of the book is in pristine condition – Geddes must have written the various proofs and calculations into another book, long since lost.

In 1952 Geddes's Outlook Tower was in a state of chaos. Lady Norah Mears extracted the Fair Book from the Outlook Tower library and presented it to Perth Museum, where it is now on display. Norah's relationship with her father, as we have seen, was not of the smoothest but we see here a kind of reconciliation in which was

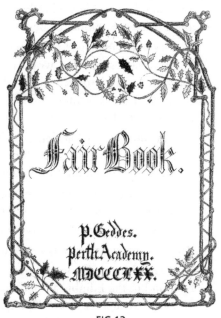

FIG.13
Fair Book of Patrick Geddes, Perth Academy.
Perth Museum

saved for posterity one of the books which helped to form the man Geddes. How appropriate it is that it should be preserved in the very building where Geddes, in 1883, took a leading part in a *Conversazione* to mark its inauguration.

Walter Stephen

Notes

1 Abraham (later Albert) Kahn was that rare phenomenon, a banker with a heart. Starting as a simple clerk he amassed a fortune in banking, moving into diamonds in South Africa and copper in the Congo, with a villa and garden in Paris and three enormous villas on Cap Martin on the Riviera. From 1906 he sent out hundreds of students to record the life and customs of endangered societies, especially in Asia. From their documentation he set up, in 1906, *Les Archives de la Planète* with 72,000 colour photographs (while Geddes was organising his black-and-white survey of Edinburgh) and 170 kilometres of film.

He lost everything in the Wall Street crash of 1929. His villa and beautiful garden by the Bois de Boulogne were bought by the department of Seine in

1937 and he was allowed to live there until his death in 1940. His Institute and garden are among the best-kept secrets of Paris.

Geddes never managed to attract a really powerful patron and Kahn, with his great interest in India, would have fitted the bill very nicely. There is scope for some research to see whether these two parallel lines ever came together, or whether the charming Geddes children were no more than a pleasant diversion one late afternoon.

2   Gerald Stanton and Alasdair were bottle-washers together. Rudmose Brown was PG's assistant. Between him and Norah there may have been a little *tendresse*. At one point Norah says that:

> On the excursions by ourselves, without the Botany Class, we used to engage in games of rough and tumble, at which he was the good-natured giant. This was a great joy for me, who had no elder brother.

Rudmose Brown re-emerges in Kenneth Maclean's chapter on Mabel Barker.

3   'Sir Frank Mears, Associates, Architects and Planning Consultants' can still be found in the Edinburgh phone book. Robert Naismith was a partner in Sir Frank Mears, Associates. He and his sister lived in 14 Ramsay Garden for 25 years, restoring 13 of the 22 murals Geddes had had painted there. On Naismith's death the flat was bequeathed to The National Trust for Scotland.

Bibliography

Mears, Norah G, *Intimations and Avowals* (The Moray Press, Edinburgh and London, 1944)

Geddes, Norah, Unpublished *Memoir* (Roger Mears)

Reynolds, Siân, *Professor Geddes Goes to the Fair: The Globe, the Assembly and the Rue des Nations at the 1900 Paris Exhibition* in *Paris-Edinburgh: Cultural Connections in the Belle Epoque* (Ashgate, Aldershot, 2007)

CHAPTER TEN

'A troublesome assistant who will not be dismissed'

Mabel M Barker (1885–1961)

Introduction

MABEL BARKER WAS Patrick Geddes's god-daughter; a key co-worker, a supportive figure throughout his diverse career, and one of his most dedicated 'disciples'. From Saffron Walden Training College to Dublin's Town Planning Exhibition, from Edinburgh's Outlook Tower to Priory School, Kings Langley, or from the *Collège des Écossais*, Montpellier, to Friar Row School, Caldbeck, her vocational paths were unswervingly committed to spreading the 'Gospel according to Geddes'. His was the message of a polymath: an intellectual generalist in the best Scottish tradition, unafraid to challenge contemporary trends towards disciplinary specialisation (PLATE 4B). Nor was Mabel any less of an academic vagrant. Like her god-father, she was first and foremost an educator; her teaching career centred on promoting the Geddesian concept of regional survey. As he put it:

> Throughout life I have been active in these two causes of survey and occupations... to bring them together as warp and woof of our fresh educational weave.

As well as her role as proselytiser of regional survey, must be mentioned her passion for mountaineering and rock climbing – activities that intersected with and shaped her concept of regional survey. Barker was one of the foremost female climbers of her day: a fearless and supremely talented climber, credited, for instance, with the first female ascent of the Central Buttress on Scafell (1925), the first female traverse of the Cuillin Ridge (1926), and pioneering fresh routes in the Lake District.

Early life and schooling

Patrick Geddes had a profound impact upon Mabel's life and career from her earliest years. She was the daughter of Harry Barker (1854–1934) a

close friend of Geddes. Born in the same year, both spent their formative years in Perth where they attended the local Academy; both shared common interests exploring and rambling in their local neighbourhood from Kinnoull Hill to the Tay and beyond – activities that significantly influenced Geddes's concept of regional survey. Their career paths deviated – Harry trained as a chemical engineer and became manager of the Maxwell Brothers fertiliser plant at Silloth. However, they maintained life-long contact, as witnessed by their letters and Barker's readiness to assist Geddes financially in such ventures as The Town & Gown Association.

Confirming his willingness to act as Mabel's god-father, Geddes enthusiastically noted that he would:

> … heartily promise to stick by the wee lassie to the utmost of my power, (and) in so far as you entrust her education to me, to do my best for it. Suppose we begin at once by suggesting for her earliest playthings as soon as she is old enough to handle things some pretty stones and shells from the beach, flowers too of course, and before she is two years old to be presented with a chunk of not too wet clay. (Horror shrieks Mamma, perhaps?) (no, I don't think so after all) to make mud pies and to begin the practice of **solid** thoughts (Geddes's emphasis). I am not joking. A philosopher of my acquaintance is doing that with much effect upon his bairns.

Such statements reflected Geddes's belief that educating young Mabel in and about her environment was the most important aim of a 'true' education, and the sooner started, the better. His basic principle of education was *Vivendo Discimus*: By living we learn. And, as Mabel remembered, Geddes put these beliefs into practice in her infancy:

> My first memory of him is one of the earliest and most vivid impressions of childhood. We walked along the sand dunes and sea-shore of the Solway. He pointed out one fascinating object after another – seaweeds, zoophytes, shells, an orange fungus glowing in his shading hands – objects he suggested for a child's museum (which was commenced forthwith).

Mabel's was a happy childhood: a born tomboy, she had liberty, with her brother, to roam, climb trees and explore derelict chemical works. Of her formal education, however, Mabel's memories were less favourable. As recalled in her PhD thesis, her conventional Victorian instruction at primary school, while not uninteresting, lacked the experiential stimulus that would have come from outdoor visits. Nor did her educational experiences improve after the death of her mother when Mabel was aged ten. She was sent to Perth to live with her father's three sisters, and attended The Ladies School, Blackfriars House, led by the Principal, Miss Alice Burton.

Here the educational atmosphere was even more stultifying; there was nothing to link textbook with the realities of landscapes, past and present: 'not the slightest connection between what I learnt and the world I knew as a child'. Relief from such tedium came from breaks at the Geddes family home, not least with his children, Norah, two years her junior, Alasdair and Arthur, and the ever-welcome holidays at Silloth with the prospect of personal rambles.

But the biggest and most welcome change came when her father sent Mabel in 1900 to Truro High School for Girls. Founded in 1880 by Bishop Edward Benson, the school aimed:

> ... to widen their intellectual life, encourage a spirit of curiosity, a habit of close observation and achieve a delight in the outdoor world.

Led by one of her relatives, Alice M Morrison, the High School provided a varied experiential education, well suited to Mabel. Academically she did well, gaining at different stages, first prizes in scripture, drawing, science, botany and even mathematics, a subject which did not appeal. Dancing and hockey were other interests; and equally important were opportunities afforded boarders like Mabel to enjoy the Cornish coastline, valleys and upland moors at weekends and holidays: wanderings for which she was awarded the prize for the Holiday Collection of Flowers. Mabel's years at Truro were a truly formative period, leaving her convinced that learning should be 'a living dynamic process, closely related to nature and the earth'. Mabel's life-long educational credo was not a matter of book-cramming confined to the classroom and pursuing externally imposed curricula; rather, her educational framework had to be experiential in the round, firmly embedded in Regional Survey.

Regional Survey and the Outlook Tower

Before discussing Mabel's career, it would be useful to say something about regional survey. She defined it as:

> ... a study made of one's environment, rustic or urban; generally of some centre of civilisation, be that village, town or city studied in relation to its region and from as many outlooks as possible.

A more concise definition came from fellow-Geddesian, Rudmose Brown. It was 'the stock taking of an area'. Both followed Geddes's conception of regional survey. This drew on his upbringing on Kinnoull Hill, his evolutionary biological outlook, his acquaintance with French geographers, notably Elise Reclus, and, in particular, mining engineer Frederic le Play's elemental notion of the basic determinates of society – '*Lieu, Travail, Famille*' – 'Place, Work, Folk'. As Barker explained:

> Survey thus seeks to use and correlate the services of all sciences, physical, biological and social.

More significantly, the Survey was the foundation stone of regional and environmental betterment.

Many will be familiar with Geddes's planning model – Sympathy, Synthesis and Synergy, where Sympathy is the initial survey of a problem – always involving the local people. Barker's constant preoccupation with regional survey is therefore more than dry accumulation of facts but is a cooperative exercise in learning with a local application.

Two main tools were developed by Geddes to elucidate inter-relationships within his famous trinity.

The Valley Section, demonstrated a longitudinal model river valley from source to sea, embracing the range of 'nature occupations' from hunter and miner on the ridge, descending in time and space through woodman, shepherd and peasant on the uplands, to farmer and townsman on the plain, and broadening out to an estuary with its fisher-folk. An ideal education, Geddes argued, should allow youngsters to experience at first hand one or more of the occupational segments of the Valley Section. This would contribute to a holistic approach to educational development, one that highlighted the 'three H's – Head, Heart, Hand' rather than the oppressive impact of the three R's.

Geddes's second tool was the Outlook Tower. Acquired in 1892, it was:

> A place of outlook and a type-museum... a key to a better understanding of Edinburgh and its region... and of the city's relation to the world at large.

These are the tools which are needed by an explorer in your place, or any other :—Ordnance Survey maps ; camera ; pocket lens ; compass; knife and string ; pencil and pocket book; coloured pencils, inks or paints ; tracing paper ; a measuring tape is also useful but, if you cannot get all these at first, begin with a note-book and pencil.

FIG.15
The Valley Section, from Exploration.
Sir Patrick Geddes Memorial Trust

This structure atop Castle Hill symbolised his vision of the region and its global context set in stone. At the top of the Tower was a Camera Obscura and a viewing gallery, affording an incomparable vision:

> … for from here everyone can make a start towards seeing completely that portion of the world he can survey.

As visitors descended, they encountered five storeys, each fittingly furnished with graphic representations and equipment, testimony to Geddes's stress upon visual thinking that integrated science and the arts. First, the Edinburgh Room housing relief models, pictures, maps, paintings and displays illustrating the city's growth from earliest times. The next storey depicted Scotland and the geographical influences upon its history; the third covered Britain and the English-speaking world, commonly called the Language Room; the fourth, Europe; and the fifth was the world room with its two large globes.

Overall, the Tower was a discursive site for the ever-voluble Geddes:

> He roamed around the sciences as around the scene and from the Tower's terraced roof he developed the most basic technique of the geographer teaching in the field, that of pointing and talking from a highpoint,

Camera Obscura

THE GEDDES EXPERIENCE
OF THE TOWER

A: "Breathless Ascent"

B: "Concentric Descent"

1. Edinburgh Room

2. Scotland

3. Britain and the
" English -speaking
World "

4. Europe

5. The World

FIG.16
The Geddes Experience of the Outlook Tower. *The late Norman Thomson.*

one of the many approaches adopted by Mabel as organiser and teacher diffusing Geddes's concept of regional survey.

Teacher Training and Training Teachers

Schooling over, Mabel, encouraged by her father and god-father, spent the next 12 years training to be a teacher, gaining her first degree, teaching in schools, assisting Geddes at Dundee, and acquiring a post-graduate qualification in geography. In 1904 she enrolled at Cheltenham Ladies College, where students could study for external London University degrees as well as the Cambridge University Teacher's Certificate. Mabel attended classes in general science, specialising in geology for her External BSc, awarded in 1907.

Three months teaching botany in Limerick at the Convent of our Lady of Mercy in 1908 conveniently finished in time for the summer term at University College, Dundee. At last she had the chance to assist Geddes (as Demonstrator in Botany) whose lecturing duties were confined to the summer term, allowing him liberty for the remainder of the year to pursue elsewhere his gallimaufry of interests, not least urban renewal and regional survey. Not all students and staff were pleased with the eclectic content of his teaching matter, ranging from Political Economy, Education for Peace and Fine Art to the structure of plants. But his course was meat and drink for Mabel, and not just her.

Session 1908–09 saw Mabel undertake her first, full time teaching position at Gowerton County School, Glamorgan, followed by the offer and acceptance of the post of Science Mistress at Saffron Walden Teacher Training College, Essex. The next three years were particularly fulfilling for the young lecturer: friendships were forged, Geddesian predilections pursued. Local historian Martyn Everett comments:

> Her arrival made a profound impact. Her enthusiasm for drama, litera-
> ture, history, country dancing and all kinds of outdoor activity but espe-
> cially nature study was rapidly communicated to her students.

A Historical and Geographical research society was set up to study the area in and around Saffron Walden. Links were made with the local museum and like-minded teachers, notably George Morris, Science and Geography Master, at the local Friends' School. An enthusiast for all forms of outdoor education, Morris organised school holiday tramps and camps for groups of pupils.

At the request of Geddes, Mabel and George initiated a regional survey of Saffron Walden, mainly using Training College students. A graphic survey was conducted, using relief models, photographs and maps to illustrate physical elements, for instance, drift geology and relict landscape features such as medieval strip fields. Many of the Survey results were displayed not only in Saffron Walden's Town Hall but at subsequent exhibitions in Ghent, London, Edinburgh, Belfast and Dublin. To accompany the Survey, a 35,000-word thesis was written by Mabel: a valuable source for descriptions of parts of Saffron Walden long gone. In Camps Yard, Castle Street,

> There were no back ways or separate yards to the houses, very little
> direct sunlight or fresh air, sanitary arrangements are very badly planned.

Recommendations for dealing with urban decay were made at the back of the Report. These and other proposals were implemented in the town during the inter-war years; testimony to Geddes's mantra of regional survey first, before planning appropriate social and environmental improvement.

Next came St Hilary's Hall (now College), Oxford where Mabel studied for the University's post-graduate Diploma in Geography during the academic year 1912–13. The Diploma was a key route to a formal geography qualification at that time. Mabel attended varied courses in regional, physical and human geography, as well as surveying, and met several influential pioneers in the educational world. She also appears to have delivered two seminar papers: one on *Saffron Walden District*, and in complete contrast, *British Trade with Russian Empire and Eastern Asia*.

Viewed in the round, possession of these academic qualifications and teaching experience would have more than satisfied any school or training college of Mabel's fitness to run one of the discrete science or geography departments that were emerging. However, apart from a period in the 1940s as Geography Mistress at The King's School, Peterborough, Mabel regularly eschewed such appointments after Saffron Walden, as typified in a letter to Alasdair Geddes, from the Outlook Tower, 18 November, 1914:

> I have applied for a geog. post in the Glasgow's High School for next term. I may not get it of course, and if I don't shall try to stick on in Edinburgh getting odd jobs of some sort – I do want to go on working here as much as possible. I am unwilling to get tied up tight because it won't leave much time for the Tower, and because I want to be free for your father when he wants me again.

The 'Tower' was Geddes's Outlook Tower and similar expressions of 'discipleship' permeate her correspondence. Basically her lifelong educational goal was to assist Geddes, where and when possible, practising and promoting regional survey by organising exhibitions and vacation meetings, and experimental teaching methods.

Organising Regional Surveys

Easter 1914 saw Mabel working with George Morris at the Outlook Tower as organising secretaries for the first Conference on Regional Survey. This was a significant conference: it established a Provisional Committee for Regional Survey, which eventually led to a national Regional Survey Association, with off-shoots such as the Scottish Regional Survey Association.

In Mabel's estimation, it was fitting that Edinburgh hosted the first regional survey conference. It was the site from which Geddes's teaching on the subject mainly stemmed; programmes of civic renewal had been initiated by him in its Old Town; and the city's environmental, historical and regional context 'made it peculiarly suitable for the beginning of regional studies'. As well as lectures, discussions and field trips, evenings often included 'At Home' sessions, given by Mrs Anna Geddes with Scottish folk songs.

The 1914 Edinburgh Conference was Mabel's most important challenge to date; within weeks she was in Dublin assisting Geddes with the Cities Exhibition and School of Civics, just as World War 1 broke out. Outings were organised within the city to outline its housing problems and beyond to better appreciate its regional context. There was also a stimulating 'synthetic' excursion, in which, from a viewpoint on the Dublin Mountains, the landscape below was described in turn by a geographer and geologist, botanist and anthropologist;

> ... and then its folk-lore and history were made to live for us by Miss Young. The sociologist (Professor Geddes) was called upon to sum up, and concluded, in characteristic fashion, by inaugurating song and dance.

In her guiding role as organising secretary for Geddes, she worked at differing times for the Regional Survey Association, the Sociology Society and the Le Play Society. Although she was: 'a girl of great energy and strength', endorsing regional survey was hard work: it required patience, tact, commonsense, and strength of character in her dealings with PG (especially) and others. The administrative load was demanding: shoals of correspondence; coping with enquiries about membership; timing meetings to suit differing Scottish and English school holiday requirements; arranging accommodation for participants; and vainly persuading Geddes to allow participants occasional breaks, but:

> ... the Prof has finally insisted on filling it up: says people needn't come unless they like etc, etc.

Overall, it is difficult to overestimate the significance of Mabel's hard work and organisational abilities promoting regional survey as an educational approach. She had absorbed Geddesian ideas from her earliest days, but it took someone practical and determined like her to assist in their diffusion. As she explained: 'the Conference cannot be said to be closed'.

A Sheffield Interlude

1916 saw an interesting, albeit short, career switch for Mabel when asked by RN Rudmose Brown [1879–1957], lecturer in geography at Sheffield University to take his junior classes for Lent term that year. 'Ruddy Brown', as dubbed by some, was one of the 'explorer geographers'; he studied Biology at Aberdeen and Montpellier Universities, and served as Geddes's assistant at Dundee. He was appointed first lecturer in Geography at the fledgling University of Sheffield.

In January 1916 a Special Meeting of Sheffield's Faculty of Pure Science was informed that: ...

> the services of Dr Rudmose Brown had been requisitioned by the Admiralty for a period of time which might extend to the end of May or even longer.

In fact his secondment was to last until the 1918–19 session. During those years, Rudmose Brown, along with other geographers, was engaged in writing Handbooks for the Admiralty, in his case on Siberia, Finland, Norway and Sweden. Arrangements were made whereby he returned once a week to take the advanced classes, but younger students were to be taught by temporary appointments. Mabel, on Rudmose Brown's recommendation, was, therefore, the first female geography lecturer at the Sheffield Department. She wrote to Geddes:

> I am feeling rather scared but he says the classes are very small and there's only about eight hours lecturing a week.

Her fears were unfounded; according to the historian of Sheffield University's Geography Department, there were only six students and she 'proved a gifted teacher'. Whether or not, she took advantage to stress, as the opportunity arose, the merits of regional survey methodology is not recorded.

For the ever-restless Mabel, however effective her university work, she felt called to aid the war effort more directly, and in April 1916 travelled to the Netherlands to assist with refugees.

Mabel and 'Peacedom'

Mabel stayed in the Netherlands from April 1916 until March 1917. Not only did she see at first hand the effects of war by assisting destitute Belgian refugees and internees, but these months afforded an opportunity to put into practice something of Geddes's notion of planning for 'Peace-dom'. Indeed war was to impact at an even more personal level. The previous year she wrote to Geddes's wife, Anna, that her brother, Arnold:

> ... has gone to France at last and he has gone as a sniper. I suppose shades and degrees of horror don't count for much in this business – but you well understand that it is a shock to me.

Far more traumatic, however, was the shattering news that he had been killed on the 28 June on the Somme, information that thankfully turned out to be false. In fact he lost a lung and had been repatriated to Aberdeen, just one of five colleagues, a 'Pals' group from the same Liverpool bank, victims of the carnage that was the Somme. In April the following year, however, she knew further pain following the death in a shell hole of Alasdair, Geddes's oldest son and her life-long friend. Perhaps it was espe-cially hurtful because she had attempted to dissuade him from enlisting. As she firmly phrased it:

> You, who see things so quickly and clearly as a rule – do you not believe that you can work for something better than even the prevention of ravage spreading across French and English and Scottish earth ? Give the earth real Peace, and she will heal even the wounds in time.

But enrol he did, and by the time of his death, aged 26, he had proved a loyal servant to his demanding father; a product of a mainly home-based education (save a year at The Edinburgh Academy) involving exposure to a range of occupational types. Despite his abhorrence of war, Alasdair's excellent reconnaissance work in the Army Balloon Corps resulted in early promotion to Major, and the award of the Cross of the Legion of Honour of France and the British Military Cross. During any lull amidst fighting, he encouraged his men to tend the plants around any requisi-tioned building, and even demonstrated how to plough adjoining fields using a borrowed plough and the artillery horses.

Alasdair's decision to enlist met with sorrow and anger from his father. Geddes was a long-time advocate of 'Peacedom' as opposed to 'Wardom'. Not that he was alone; the peace movement was being promoted by many active citizens, frequently through peace societies of which over 400 existed in Europe and the USA by 1900. Such societies were a response to the industrialisation of warfare, mass conscription and growing state-na-tionalism that came to a head in the butchery of World War 1. Mabel's god-father was long aware of the evils of war and militarism in his life-time, from the 1870–71 Franco-Prussian War to the bloodshed at the cusp of the century: the Armenian massacres, the Spanish-American War, the Russo-Japanese War and the Boer War, as well as the growing rivalry between European powers. War, according to Geddes the biologist, was a Darwinian struggle between contrasting occupational types, with their differing social structures, of the Valley Section. Historically, this was illustrated by conflict between the belligerent hunter and shepherd against the peaceful peasant with resultant agricultural deterioration, deforestation and soil erosion. And superimposed upon these long-term rural ills were those of what he termed the Palaeotechnic era: urban squalor, the economic injustice of capitalism, disease and slums. For Geddes, the militant pacifist, the preferred solution to such rural decay and urban decadence was 'an adventurous, constructive peace... that can compete with war and its glory'.

Such idealism was replicated by Mabel in her address to the 1915 London meeting of the Regional Survey Association. Drawing on her notes made at one of Geddes's ever-eclectic Botany classes in 1908, she suggested that, for the coming generation, education for peace through regional study was the answer. Knowledge, ideally at first hand of each of the occupational groups, was the way forward, but conceded: 'We do not all live in favoured regions where all occupations can be studied'. Nonetheless, outdoor experiences should be encouraged, thereby making life 'much more adventurous and exciting... We want more courage and power of enduring hardships'. While accepting that it was difficult for individuals to work-shadow (to use modern terminology), for example, a shepherd, at least something of the elements of his work, place and the dangers faced can be experienced through climbing real hills, while acknowledging that some element of risk was involved. Similarly, not all youngsters could actually experience the activities of a hunter, but teachers could substitute role play or use literature such as Kipling's *Jungle Book* to stimulate youthful imaginations, and:

> Surely one can hunt the biggest or smallest game, in exciting manner and places, with a camera. Every keen naturalist is something of a hunter, though the best of such kill but little.

Ultimately, war for Mabel was a tragedy; it was a conflict of attrition, a misspent application of the best scientific brains in the service of 'Wardom' rather than 'Peacedom', as revealed in this letter to Alasdair Geddes, 15 March 1915.

> It's not a deadlock but something even more terrible I'm afraid – a definite policy of 'attrition'... They are not trying to break the lines and drive

them back but to wear them thin: a thing I find it horrible to realize...
but I certainly do not see the conduct of this war as stupid: on the
contrary it seems to me that a perfectly amazing amount of brain-power
and organisation and application of all sciences has been involved. It is
the more awful that that they can be brought out and co-ordinated by
war and not as yet geotechnic activities.

Mabel's use of the word 'geotechnics' is apposite. It was defined, by an
American acolyte of Geddes, as the applied science of making the earth
more habitable. For Patrick and Anna Geddes in 1897, geotechnics
involved a six month sojourn in Cyprus initiating rural schemes to create
jobs for Armenian refugees; for Mabel in 1916, it involved working for
the War Victims' Relief Committee of the Society of Friends to improve
the lot of Belgian refugees and internees.

When Germany invaded Belgium on 4 August 1914, thousands fled
to neutral Netherlands, a restless flow peaking after the fall of Antwerp.
Initially Mabel was placed at Uden, a camp for civilian refugees sited in
the less-densely populated heathland (*Geeste*) areas of South Brabant.
Although she made return visits to Uden, she was mainly based near
Amersfoort, at Elizabethsdorp, a camp for the wives, children and elderly
relatives of Belgian soldiers, interned close by at Zeist.

The methods by which Mabel and her co-workers assisted these refugees were threefold. First, they provided employment. Workrooms or
'*Zals*' were established, craftwork skills were demonstrated and workers
made a wide range of items: brushes, mats, shoes and slippers, baskets
woven from local reeds at Uden, and woollen rugs and cushion covers
produced in the female workshops at Elizabethdorp. At Uden, by way of
payment, 'points' cards were given to the refugees for their end-products,
which could be exchanged for goods in the camp shops. Secondly, evening
classes were offered on a range of topics including English lessons and
country dancing, socials and concerts, and – not unexpectedly from a
Geddesian 'disciple' – gardening classes.

Thirdly, programmes of outdoor activities were initiated, sometimes
organised through newly-formed scout troops. Mabel, like Geddes, approved
of the opportunities that scouting offered youngsters. It was a means of
developing the physical and mental life of boys through outdoor education
and training in woodcraft and camping; of fostering a hunting as opposed
to a militaristic attitude; and assisted in the promotion of citizenship. At
Uden and Amersfoort, she assisted with scouting activities for boys and
girls: tracking and fire-making; demonstrating cooking and camping skills;
undertaking hikes through the pine forests and heather moorland;

FIG.17
At Elisabethdorp Camp, Holland, in June, 1916. Mabel third from right.
(from *And Nobody Woke up Dead*).
Williamina C Barker

building canoes and organising swimming parties. For Mabel, it was a
fruitful period, aptly summed up:

> She felt that she was able to give some measure of interest and happiness
> to the life of the refugees and to help some of the lads and lasses through
> their broken times, providing hope for the future.

Mabel sustained her interests in scouting after the war, including supporting an off-shoot organisation called Kibbo-Kift. It was founded in 1920
by John Hargrave (1894–1982). He grew up in the Lake District, had a
negligible amount of formal schooling but showed a precocious talent as
an illustrator of books by authors such as John Buchan. In its foundation
year, 1908, he had joined the Boy Scouts, soon forming his own troop of
irregular Boy Scouts, possibly the inspiration for a comparable troop – the
Gorbals Diehards in Buchan's novel, *Huntingtower* (1922). As a Quaker
pacifist, Hargrave enlisted in the Royal Army Medical Corps, serving as
a sergeant of stretcher-bearers in the Gallipoli campaign until invalided
out with malaria. An able leader and organiser, he rose through the ranks
of the Scout Movement, contributing articles under the name 'White Fox'
on Woodcraft for their popular magazine *Trail*, and appointed Boy Scout
Commissioner for Woodcraft and Camping by Baden-Powell after the war.

Hargrave, however, become disillusioned by what he perceived to be an increasingly militaristic tendency in the Scout Movement, and, with like-minded, pacifist scoutmasters, developed an alternative movement. Open to all regardless of sex, age or race, Kibbo-Kift appealed to Mabel; and in her thesis, the final chapter – *'L'Education Par L'Experience de La Vie'* – outlined the aims of Kibbo Kift:

1   To camp and live in the open air as much as possible, and to strive for perfection in the human body.

2   To be ready to give practical assistance to everyone; to learn, therefore, the skills of practical work as much as possible.

3   To work for peace in the world, and the fraternity of humanity.

Aspirations such as these matched her own educational outlook because of their emphasis on outdoor education and a quest for a universal state of 'Peacedom'. As well as participating in Kibbo Kift camps, Mabel collaborated with Hargrave – a devotee of Geddes, and prolific writer – in several educational pamphlets such as *Discovery* (1926). Another, also published by Le Play House, and written by Mabel herself was *Exploration* (1939). Its title page encouraged readers to 'Get to know your own Place and Work and Folk'. After a familiar valley section, she provided a series of prompts, questions and techniques organised under 15 headings, beginning with 'walk all over your region till you know it well enough to draw a sketch map from memory'. Later sections covered geology, weather and climate, history and modern conditions, concluding with camping and rambling.

Arguably, the key feature of *Exploration* was that its

EXPLORATION

REGIONAL SURVEY
Get to know your own Place and Work and Folk

" Every Village, Town or City is not merely a Place in Space, but a Drama in Time."   " All Time has gone over all Places,"and " Every Place is the centre of the World."—PATRICK GEDDES.

The place in which you live has largely determined the nature of the work which is done in it. This work in its turn has influenced the lives of the people. Try to know all you can about your Place, in the Present and the Past, and so help to make for it a great and happy Future. *BEGIN WHERE YOU ARE.*

If you learn to know your own place well, and in so doing learn to love it more, it will help you to understand and appreciate other places, and to sympathise with their problems.

THE
LE PLAY SOCIETY

Published by
THE LE PLAY SOCIETY
Late of 1 GORDON SQUARE, LONDON, W.C 1

ALL COPYRIGHTS RESERVED.

POCKET EDITION

Temporary Address: The Birlings, Birling Gap, Nr. Eastbourne, Sussex.

FIG.18
Exploration: Regional Survey.
Sir Patrick Geddes Memorial Trust

questions were not just about local knowledge *per se*; rather they were part of a life-long learning experience, capable of being used in fresh contexts. One touching instance of a wartime setting is illustrated by Ernest Young. He was a London headteacher, a well-known textbook writer and scoutmaster. Writing about the merits of regional survey, he recalled taking a party of scouts in 1916 to pick fruit at Pershore, Worcestershire, where the village headmaster incorporated the methods of regional survey into the curriculum and established a school museum replete with specimens collected by the youngsters, some of whose enthusiasm extended into adulthood. Young recalled:

> During my stay in the village the schoolmaster received a parcel from a ploughboy who was serving in France, and the parcel contained specimens of insects, flowers and rocks picked up in the trenches. This was by no means an unusual experience.
>
> ... testimony to the potential worth of regional survey taught by dedicated practitioners and promoted in publications such as *Exploration*.

Like so many of her generation, war impacted on and tested Mabel; yet she rose to its physical and mental challenges, well demonstrated in her dogged commitment to her Belgian charges. War more than affirmed her belief in the need for an alternative education system that promoted 'Peacedom', one embedded in regional survey, a methodology she was free to develop at Kings Langley.

Regional Survey at the Priory School, King's Langley

> But the really interesting thing is the working of the school. There are about 40 children, girls and boys, aged 4 to 18, and all the work of the school is done by staff and children – there are no servants. The work is all marvellously organised (perhaps a little too much so even). They are vegetarian and grow practically all their own vegetables and fruit. The place is surrounded by orchards – apple, cherry, walnuts etc and has a good deal of cultivated garden. There are goats and ponies, fowls and pigeons, dogs and rabbits, all immaculately kept. Inside the place is spotlessly clean and perfectly tidy. The tiled passages get washed twice a day and when helping to 'dust' one is quite pleased to find little... the place is rather too cold and the children get chilblains, though no other ailments it seems. The children are delightful, lively and friendly – in fact by the end of one week they were most affectionate and I shall be glad to

see them again, for I am to go back for a week in May, probably. We have got the Survey started all right, but I don't quite know how they will get on alone – their time is so very full.

It was an excited Mabel who wrote these words to Alasdair Geddes in March 1915, enthusing over her initial contact with the Priory School, a progressive private school in King's Langley, Hertfordshire. Sited on the southern slopes of the Chilterns, the settlement lies strategically beside the M25 and the Watford Gap, part of London's commuter belt; in 1922 she described it as a 'one-street' village on the trunk road to Tring, on the main London and North-Western Railway to Birmingham and on the Grand Junction Canal. This was the first opportunity to conduct regional survey since her experimental work with Edinburgh children the preceding year. Encouraged by the headmistress, Miss Cross, a proponent of survey methodology whom she had met at the Easter 1914 meeting, Mabel initiated survey methods. On day one of a preliminary visit, she took pupils on a walk to a high point in the chalk hills; day two saw her discuss the 'moral and social grounds' for survey methods with pupils, staff and interested adults.

Advice was given, topics were chosen, and were investigated over the next two years by pupil volunteers – mainly seniors, responsible for mentoring younger ones. Local industries – a popular choice – were studied, including paper, flour and brush mills, and possibly the expanding Ovaltine factory beside the Grand Junction Canal. Geology and vegetation studies were initiated; local housing conditions were surveyed and mapped. Study of the village's history and architecture such as the medieval priory involved cycle rides by senior girls to Watford or St Albans to study appropriate maps and documents. Only a few return visits were possible, given Mabel's other commitments over the next two years, but it was more than gratifying for her to see the successful application of regional survey methods. Mabel stayed for eight years until 1925: interspersing regional survey teaching with further vacation conferences, publishing pamphlets and pursuing her passion for climbing whenever possible.

Initially, there was no definite place for survey as a separate subject on the Priory's timetable, instead, children volunteered for after-school work. After two or so years, more staff assisted, and 'Survey' was given a place on the timetable. Work was now less individual, more of a class affair; allowing a greater synthesising of subjects. Outings were organised to show the connection between contour patterns and gradient; view the relationship between relief, settlement and transport links. Farm and factory

FIG.19
Dramatisations of History by Patrick Geddes.
Sir Patrick Geddes Memorial Trust

visits were arranged; wells sunk into the Chiltern chalk were measured for depth and water level to illustrate the water table; prehistoric artefacts, flints and fossils were examined.

Outdoor survey was reinforced by classroom activities. Mabel followed the example of 'PG' and organised pageants – Dramatisations of History – to illustrate historical events.

Role play was useful during bad weather:

One day we were to have gone to St Albans but it snowed... Miss Cross suggested that I should dramatise some ballads with them. They had never met the ballads before and attacked them vigorously. I suggested Kinmont Willie to the middle classes... They had perhaps an hour all told to get it up. I suggested the scenes and they did the rest. They spoke – not in the words of the ballad, except where they remembered them... but in dialogues which they made up themselves. You should have seen them swim the Liddel and the Eden (chalked on the floor) and storm Carlisle (which was an old loom strong enough to climb in). It was great fun.

Prehistory, in particular, held a special appeal for Mabel. Writing from Le Play House, 27 June 1924, she informed 'Dearest Uncle Pat' that:

Your welcome and jolly letters about caverns and lake-dwellings reached me a few days ago on K(ings) L(angley)... a girl member of the KK (Kibo Kift) has written quite a good lake-dwellings story (early Bronze Age, Phoenician trader etc) which I lately used for my children at Kings Langley... although not particularly well written, the plot is good and full of action and the archaeology seems to be correct – it struck me as a fine idea to construct a lake village and get all the Bronze details right and act her story and film it.

Such extracts give something of the flavour of Mabel's teaching during, what were for her, seven fulfilling years at Kings Langley. That her work came to an end was partly because Miss Cross was converted to 'Anthroposophy', the underlying philosophy of Rudolf Steiner schools. As she informed Geddes:

> I think it is no use struggling with anthroposophical developments at school – one can't assimilate two quite different outlooks and run the two methods in the same regime. I have tried to tell Miss Cross so, and pleaded with her to let me go for a term at least, leaving my return optional... But Miss Cross is ageing pretty rapidly and is in difficulties all the time and in some ways needs me more than ever. It is a dilemma, for her new anthropomorphically methods can never get going while I am there. These conflicts all round... are making me 'nervy' and that is a pity.

Another reason for leaving was to join her god-father in France.

Montpellier and the Collège des Écossais

Mabel departed in September 1925 to assist Geddes and to complete a thesis for her PhD at the *Collège des Écossais* in the Mediterranean Midi at the medieval university city of Montpellier. The previous year, on medical advice, Geddes had relocated there to establish a Scots College on the arid, hilly *garrigue des Brusses,* north-west of the town. For Geddes it would be a concrete reminder of Franco-Scottish links, and mark a return to Montpellier – with its benign Mediterranean climate – where he had spent happy times. From the remodelled College's outlook tower, views embraced the low plateau and coastal plain of Languedoc; vines and *garrigue* rising northwards to the Cevennes; the Golfe du Lion with its sand bars enclosing the long line of lagoons, salt pans and fishing villages. Such variegated geographical sites would admirably lend themselves to regional survey. Aided by his younger son, Arthur, hastily summoned from India, and a loyal group of devotees, including Mabel, he redeveloped and redecorated the College, acquired the nearby *Château d'Assas*, planted gardens and created walks on the stubborn *garrigue*. It was his final venture, aimed at establishing an international hall of residence that would attract students at the University of Montpellier who would promote world citizenship.

Numbers did not live up to expectation, and the College had limited success, though it later served as a base for field work for British students of geography. Among its post-graduate students were Arthur Geddes and

Mabel. Supervising their research was Jules Sion (1879–1940), an authority on Monsoon Asia and the Mediterranean lands, and Professor of Geography at Montpellier University from 1910. For Arthur, it was an angst-ridden time: tensions existed between himself and his domineering father over 'the severe demands made... on his time and the work on his thesis' on Bengal. As a consequence, Arthur sought refuge in Sion's house; an outcome that fostered ill-feeling between PG and Sion to such an extent that Sion told him 'in no uncertain terms that he was an unreasonable and harmful father'. Whether or not Mabel was involved during her ten- month stay is unknown, but it is unlikely, given her close links with the Geddes family, that she would not have been aware of the stresses.

Arthur's thesis – *'Au Pays de Tagore'* – was well received, as was Mabel's *L'Utilisation du Milieu Geographique pour l'Education*, (*The Use of the Geographical Environment in Education*). After initially developing her belief that education should be focused on children experiencing their environment as directly as possible, she outlined the concept of regional survey, its evolution and main proponents from Rousseau's *Emile* and his emphasis on the importance of the natural environment through to the implementation of nature study in schools' curricula (1899 in Scotland, 1900 in England), thanks to Geddes and his collaborator, J Arthur Thomson. Exemplars of regional survey from primary and secondary schools were then given, including familiar figures such as George Morris at Saffron Walden and Valentine Bell, and Norman M Johnson, headmaster in the Fife mining village of Kinglassie: a markedly contrasting school environment compared to those experienced by Mabel. It is likely that Johnson met Mabel through membership of the Scottish Regional Survey Movement and at Survey meetings in Edinburgh and Durham; and like her, he vigorously promoted its merits in varied sites and sources, including *The Geographical Teacher* (1922), *Observation* (1926), and the *Scottish Educational Journal*, a significant source for Scottish teachers.

A second section of her thesis dealt with the process of human evolution. Using the Valley Section as her model she stressed the significance of primitive occupations maintaining that they underpin the connections between mankind and the earth. Adapting the American educationist, G Stanley Hall's *Theory of Recapitulation*, Mabel suggested 'that the spirit and character of the child follows the route of our ancestors as they evolved towards civilisation'. Children, she suggested, needed a recapitulation of the occupations of prehistoric people, not just by reading about them but by doing practical work; as Geddes would say: 'Vivendo Discimus', education is life, not just a preparation for life. Mabel's thesis also emphasised the importance of large scale maps, stressed the value of employing works of literature to foster a sense of place and the past, and concluded with a short account of Alasdair Geddes's life.

Her thesis was accepted in 1926, published by Ernest Flammarion, Paris, and reproduced by the Le Play Society in 1931. Typical of its reception in Britain was that by HC Barnard, Headmaster of Gillingham County School, Kent:

> Miss Barker has shown us how a whole syllabus can be woven around a school regional survey, but she was working with small groups of children in a private school. In the secondary school where a certificate examination is taken at about the age of 16, the requirements of the geography syllabus make it difficult, if not impossible.

One solution, he suggested was to set up a Regional Survey Club as an after-school or half- holiday activity – 'if the games master does not object'. Arguably, this was a common response from schools understandably faced with pressures of syllabi and examinations; a majority rejoinder incompatible with Mabel's educational philosophy – the solution was to found her own school.

Regional Survey as 'the Portmanteau': Friar Row School

Dr Barker's thesis finished by suggesting the ideal location for any future school focusing on regional survey was proximity to mountains. Arguably, Mabel had in mind the site of her own school – Friar Row – in the Cumbrian village of Caldbeck, some 11 miles south-west of Carlisle. For a start, there was the critical pull of the Cumbrian Mountains. In an earlier letter to 'PG' from Kings Langley, she wrote:

> I always go south with regret and north with the joy of an exile going home. The chalk hills are fair and alluring in their wonderful contours and thrilling with the appeal of the past – and I feel all that and yet in some way they tire me spiritually as it were, and I leave the chalk with relief – Limestone is better, but full ecstasy belongs only to the rugged hills of Cumbria and the Highlands.

Additionally, as stated in a prospectus for the school, Caldbeck was:

> ... a village of ancient traditions, deep in the country between the Cumbrian Mountains and the Solway Plain, and affording ample opportunity of exploration and varied occupational experience from hill to sea.

Caldbeck, in modern parlance, ticked all her boxes: accessibility to contrasting environmental and occupational types of the valley section; a
village surrounded by extensive park, woodland and streams; a school
with south-facing gardens and orchard, sloping to a tributary of the
Caldew; opportunities for outdoor rambling and climbing in the Fells;
relative proximity to Seathwaite for an annual camp. Caldbeck was her
locational apotheosis for regional survey.

That Mabel was able to fund and start her own school in 1927 was
thanks to a fortuitous legacy from her aunt, Kate Barker, in Perth. Three
thousand pounds was then a very large sum: it allowed her to purchase
several cottages adjacent to the derelict mill in Friar Row; renovate and
adapt the buildings to contemporary school requirements, guided by her
architect friend, Frank Mears, Norah's husband.

When the school opened in September 1927, it was on a fairly small
scale but it grew steadily. There were three members of staff: Mabel,
responsible for nature study, science, history and geography; her friend,
Gertrude Walmsley, who covered maths – though it did not seem to loom
large in the school's curriculum – English, handicrafts, music, housewifery
and kindergarten work. A third staff member, a French girl, Yvette,
appears to have eschewed conventional methods of language instruction
and used nursery rhymes to teach French. Although advertised as a co-ed-
ucational school for day and boarding pupils, her initial intake was
confined to boys. Mainly local, they included her three nephews, Lindsay,
Chris and Morris, sons of her brother Arnold, now married and multi-
tasking – running a pub, post office, the local garage and bus service to
the nearby market town of Wigton.

Something of the flavour of Friar Row was conveyed to this writer
when he spoke in September 2011 to Mabel's nephew, Lindsay Barker,
aged 91: school memories matching those detailed in Levi. It was a happy
schooling with inbuilt flexibility in the daily curriculum: when it snowed,
pupils built an igloo, followed by appropriate readings on Inuit lifestyle
and environment; likewise, Hiawatha was read, all pupils seated round a
large wooden table, followed by constructing a wigwam. Gardening, tree
climbing, making dams across local streams, nature walks and collecting
plant specimens and berry picking were an integral part of the curriculum,
and understandably were fond memories. Likewise, given Mabel's predilections, camping and climbing were core activities. This was at a time when,
unlike today's schools, Mabel and like-minded teachers did not encounter
current bureaucratic formalities of risk assessment; doubtless, had they been
in force, she would have ignored them! Descending a fog-ridden Great

Gable, eight-year old Lindsay and five others were cautioned by Mabel to scrupulously follow her footsteps – there was a 300 foot drop and they were on the edge of it: confirmation of her belief, noted earlier, that adults should accept that risk-taking was part of a child's education and life.

Not all local children went to Friar Row, for some adults it was too unconventional and risky. Lindsay, however, felt that it gave him an excellent start in life and made him a good citizen. At Secondary School, he gained top prizes in French, Latin and Geography; only in Maths did he initially struggle, but the two-year gap was bridged, and in the longer term, an engineering career not hampered. Another former pupil, Graham Wilde, acknowledged Mabel's

> … lasting impression on the pupils. So many years on, the powerful personality of its principal is still remembered in terms of her enthusiasm and teaching ability.

For Mabel, her enthusiastic teaching stemmed from the opportunity afforded curricular freedom at Friar Row, and earlier at Kings Langley, to pursue a programme shaped by regional survey: she was

> realising in practice what we along knew in theory, namely, that Regional Survey is not a new thing to put into a full portmanteau; it is the portmanteau!

FIG.20
Evacuees from Leeds at Friar Row, 1939 (from *And Nobody Woke up Dead*).
Williamina C Barker

After World War II, Mabel retired and followed a simple, non-material-istic life in Caldbeck. Friar Row was divided up, and she lived in one of the cottages with her pets, continued writing, and was ever-delighted to meet friends and their children. Eventually, after 'many years of smoking took their toll', she died peacefully in hospital in 1961.

Conclusion

David Matless (1992), discussing the period 1918–39 in British geography, dismisses the notion, held by some historians of the subject, that these inter-war years marked a 'geographical Dark Age'. Rather, he argues, it was a period during which regional surveys, the consequent increasing awareness of local knowledge, and the promotion of citizenship nurtured a vigorous form of '*outlook geography*': developments which 'took their cue from Patrick Geddes'.

This chapter has discussed how his god-daughter Mabel Barker more than took her cue: regional survey was almost a pre-natal imposition that grew up with her, and was developed by her as she promoted its diffusion as school teacher, lecturer, organising secretary, aid worker and writer at variegated sites from the Outlook Tower to Friar Row. Like other women in Geddes's circle, she found that it was a challenging vocation, not least because he could be demanding, domineering, a 'driving force which made his milieu exhausting at times to those of lesser fibre', and, at times, unappreciative. Geddes was lucky: Mabel did not lack fibre. Like other promoters of regional survey, she was ever-determined to promote his credo, though with her own take: hers was a particularly active interpretation, taking advantage of progressive schools such as Kings Langley Priory and of generally small groups of youngsters as at Friar Row, a situation rarely found in the state sector. Indeed, her interpretation of regional survey surely marks her out as one of the

FIG.21
Mabel on Dovedale Slabs (from *And Nobody Woke up Dead*).
Williamina C Barker

key founding mothers of outdoor education; like Geddes she was ahead of her time.

A final thought for discussion: Mabel worked slavishly, but does this final extract, from a letter (written from the Outlook Tower, 25 February, 1915) to 'PG', suggest that she was enslaved?

> I've just had the offer of work for next term in an Edinburgh school – science mistress – but I don't want to take it... I don't feel like cramming children for exams in chemistry and botany on the wrong lines. I want to remain free for you, whenever and wherever you want me. On the other hand I'm rather afraid of making you feel that you **must** find work in order to provide for me – a troublesome assistant who will not be dismissed!

Kenneth MacLean

Chronology

1885	Born 14 December in Silloth, one of four siblings, of whom two survived
1897–1900	Blackfriars House School, Perth
1900–04	Truro High School for Girls
1904–07	Teacher Training at Cheltenham Ladies College
1907	BSc London University (External)
1908	(January–April) Lecturer on Botany at Nuns of Mercy Convent, Limerick
1908	(April–June) Demonstrator in Botany, University College, Dundee
1908–09	Science Mistress at Gowerton County School, Glamorgan
1909–12	Saffron Walden Teacher Training College, Essex
1910	Cities and Town Planning Exhibition, Dublin
1912–13	St Hilda's Hall, Oxford University
1913	Post-graduate Diploma in Geography
	Summer – Cities and Town Planning Exhibition at Ghent
1914–15	Easter – Outlook Tower, Edinburgh – first Regional Survey Conference
	Provisional Committee for the Development of the Regional Survey initiated
	Summer – Civic Exhibition, Dublin
1916–17	Spring – Temporary lecturer in geography, Sheffield University
	Belgium – Uden /Elizabethdorp
1917–25	King's Langley School

1924	First female ascent of Central Buttress, Scafell
1925–26	*Collège des Écossais*, Montpellier
1926	First female traverse of the Cuillin Ridge, Skye
1927	Friar's Row School, Caldbeck, opened
1927–42	Resident at Caldbeck, Cumberland
1933	Joined the Pinnacle Club
1942–46	Geography Mistress, The King's School, Peterborough
1946–61	Resident at Caldbeck
1961	Death at Carlisle, 31 August

Acknowledgements

Sian Astill, Oxford University Archives, Bodleian Library, Oxford.

Mr Lindsay Barker, Friar Row, Caldbeck.

Helen Burton, Special Collections and Archives Administrator, Keele University Library.

Steve Connolly, Principal Archivist, AK Bell Library, Perth and Kinross Council

Kate Hanlon, Enquiry Officer, Saffron Walden Library.

Marianne Inskip, Secretary, Truro High School Old Girls Association.

David Powell, Project Manager and Archivist, Tasglann nan Eilean Siar, Sternabagh.

Rachel Roberts, Archivist, Cheltenham Ladies College.

Staff of the National Library, Scotland.

Matthew B. Zawadski, University Archivist, University of Sheffield.

Bibliography

Barnard HC, *Observational Geography and Regional Survey* (Le Play Society, London, 1933)

Barnard HC, *Principles and Practice of Geography* (University Press, London, 1948)

Branford V and Geddes P, *The Coming Polity* (Williams and Norgate, London, 1917)

Fagg, CC and Hutchings, GE, *An Introduction to Regional Surveying* (Cambridge University Press, Cambridge, 1930)

Flint, C, *Introduction to Geopolitics* (Routledge, London, 2011)

Freeman TW, *A History of Modern British Geography* (Longman, London, 1980)

Geddes P, *Cities in Evolution* (Williams and Norgate, London, 1915)

Hysler-Rubin N, *Patrick Geddes and Town Planning: A Critical View* (Routledge, London, 2011)

Levi, Jan, *And Nobody Woke up Dead: The Life and Times of Mabel Barker – Climber and Educational Pioneer* (The Ernest Press, Bury St Edmunds, 2006)

Livingstone, DN, *The Geographical Tradition: Episodes in the History of a Contested Enterprise* (Blackwell, Oxford, 1992)

Mackaye, B, *From Geography to Geotechnics* (University of Illinois Press, Chicago, 1968)

Novak Jr, FG, (ed.), *Lewis Mumford and Patrick Geddes: Their Correspondence* (Routledge, London, 1995)

Stoddart, DR (ed) *Geography, Ideology and Social Concern* (Oxford: Basil Blackwell)

Stoddart, D R, *On Geography* (Basil Blackwell, Oxford, 1987)

Tyrwhitt, J, *Patrick Geddes in India* (Lund Humphries, London, 1947)

White, P, *To Understand Our World: 100 Years of Geography at the University of Sheffield* (Department of Geography, Sheffield, 2008)

Withers, CWJ, *Geography, Science and National Identity: Scotland since 1520* (Cambridge University Press, Cambridge, 2001)

Withers, CWJ, *Geography and Science in Britain, 1831–1939: A Study of the British Association for the Advancement of Science* (Manchester University Press, Manchester, 2010)

CHAPTER ELEVEN

Marie Bonnet and Jeanne Weill (aka Dick May)

Two Women from the Geddes French Circle Before 1914

PATRICK GEDDES WAS a frequent visitor to France, particularly during the Belle Epoque (1890s–1914), and again from the 1920s until his death in Montpellier in 1932. His first field trip to Brittany in 1878, at the age of 24, had brought him friendship with scientists from several universities, including Montpellier, and he later made the acquaintance of leading academics, social thinkers and politicians in Paris. Over time, he accumulated a strikingly large network of French contacts, and was responsible for several cross-national projects: he was one of the founders of the Franco-Scottish Society(1895), and another high point was his International Assembly or Summer School at the 1900 Paris World's Fair.

FIG.22
The Palace of Navigation, Exposition Universelle de 1900.
Siân Reynolds

Unsurprisingly, given the structures of French academic and public life, most of his contacts were men – the professors, social scientists and public figures who dominated cultural life at the turn of the century. French women at the time faced many restrictions in both public and private life, and the modern feminist movement was still in its early days. Geddes, although not a supporter of *political* feminism, believed that women had a major contribution to make to society, albeit through their 'traditional feminine' qualities: in practice, paradoxically, he offered opportunities to women of various nationalities to become involved in his educational, publishing and social schemes, in ways that might encourage them to greater assertiveness and independence. This chapter considers two French women from among his contacts, who represent, in their rather different ways, some parallels to Geddesian ideas in France.

Marie Bonnet (1859–1925)

Marie Bonnet belonged to the Geddes circle in Montpellier. Through their early acquaintance with the botanist Charles Flahault, Patrick and Anna Geddes had met several academic families in this ancient university city in south-west France, and kept up warm relations with them for years. In the winter of 1889–1890, the couple spent several months in Montpellier and Anna Geddes wrote an article about the university's 600th anniversary celebrations. Their contacts included the historian Ernest Lavisse (1842–1922), the economist Charles Gide (1847–1932), and the entire Bonnet family. Max Bonnet, son of a Protestant pastor, was professor of ancient languages in the university arts faculty and, with his wife Charlotte, held open house at their home, *L'Enclos Laffoux*. Their daughter Marie, one of five children, was born in 1874. She studied English and German, and was in her teens when she first met the Geddes couple. By 1895, she was in regular touch with them, and began visiting Edinburgh, attending the Summer Meetings several times before 1900. As well as some letters from other members of the Bonnet family in the Strathclyde Geddes Archive, there is a particularly rich collection of letters from Marie to Anna Geddes in the National Library of Scotland, from which we can follow their relations. (The letters are in French: extracts here are all in my translation).

This correspondence makes it clear that *L'Enclos Laffoux* was a centre of like-minded spirits, including among others the Gides, Professor Flahault, and the family of Gabriel Monod, another Geddes contact. As Marie wrote to Anna in January 1898:

This may sound silly, coming from a girl, but I can be open with you: I really think that the elite of the university has gathered round my parents. Our social circle is the most agreeable possible and we treat each other with the simplicity of the patriarchs (i.e. of the Old Testament), in absolute freedom.

From 1895 onwards, the Bonnets and most of their friends became closely concerned with the Dreyfus Affair, a crucial background to Patrick Geddes's networking in France. Virtually all the French people he associated with in the late 1890s were 'Dreyfusards' – that is supporters of the Jewish Captain Alfred Dreyfus, whom they regarded as wrongly convicted by a French court-martial of spying on behalf of Germany. The press campaign for his retrial raged particularly between 1897 and 1899, when he was brought back from Devil's Island to stand trial again. The army once more convicted him, but he was first given a presidential pardon, and finally, in 1906, acquitted. The Affair pitted defenders of the army, and increasingly its defenders from within the Catholic Church, against liberals, including many Protestants and Jews, who argued for Dreyfus's human rights. It seriously divided urban French society for years.

The Bonnet family arranged and attended public meetings addressed by pro-Dreyfus speakers campaigning in Montpellier, and Marie was apparently among those who joined the *Ligue des Droits de l'Homme*, an organisation formed to fight for human rights in the wake of the Affair. Her letters to Anna throughout these years are full of enthusiasm

The intellectuals who have joined the fray are taking up social causes and vital issues for the people at last – that is at least one benefit derived from this terrible struggle,

she wrote on 4 December 1898.

Marie herself had an awakening social conscience, and expressed feelings of guilt at being a comfortable young bourgeois woman. Evidently both Patrick and Anna Geddes gave her encouragement, inviting her to the Summer Meetings, where she overcame her considerable shyness in order to give classes in French language and literature. 'You gave me the opportunity to appear in public', she later wrote. Marie took kindly to the elder Geddes children, Norah and Alasdair (*'mes marmottes'*), and formed a strong bond of affection with the whole family. Clearly, the freedom of the young British women whom she had seen in Edinburgh impressed her (as it did other French visitors) and made her chafe under the more conventional restrictions imposed on their contemporaries in France.

All the same, Marie Bonnet appears always to have been uneasy about speaking in public or to large groups, especially mixed audiences. She continued to help out at the Meetings, while indicating that she would be happier with an all-female class. Her main occupation for much of the later 1890s (about five years) was at home in Montpellier, as full-time governess to two young girls: her sister Gertrude and a family friend Suzanne Charmont. She was also called on to stand in for her mother to entertain their many guests, as well as hospital visiting and carrying out 'good works' among young women of the working-class.

Marie Bonnet turned 26 in 1900, the year that marked a high point of Patrick Geddes's French initiatives. His Paris International Assembly was an ambitious Summer School for visitors to the World's Fair, during which Geddes recruited many leading figures in French public and academic life to act as patrons or lecturers. Marie Bonnet declined to give any lectures ('the audience is unpredictable and you will have many other people!') – and indeed expressed doubts that the Assembly would succeed among French people. But she was prepared to help unstintingly behind the scenes, advising on publicity and, most importantly, staying with the Geddes family for the two months they spent in the French capital, acting as a general factotum. This time was a difficult one for them, and her help was valuable: Patrick was engaged massively in the summer school; Anna

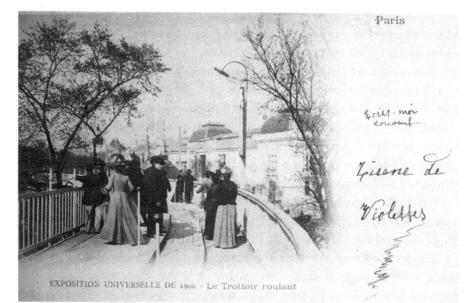

FIG.23
Exposition Universelle – the latest in traffic management – the moving pavement.
Siân Reynolds

Geddes suffered a miscarriage while in Paris, and the family received news of two sudden deaths, those of their friend Mary Hill Burton, and of Robert Smith (Patrick's young replacement at Dundee University, who died of appendicitis).

So far, Marie Bonnet had lived a life of modest and fairly conventional obscurity: she had a close circle of family and friends, and was more open to progressive ideas than many well-off women her age; but her feelings of admiration and affection for the Geddes couple were special, and prompted her to think seriously about her future. She often remarked that she did not have their strength and audacity ('I'm not a Geddes'). Her mother, Charlotte, wrote to Anna saying: 'you probably do not realise the influence you have had on (Marie's) entire existence.' Once Marie's young pupils were old enough to dispense with her tutoring, the Geddes influence began to interact with her social conscience in a more galvanising way, allowing her to reconcile her preference for single-sex milieux with a strong desire to help people in need. In December 1902 she wrote at length to Anna, saying she regretted – in a context of much anticlerical feeling in France and the rise of feminism – that

> … we (the French) are wrong to let the monastic spirit disappear, at least the good aspects of it, and in particular, the notion of celibacy for women although this may seem paradoxical at the very time when feminism is being developed.

Marie went on to say that she approved of feminist claims for women's rights and for their entry to the professions, but – rather like Geddes – she felt something was lost if the fight was only for 'equality'. 'In England, woman is liberated and educated, but by identifying her with man'. She had therefore devised, as a practical application of her ideas, a rather 'Geddesian' plan of her own to create a special sort of lodging – part hostel, part hotel, part convent – for girl students. She imagined that such girls/young women would be foreigners, since they would be particularly in need of a place to stay, but in any case her idea was to provide protection and guidance for what she saw as a vulnerable group. Her initial scheme was to set up something like this in Montpellier near her parents' house, so that the lodgers could benefit from their social contacts.

We do not know whether she managed anything of the sort at first. Some sources suggest earlier dates, but it seems clear from her correspondence with Anna Geddes that it was only in 1906 that Marie Bonnet – by now in her 30s – embarked seriously on the career as warden of lodgings for young women, and later still as administrator of women's organisations. Her role was not unique: there were a number of *pensions* and hostels for young women at the time but, as indicated above, Marie Bonnet aimed to do more than simply run a boarding house.

In spring 1906, she was approached by a committee who planned to open a residence for female students of limited means in Paris. Her name had been mentioned – probably through the Protestant grapevine – as a potential warden. It was to be 'a convent. Yes, literally a convent!' in the rue d'Amyot, a street behind the Pantheon – recently vacated by one of the Catholic teaching orders barred from practising after the Separation of Church and State in the wake of the Dreyfus Affair. The buildings turned out to be very austere, but it was a first chance really to run something, and for two years this became Marie's home. The students were all French girls in the event, as the funds had been provided by provincial *lycées* for their ex-pupils going on to higher education – still very much a minority.

Two years later, again through a committee, Marie was promoted to run a larger and more comfortable student hostel in the rue Saint-Sulpice, from which her later letters mostly come. Evidently she was much happier here, and had found her *métier*, organising the practicalities of lodging, but also trying to see to the emotional and even spiritual needs of the students. There are signs in the letters that she became very attached to them. It was also possible to lodge foreign students, as she had originally hoped – girls more in need of a helping hand. It was now that Marie first became friendly with Marguerite Pichon-Landry (1877–1972), a well-connected woman closely involved with the hostel, as well as with many other all-women organisations.

The Paris educational world was thrown, like everything else, into turmoil by the declaration of war in August 1914. With the military threat to the city, no students arrived and classes were suspended. Letters to Anna Geddes in 1914 recount how both Marie's brothers were mobilised, and she too felt she should engage in war work. As the war progressed, some degree of normal life behind the front returned and the hostel re-opened. Marie's letters to Anna after 1914 recount details of the many losses in their circle, her fears for her brothers and the dislocating effect of the war on every aspect of life in France. On the Geddes family, the impact of the war was of course devastating: first came the sinking by enemy action of the ship carrying the Cities Exhibition to India. Marie, like many Geddes friends, wrote sympathetically asking what she could do to help, and before long she was searching out documents and pictures to help reconstitute the exhibition. Worse was to come: in 1917 Anna

Geddes died of fever in India, not knowing that her son Alasdair had recently been killed in action.

After Anna's death, there is very little correspondence in the archives. Marie Bonnet's contact with the Geddes family had always been through Anna: presumably she felt it was most appropriate to write to the wife rather than the husband – and the revealingly large collection of letters to Anna in the NLS shows how many people felt the same.

But Marie Bonnet herself went from strength to strength after the war. In 1920, at the initiative of Marguerite Pichon-Landry, the Saint-Sulpice hostel amalgamated with two other Parisian associations: the *Foyer universitaire féminin* and the *Société des amis de l'étudiante* under the umbrella name *Maison des étudiantes*, located at 214 boulevard Raspail. Marie Bonnet, who presided over it, also made contact with the US-based *Foyer international des étudiantes* on the boulevard Saint-Michel, and Reid Hall, a centre for American students in the rue de Chevreuse, still in existence. By her later years, Marie had developed a truly Geddesian networking talent, always among women, and largely among Protestants. With her exact contemporaries, Marie Mespoulet and Marie Monod, who had married into the Monod clan, Marie Bonnet helped found the French branch of International Federation of Women Graduates, also located in Reid Hall. The French branch had several names before settling on AFDU – *Association des femmes diplômées de l'université*. It was intended to unite 'an avant-garde of graduate women who are well-informed and competent, in order to defend the cause of women.'

These moderately feminist organisations, clearly elitist, have to be seen in the context where women had had a struggle even to be allowed to study for the qualifying exam for university (the *baccalauréat*) and where women were still a minority as students, let alone lecturers. Marie Bonnet became the AFDU's first secretary-general. One close friend was Louli Sanua, later Mme Milhaud (1886–1967), who founded the first association of state-trained women primary teachers, and was among, other things, a major promoter of Russian music in France. Marie Bonnet was, as a result, closely involved with the Russian section of the International Federation of Women Graduates – although we don't know whether she travelled abroad. She was awarded the *Légion d'honneur* in 1933, a year after Patrick Geddes had died at Montpellier. It is quite likely that through her family she had been in touch with him during his later years at the *Collège des Écossais* there. Marie herself died in Montpellier in 1960.

'Dick May', a Strong-minded Woman

The other woman whom this chapter considers was also a great networker, and she too moved in Dreyfusard circles. But she was in most respects very different from Marie Bonnet, although we know they had met. Closer in age to Patrick Geddes, Jeanne Weill was born in 1859 in Algiers, where her father Michel was the chief rabbi of the Algerian Consistory. Her mother, a distant cousin of Karl Marx and an active philanthropist, was involved with early feminist associations. Her brother Georges, who received a good education not available to his sister, later became a reputed historian.

The family eventually settled in Paris in 1885, and after the death of her father (an overpowering figure) Jeanne launched herself into a writing career. She took the rather odd pen-name 'Dick May', by which she was later known. It seems that this was in homage to two English writers whom she admired, Charles Dickens and Henry Mayhew, the author of *London Labour and the London Poor*. These choices might indicate a determination to tackle the problems of the disadvantaged working classes, though this was not immediately apparent. 'Dick May' published several short stories and serials in reputable French newspapers (*L'Illustration, Le Temps, Le Journal des Débats* etc) and a novel *L'Alouette* (1890) about a young woman's struggle for a career.

Despite a measure of success, her writing does not appear to have brought her either fame or wealth, nor, given the restrictions of her background, could she really emulate writers like Emile Zola, who had shone a spotlight on the lower depths of French society. But Dick May was well-connected through her journalism, and acquainted with progressive Parisian society at the time of the Dreyfus Affair.

The breakthrough moment for her took place when she was already in her thirties and, like Marie Bonnet, unmarried. She became secretary in 1889 to the Comte Aldebert de Chambrun (1821–1899), a wealthy aristocrat, industrialist, and philanthropist, interested in ideas of social justice. In 1894, he provided the money to found the *Musée Social*: a kind of 'social laboratory' or research centre, in which he interested a certain number of eminent men from various horizons, including Charles Gide and the prominent reforming politician Jules Siegfried (1837–1922), both important members of Geddes's circle. The ideas of social thinker Frédéric Le Play, an early influence on Geddes too, had helped inspire the foundation, which still exists. Its early members were mostly moderate-to-liberal republicans, opposed to the 'collectivist' and Marx-inspired socialist parties then in the ascendant in France. The Musée Social group favoured instead reform through class cooperation, and the philosophy of 'Solidarism' associated with the leading politician Léon Bourgeois, another Geddes contact. Dick May, too, although closer to the radical end of the spectrum, seems to have stopped short of identifying with socialism (as represented by Jean Jaurès for example.) But she became disenchanted with the founding fathers of the *Musée Social*, whom she knew well, for what she saw as the institution's ivory tower position, ensconced in its 'cosy nest' in the bourgeois west end of Paris.

The following year therefore, 1895, she joined forces with a sociologist and philosopher, Théophile Funck-Brentano and others to create a more practical institution, the *Collège libre des sciences sociales*. This was a state-subsidised, though not state-directed 'free college', offering courses on *le social*, i.e. sociology, without being tied to any particular current of thought. Dick May described it as a 'living library', recruiting eminent lecturers from different horizons, and offering a supplement or even a counterpoise to official teaching at the Sorbonne, and other formal places of learning in Paris. The College was launched, it seems, simply by formidable networking among a certain liberal elite, including important figures like historians Lavisse and Charles Seignobos. The support of Léon Bourgeois must have been acquired, but Henri Hauser later wrote that the college 'was above all the work of Dick May'.

Space forbids a full description of the College, but enough has perhaps been said to indicate that, in certain respects, it could be said to parallel Geddes's intentions at the Summer Meetings and later at the International Assembly. For all that however, there is no evidence that Geddes and Dick May had actually met before 1895 (or indeed until 1899), although they both moved very much in the same circles, which included for example Charles Gide and Alfred Croiset. Croiset (1845–1923), a classical scholar and liberal Catholic, was a supporter of Léon Bourgeois and a friend of Lavisse, and it was probably through the latter that he became involved with the Franco-Scottish Society. He was certainly present at its meetings in 1895 and 1898, and must have met Geddes. A member of the *Académie des Inscriptions et Belles-Lettres*, and Dean of the Literature Faculty at the University of Paris, the widowed Croiset became a close friend of Dick May – so close indeed that Parisian gossip assumed they had an affair. They travelled to Italy together more than once.

Dick May/Jeanne Weill was undoubtedly not a woman to be trammelled by the conventions of the day. All the scattered references to her suggest a woman of formidable presence – even though they are rarely complimentary. Apparently she cultivated a rather bohemian appearance. The first indication of her having any contact with Geddes comes, in fact, from the more strait-laced Marie Bonnet, who was unfailingly censorious of her. Marie wrote to Anna Geddes in December 1899, saying that she knew Patrick had arrived in Paris, because Célestin Bouglé, a rising sociologist, had met him 'at Dick May's house'. Was Dick May going to be part of the Geddes's Assembly, she wondered?

> Between ourselves, I wouldn't receive her at home for any money, and many women would not want to be associated with a woman like that... A witch, if you like as Monsieur G. called her. But frankly, she seems too like an adventuress from who knows where. If you want to attract a female audience you would need to offer it some ladies who wash, and comb their hair...

Jeanne Weill's unconventional manner and appearance might be less shocking to the British than to the French, in the age of the suffragettes. At any rate, Patrick Geddes recognised in 'Dick May' a good organiser, since he was still in contact with her during 1900. She does not appear to have given any lectures in his Assembly (lecturing was probably not her forte, although she wrote copiously) but we know for sure that they were collaborators at the International Congress on the Teaching of Social Sciences, held during the World's Fair from 30 July to 3 August 1900. It was at this five-day conference which she organised virtually single-handed, recruiting people from many countries, that Dick May launched what was to be a slightly breakaway institution vis-a-vis the College, the *Ecole des hautes études socials* – inspired by a greater sense of urgency, of moral crisis arising from the Dreyfus Affair. The EHES tended towards more practical cooperation with organisations like the *Universités populaires*, idealistic centres for working-class adult education.

At the end of the conference, an 'international committee on teaching social science' was formed, with Dick May as its secretary, and Emile Duclaux (of the Pasteur institute, another close Geddes friend) as president. Alfred Croiset and Charles Gide represented France, and Patrick Geddes, James Bryce, Horace Plunkett and Michael Sadler represented Britain. Curiously enough, this was the first of two conferences covering much the same ground, held in Paris that summer. They are sometimes described as 'rival conferences', in the sense that the emphasis insisted on by Dick May was what would today be called 'outreach', something we can assume Patrick Geddes agreed with, whereas the 'rival' *Congrès International d'Education sociale* (25 to 30 September, drawing on some of the same people), was retrospectively more famous because of the role played by the eminent sociologist Emile Durkheim. He insisted on the teaching of sociology as a scientific and academic subject based on university degrees and formal qualifications.

We do not know whether Geddes and Dick May had any further meetings in the context of their committee, which was supposed to coordinate thought on social sciences across national borders – admittedly a rather vague remit. They had plenty of mutual friends, and it is reasonable to suppose that there were some contacts, although Geddes was to be absorbed with various other activities, mostly in Scotland, over the next few years.

But Dick May continued to lead a very active role in the College, the EHES, and on the journal *Athena*, to which she contributed many articles, including reflections on the problems faced by women in the academic world. She also launched yet another school, the *Ecole du journalisme* – having grasped during the Dreyfus affair the power of the press. This had varying fortunes in the period up to 1914, again being relatively unstructured, but offering much-valued open lectures and practical advice, both to would-be journalists and students looking for general studies.

Although there do not seem to be any letters from Dick May in the Geddes archive, she was still kept in mind. A letter from Marie Bonnet to Anna in 1909 makes a surprising reference to her, combining malicious gossip with real appreciation:

Do you remember the horrible Dick May? Her college of social science (sic) is worth ten times the Sorbonne for the flexibility of its ideas and the originality and variety of its programmes. I am waiting for her to die. Then I would write her biography. But I would want to write what cannot be said during her lifetime. I find her role in the Latin quarter very piquant. She doesn't even look like the little cocottes the students take walking down the boulevard Saint Michel, because they wouldn't want to step out unwashed and without combing their hair, like this woman. People say she is Croiset's mistress, and it certainly looks like that, which is of no concern to me, indeed it's amusing, and picturesque. Croiset makes up for it by preaching morality to the young. People say it's hypocrisy, but I think on the contrary that he puts into it all the passion of a poor man who doesn't wish his misfortune on others. Meanwhile she (Dick May) undulates like a serpent among the intellectuals who are all captivated by her incomprehensible charms... Why on earth did this woman use all the genius of an adventuress to found such an austere college? At any rate, she has succeeded very well. Through Croiset, she has access to the university and the administration, and her indecent style and equivocal attitude do the rest. She employs excellent lecturers, but she is the organiser.

Other people were impressed with Dick May's networking and organisation as well, but towards the end of the pre-war period, she seems to have run out of energy. And as with Marie Bonnet, the outbreak of war came as a bitter blow to Dick May's idealistic schemes for regenerating the youth of France through education. She had already become somewhat embittered. During the war, she worked on various humanitarian, war-related projects, but after the armistice she seems to have faded from the scene. Much affected by the deaths of her mother in 1919 and of Croiset in 1923, Dick May died in the Alps in 1925, in what the papers described as a mountaineering accident, although some references appear to hint at suicide.

Conclusion

These two women, although chalk and cheese in many ways, form part of a cohort of women in France around the turn of the century, who were reacting against restrictive French society, and choosing to pursue their own projects. The obstacles were both legal (the provisions of the Napoleonic code) and informal: the practices of French bourgeois circles from which both women came. Crucially perhaps, they were unmarried. Marriage was not necessarily a drawback – many of the women active in related activities at the time were married – like Marie Monod, or Marguerite Pichon-Landry. But it depended who one was married to: a sympathetic husband was an advantage. In Marie Bonnet's case, her devotion to running her hostel was something probably only possible for an unmarried woman. In the case of Dick May/Jeanne Weill, her disregard for the conventions enabled her to ride out the whispered criticism around her, and she was evidently built of very stern stuff.

Their relationships to Patrick and Anna Geddes were very different too. They were by no means the only Frenchwomen who came within the Geddes circle, but they are perhaps the two who come closest to being 'Geddesians'. Marie Bonnet was, by happy accident, a close family friend, who over a period of years saw what was possible in Britain, and overcame her sheltered background and lack of confidence, largely thanks to the encouragement and advice of the Geddeses.

Patrick Geddes had of course long been concerned with student lodgings, both in Edinburgh and in France, where he had dreamed of reviving the ancient *Collège des Écossais* in Paris, and this must have been a major influence in a general sense. Marie Bonnet's particular concern for women's education was surely prompted by the presence of young women at the Edinburgh Summer Meetings, and also no doubt inspired by the particular way in which Anna Geddes contributed to make the experience a welcoming and hospitable one for the students. What was more, as a younger woman herself, she was able to continue her activities into the post-war world, and to witness her horizons widening.

Dick May did not need Patrick Geddes to prompt her into action, although it is possible to suppose that she had heard, via mutual acquaintances, about the Summer Meetings. She evidently did receive an impetus from the Comte de Chambrun, Croiset, and other men in academic and republican circles. But we do know that she met and worked with Geddes, and although we have very little first-hand testimony about their relationship, it seems fairly clear that they shared some similarity of approach. All the enterprises on which Dick May embarked could be said to parallel in some sense those of Geddes: they include her interest in social science as a new field of research and action, a willingness to experiment with flexible ways of teaching, and a keen sense of the need to moralise society (not unlike that of another friend of Geddes, Paul Desjardins, whose Union pour l'action morale was contemporary with Dick May's projects in the 1890s).

Although the Great War marked, as indeed it did for Geddes himself, the end of Dick May's most productive years, and although her initiatives ran into the sand in some respects, they proved prophetic and inspirational for later developments. She has only just started to be discovered and taken seriously by historians. In the context of the present collection, the lives of these two very different women illustrate the degree to which Patrick – and Anna – Geddes were part of the complex and changing world of the dawning 20th century: a world in which, on both sides of the Channel, women were increasingly asserting their right to pursue their dreams alongside men.

Siân Reynolds

Bibliography

Diebolt, Evelyne (ed), *Militer au XXe siècle: femmes, féminismes, Eglises et société: dictionnaire biographique* (Houdiard, Paris, 2009)

Foley, Susan, *Women in France since 1789: The meanings of difference* (Palgrave Macmillan, Basingstoke, 2004)

Fowle, Frances and Thomson, Belinda, eds, *Patrick Geddes: the French Connection* (White Cockade Publishing, Oxford, 2004)

Horne, Janet, *A Social Laboratory for Modern France: the Musée Social and the rise of the welfare state* (Duke University Press, Durham NC, 2001)

Prochasson, Christophe, *Dick May et le social* in Colette Chambelland et al, eds, *Le Musée Social en son temps* (Presses de l'ENS, Paris, 1998)

Reynolds, Siân, *Paris-Edinburgh: Cultural connections in the belle époque* (Ashgate, Aldershot, 2007)

CHAPTER TWELVE

The Noble Patroness
Lady Aberdeen (1857–1939)

Introduction

LADY ABERDEEN, born Ishbel Maria Marjoribanks on 15 March 1857, embarked on a life of public service, both at home in Aberdeenshire and abroad, when she married the 7th Earl of Aberdeen (later the 1st Marquess of Aberdeen and Temair) at the age of 20. She was particularly interested in improving the lives of women, but her passions and drive encompassed many areas and new ideas.

Unlike many of the other women in this book, she was not employed or inspired by Geddes to implement the detail of his projects. Indeed, it was Lady Aberdeen who enlisted Geddes's support and ideas, to improve the health and, associated with that, the general environment of early twentieth century Dublin. Along with her husband, twice Viceroy of Ireland, she ignited the flame of town planning in Ireland and saw it as a way of solving many of the problems of poverty, while at the same time encompassing the issues associated with Home Rule.

This chapter is in three parts. It provides an overview of her quite extraordinary and influential life. It then focuses on the second period of the Aberdeens' residency in the Viceroyal Lodge, as this is the time when they invited Patrick Geddes to Ireland. It concludes with a brief consideration of the relationship and the legacy of the meeting of these two formidable personalities.

Part I: Lady Aberdeen: An Overview

Early life
There is more than a whiff of romantic fiction or Sunday night costume drama about the first encounter of Lord and Lady Aberdeen.

The Gordons provided the cavalry for Montrose's army in the so-called English Civil War and forfeited their lands as supporters of the Jacobite cause. George Hamilton Gordon, the 4th Earl of Gordon, was Prime Minister of the coalition government at the time of the Crimean

War, but dedicated much time and care to his Scottish estates, including Haddo, in Aberdeenshire. Queen Victoria and Prince Albert were regular visitors to Scotland, including to Haddo, and Albert acquired the lease for the Balmoral Estate in 1848 from the 4th Earl.

George Hamilton Gordon was succeeded by George John James (the 5th Earl) in 1860 who, never having been in good health, died four years later. The eldest brother (the 6th Earl, known as the sailor earl) was swept overboard while working under the assumed name of George Osborne, in the American merchant navy in 1870; his second brother having already died in a rifle accident in his rooms at Cambridge in 1868. John Campbell Gordon (Johnnie) was therefore confirmed as the seventh earl of Aberdeen in 1872, after extended judicial proceedings to confirm the death without heirs, of his oldest brother and then to settle on him the title and estate. 'Four deaths in the space of ten years brought John Campbell Gordon to the peerage' said the Ulster Medical Journal. At that time, he was yet to marry, but he already knew his wife to be.

Educated at St Andrews and Oxford, the long vacation of 1868 provided Johnnie the opportunity for a romantic first glimpse by the 14 year old Ishbel. Johnnie had apparently lost his way journeying around the Highlands on horseback. The traveller, however, was welcomed at Guisachan, the highland home of Sir Dudley Marjoribanks, Ishbel's father. She viewed him only from the hall above, as he went into dinner. Nevertheless, in due course there followed a friendship, then almost reluctantly a proposal. They married in St George's, Hanover Square, London in 1877. She and her husband, who was by now a regular at the House of Lords, shared a strong sense of duty, rooted in Christian philosophy and belief, as well as a love of the outdoor life – both typical of the aristocracy at the time, with part of the year being spent in London and part in Scotland. They resolved to devote their lives to solid useful work, which should do something of good in the world.

Lord and Lady Aberdeen have been described by Leon O'Broin as contrasting, he bearded and small and polite, she disproportionately large, matronly and masterful. She apparently also had an aptitude for getting things just a little wrong; for interfering with things that had nothing to do with her and for an apparent inability to recognise a rebuff. A well known anecdote from her first period as Vicereine, at the time of Gladstone's initial Home Rule Bill, was her remark to the Chief Justice, 'I suppose everyone but yourself is a Home Ruler here tonight?' 'Not at all your Excellency, he replied frostily, 'Barring yourself and the waiters, there's not a Home Ruler in the room.'

Lord Aberdeen required a strong woman at his side, as he had not been anticipating his viceregal role.

Haddo House and Estate, Aberdeenshire, Scotland

The couple first arrived at Haddo House and the 1,700 acre estate at Methlick, Aberdeenshire, after a seven month honeymoon abroad, as it would be more acceptable to the new wife, to first be exposed to the North East of Scotland in the summer. The tenants turned out in full and accompanied them the last mile of the journey. There followed celebrations that lasted a week, concluding with a banquet for over 900 tenants and wives. Haddo House itself had been built during the time of William, the 2nd Earl, designed by William Adam. The new Lady Aberdeen soon began making her mark on her new home, ordering renovations, extensions and alterations with redecoration by London's best interior designers. These were soon filled with children – George (1879), Marjorie (1880), Dudley Gladstone (1883) and Ian Archibald (1884).

Ishbel's talent for good simple and practical ideas to improve the lives of others, plus excellent organisation, started at Haddo House. She took a keen interest in the education, development and even entertainment of their servants, providing 'hops', special holiday meals, followed by treats such as magic lantern shows. She started a Household Club, with regular classes. A singing class was led by the head forester, a carving class by the governess, a drawing class by the nurse and a home reading circle led by a neighbouring school master. There were fortnightly social evenings of music, singing, recitation and short lectures. The Aberdeens usually attended these meetings.

Unfortunately, this interest in the household staff was ridiculed and JM Barrie's play, *The Admirable Crichton,* was popularly believed to reflect the radical notions of the Aberdeens. Lord Aberdeen sought, and was given, an apology by the author, nevertheless, the Aberdeens had to contend with persistent reports that they ate with the servants, even to the extent that Queen Victoria made enquiries as to whether this was true.

In the early years of her marriage, Lady Aberdeen had yet to embark on a public role, although she was very much part of London society. At that time she regarded teas, balls and parties as bearable due to the opportunity for 'influencing for good' the people of wealth and power in Britain.

The Aberdeens continued their good works at home, endowing a cottage hospital, at Tarves, providing an institute for education for young men in Methlick and arranging hot lunches for school children, for a penny, throughout their estate area.

Lady Aberdeen, however, began to focus on female needs, with working parties where farmers' wives and their daughters met to sew for the destitute, have tea and listen while a worthwhile book was read aloud. She also built on the ideas of the Household Club with the creation of the Onwards and Upward Association, designed for servant girls. They took postal courses on various subjects such as history, geography, bible studies, literature, domestic science, needlework and knitting – with prizes and certificates being awarded annually. Eventually it had 115 branches and 8280 members across Scotland before it was absorbed into the Scottish Mothers' Union. The desire to do good in their immediate circle was definitely being implemented by both Aberdeens. To think global, act local, as it were.

Politics, public life and Ireland

Lady Aberdeen was clearly emerging as the organiser and implementer of the union and although she had lavish personal tastes she appeared to be a generous benefactor. Her husband was also generous, but somewhat impractical and whimsical in his schemes for the estate, such as a branch railway through their properties.

Politics, for both of them, however, provided focus, excitement and drama. Lady Aberdeen began to fulfil a role as consort and hostess. He was traditionally a Tory, she from a strong Liberal family, although their political views largely coincided. Inevitably, however, he became a supporter of Gladstone and from March 1880 took his seat on the liberal benches. By that time Haddo House was already regarded as a hot bed of Liberalism. Lord Aberdeen's first public office was to represent the British Government in Edinburgh at the General Assembly (as Lord High Commissioner to the Church of Scotland), it being noted by Lord Rosebery, that not the least of his qualifications for the position was the Lady High Commissioner. Lady Aberdeen relished the opportunity for entertaining and the increasing public profile.

Much greater opportunity arose for public service in 1886, however, when following his election as Prime Minister, Gladstone announced his intention to introduce Home Rule to Ireland. Indeed there were expectations on both sides of the Irish Sea at that time that a limited level of political independence could be implemented. To that end, he invited Lord Aberdeen to be the Irish Lord Lieutenant or Viceroy. This he accepted, without consulting his wife. In fact, when he met her with the news at Waverley Station, Edinburgh, she was initially horrified and refused to cross the Irish Sea. She soon embraced it and ultimately their first period of office was regarded as a brief, but triumphant stay.

Lady Aberdeen, had in fact, found a fitting cause for her energies and threw herself wholeheartedly into projects, schemes and plans for the development and improvement of Ireland and its people. Both Aberdeens aimed to promote Gladstone's Home Rule by addressing the real problems and issues of Ireland. For Lady Aberdeen in this first period of office, this took two distinct strands: firstly mitigation of the terrible poverty, appalling living conditions and disease in the urban areas and secondly by promoting Irish industries and fashion.

During the first period in Ireland she particularly focused on Irish craft skills. Her practical approach was quickly apparent as she used the opportunity of the Women's Home Industries section of the Edinburgh International Exhibition, opening 1 May 1886, to exhibit Irish lace, embroideries, poplin and other handicrafts. Lady Aberdeen sourced these from all over Ireland and drew up an accompanying catalogue, containing detail about the origins of each craft and the role that these cottage industries played in economic and social life of Ireland.

Lady Aberdeen quickly hosted a garden party at the Viceregal Lodge, to which all the guests were required to wear clothes made of Irish materials, including the children, who were to wear fancy dress. An exhibition was held on the Viceregal tennis courts with Irish manufacturers invited to display their goods, and milliners, tailors and dressmakers to view the show. The result was a huge success, with the men wearing white flannels or homespun suits and soft hats and the ladies in linen, laces, embroideries, poplins and woollens. The garden party caught the public's attention and Dublin newspapers issued special supplements. This clear interest in local crafts and industry developed into Lady Aberdeen becoming the Chairman of a newly formed Association of Irish Industries. During this first term of duty in Ireland she was also a founder member of the Mansion House Ladies Committee for the relief of distress.

The defeat of Gladstone's government later that same year (1866) meant that her husband's term of office had lasted less than six months. They had so endeared themselves to the people of Ireland that their departure was cause for general national regret, not only because the Aberdeens had proved so popular, but also as their leaving put an end to hopes of Home Rule. The farewell procession on 7 August was described as the most memorable manifestation ever witnessed in Dublin. It was an expression of affection for the friendly ex-Viceroy and his amiable wife and was 'enormous, stately and never to be forgotten'.

Lord and Lady Aberdeen were bitterly disappointed to be recalled so quickly with Lady Aberdeen taking it particularly badly. She was, in fact, physically and mentally exhausted by her efforts in Dublin, to the extent that she was seriously ill and prescribed foreign travel as a means to convalesce. This took them for the first time to North America. Lady Aberdeen was disturbed by what she regarded as the desolation of the prairies, as well as the general bleakness and poor quality of the women's lives. Her solution was the distribution to these women of magazines through a charitable organisation. She suggested that where possible a small token could be included, such as a packet of flower seeds to enable the women to brighten their surroundings. Patrick Geddes would have approved.

This travel and activity not only restored her health, but provided a vehicle for her to promote Irish industries abroad. In due course, sales of Irish industries were instituted twice a year, one in London and one in another city. Depots for distribution of the goods were also created in Dublin and Chicago, where Lady Aberdeen was spectacularly successful with the creation of an Irish Village at the World's Craft Fair in Chicago in 1893, which brought Irish crafts to the notice of Americans. It was one of the main financial successes of the exhibition and created a good deal of interest and orders for Irish goods in America.

Canada and after

The Earl of Aberdeen was appointed Governor-General of Canada, 1893–1899. This was a successful period for the Aberdeens with many achievements and developments. Lady Aberdeen in particular flourished and among many other initiatives founded the Victorian Order of Nurses and the National Council of Women in Canada of which she was President, as well as being President of the International Council for Women.

After leaving Canada, Lady Aberdeen resumed her active home life in Scotland. She consistently took a leading role in many philanthropic movements, particularly those dedicated to improving the health and lives of women and children. Soon after returning from Canada, Lady Aberdeen was re-elected to the presidency of the Women's Liberal Federation of England and also that of the Scottish Women's Liberal Federation. In 1899 the International Council of Women met in London (their first meeting in Europe). This consisted of the representatives of the National Councils of Women of 22 countries. She had by that time been President of the International Council of Women since 1893 and was in fact to be the only

President until 1936. Many more difficult and exciting challenges lay ahead, however, with a return to Ireland

Part II: *Ireland 1905–1915*

Changes in Ireland since 1886 and a context for the second period of office

At the beginning of 1906 the Aberdeens returned to Ireland, Lord Aberdeen having been appointed Viceroy for the second time. Their period of office was to last until 1915, and therefore, to cover the turbulent years leading up to the 1916 Easter rising in Dublin. In 1906, however, it was considered that there was once again a strong possibility of Home Rule. There had been some distinct changes since the Aberdeens' last occupancy of the Viceregal Lodge in 1886. In particular, there had been a social and legal transformation, with the transfer to tenants of much of the land previously held by landlords. This gave a new sense of pride and personal independence to the former tenants. It also appeared to reinforce a fresh awareness of Irish culture. The terrible living conditions and extreme poverty in the towns and particularly in Dublin city, however, led to serious discontent, Unemployment was higher than ever and the slums were more overcrowded and unsanitary. Infant mortality was extremely high and tuberculosis had joined the other diseases of typhoid, typhus, scarlet fever and small pox that were rife at that time.

Politically it was complex, with Home Rule being both promoted and vigorously opposed, particularly in Ulster, all with the backdrop of the rise of Sinn Fein. There was also a growing unrest among workers supported by strong union leaders. It was into this difficult and changing Ireland that the Aberdeens came, still determined to do good. Lady Aberdeen, by this time, however, had an excellent track record in organisation and leadership and was well equipped to do more than wear and promote Irish fashion.

The fight against tuberculosis in Ireland

The most desperate need was in health and hygiene. Her crusade against tuberculosis in Ireland was truly remarkable and is well documented. She was approached for help in 1906 by the National Association for the Prevention of Tuberculosis and this resulted in the foundation of the Women's National Health Association of Ireland (WNHA), which was launched with Lady Aberdeen as its patron on 13 March 1907. This organisation, arranged on a district basis throughout the country, was committed to the eradication of disease, especially tuberculosis. In due course, it founded the Peamount and Rossclare Sanatoria, and the Sutton Preventorium, together accommodating over 300 patients.

Other work included the after-care of sanatorium patients in their own homes, Child Welfare Work, Infant Mortality Work, Babies' Clubs, School Children's Dental Clinics and the Maintenance of Visiting Nurses. It also extended, over time, to the provision of playgrounds and school gardens, the organisation and staging of exhibitions, including Health and Housing, Child Welfare, and Food, which travelled round Ireland as part of an intensive campaign against tuberculosis. There was the publication and distribution of Health Literature. Health Lectures, illustrated by lantern slides, were sent to Local Districts and Local Milk Depots. There were Meals for School Children and Folk Dancing. Some of these activities were directly linked to the influence of Patrick Geddes and are considered in more detail below.

It is clear that she was fully engaged in all that she took on. She was not a distant patron or mere figurehead. She really got involved. In fact Lady Aberdeen's own power of work was so amazing that she did not realise when others could not keep up with her. She would sit up until the early morning rather than leave anything undone. Her companions could not keep up. Her energy was more than physical, it was fuelled by an inner compulsion to be up and doing and Maureen Keene observes that it may have been derived from a need to escape her own private sorrows. Her youngest son, Archibald Gordon, (Archie) was killed in 1908, one of the first persons in Britain to die in a car accident.

The excellent work tackling TB was recognised by the award to the Women's National Health Association of Ireland of a prize of $1,000 for the best anti-tuberculosis work by volunteers (awarded jointly to the New York Charity Organization Society) by the International Tuberculosis Congress in 1908. But even successful health improvements could only have limited success. The WNHA was well aware of this and the frustration felt by its members was vented in a speech by Lady Aberdeen who, despairing, said:

> What is the point of spending money fighting TB if sufferers come back from sanatoriums to crowded unhealthy dwellings? What's the use of rescuing children if their Mothers have to live in overcrowded, contaminated dwellings?

From tuberculosis to town planning

The WNHA, under the leadership of Lady Aberdeen, was therefore, instrumental in bringing social and physical reform together in a single concerted effort. There was a realisation that healthcare in isolation was not enough. Indeed, it was Lady Aberdeen's frustration about the poor living conditions, exemplified by this sentiment,

> If we could have persuaded some of the Cabinet Ministers to come across to see things for themselves, the result might have been different ... To turn from rural to the urban districts of Ireland would have surely convinced (them) that the housing conditions of the cities and towns of Ireland remained a blot and a menace, culminating in Dublin ...

that prompted her to explore the wider ideas of town planning and civic survey, and therefore, involve Patrick Geddes. She recollects in her autobiography that she (and her husband) endeavoured to stir up public feeling on this subject and therefore invited Professor Geddes to bring his City and Town Planning exhibition to Dublin. This had first been exhibited in Chelsea in 1910 and had been touring since then. He came, not once, but twice, and his two Exhibitions made a deep impression on a small circle of earnest students. This was the Aberdeens using their position and in particular, her insight and belief in positive action. She recognised that notwithstanding the strides made since 1906, on health care, particularly in relation to the fight against tuberculosis, the real problems were poverty and bad housing. Until the links between these issues were addressed properly then no real solution would be found.

1911: a summer of planning exhibitions in Dublin

In 1911 Patrick Geddes staged his Cities and Town Planning exhibition, with accompanying lecture series, in two Dublin locations over the summer. The cost of transferring the Edinburgh exhibition was £300.00 and was met by the Aberdeens. Patrick Geddes was their guest while in Dublin. The Exhibition was mounted first at the Royal Dublin Society premises at Ballsbridge from 24 May to 7 June 1911. It closely followed the arrangement of Geddes's Edinburgh exhibition earlier in the year and Frank Mears, his future son in law, was appointed assistant director and oversaw its installation. In a lecture to promote this first exhibition, Mears emphasised that town planning was no mere fad, indulged in by reformers, but a means of bring open space back into the cities and to ensure that, with wise and orderly development, a town would be convenient, prosperous and healthy.

The exhibition was divided into four sections

1. Geographical and Historical: tracing the main geographical and social forces which have determined the present form of Western European Towns
2. Examples of continental official town development plans, including some garden village examples
3. Illustrations of the principle of survey work already undertaken in Edinburgh
4. Survey material on Dublin and other Irish towns, with particular reference to the intimate relation of town and country (but explicitly stated that the Irish material had been assembled in a few weeks and was therefore very incomplete).

A series of lectures dealing with planning and the development of Dublin was organised to run alongside the exhibition and held in the conference hall of *Ui Breasail,* RDS. It appears that Lady Aberdeen had a keen interest in and may even have been an instigator for the accompanying lecture series. Correspondence between the two in 1911 includes names of speakers, with Geddes indicating their main area of interest and also whether they are good speakers. William H Lever, Chairman of Lever Brothers, Port Sunlight is certainly approved of and subsequently delivered a lecture on Planning, Place and Industrial efficiency. Other speakers included WG Strickland, Director of the National Gallery, on the City of Dublin, its development and growth, illustrated with lantern slides. Geddes, however, gave the opening lecture, entitled *Dublin and City Development,* in which he alluded to the potential of the emerging neotechnic industries. With specific reference to Dublin he said:

> The cultural resources of Dublin, its vast scientific equipment, its magnificent museums, its universities, all expressed increased possibilities of development, not only for the metropolis but for the greater part of Ireland, thus affording a promise that this country would once more recover its world influence throughout European civilisation.

He also spoke of the influence of the city's cathedrals, which he described as a vast system of cultural institutions devoted to the study of all the history and of all the sciences and of all the industries and of all the activities which it was the function of the cathedral to idealise. In short, the true cathedral was the expression of a city's fullest and most vivid life.

These ideas are augmented in an interview given by Geddes and reported in the *Freeman's Journal* about that time. He clearly illustrated the type of improvement that might readily be undertaken in Dublin, but with a caveat that he needed to study Dublin more carefully.

> I would venture upon things that are simple, easy and obvious and things that everyone would approve of. I would tackle things like mending and cleaning and brightening of derelict corners and tumble down houses, and especially the letting out of little bits of garden, that the casual labourer in the work house should be absorbed by your garden. I would have two types of garden, small patches in the crowded areas and the larger gardens where the population is not so crowded.

This early importance of gardens and parks is echoed by Lady Aberdeen in her Presidential report of 1912. Bannon observes that in this interview he is also demonstrating the practicality of his 'conservative surgery approach' which so marked him out from most of his contemporaries. Geddes was keen to explain that his town planning exhibition was about the concrete study of human communities struggling towards betterment. This first exhibition was a great success with a total attendance of 160, 000 over the two weeks.

The exhibition was re-erected at Trinity College Dublin in August 1911, along with another accompanying lecture series as part of the Royal Institute of Public Health Congress. The *Irish Times* reported that this proved to be a joyous and ceremonial occasion despite the wider social backcloth of serious disruption and upheaval in Dublin. Notwithstanding, that the main focus of the congress was medical issues, there were sections on engineering and architecture. Section F dealt with Housing of the Working classes, Town Planning etc. and this was Patrick Geddes's Cities and Town Planning Exhibition. It later toured Ireland as a Health and Housing Exhibition.

Helen Meller observed that in Dublin, Patrick Geddes grasped the nettle of religion and politics. He did so both at Lady Aberdeen's dining table, where Dublin society was invited to meet the professor. But, also by walking the streets of the city and from his insistence on meeting Jim Larkin (the charismatic union organiser sent over from Liverpool to lead the striking dockers) to discuss the dockers' housing. He had previously met Larkin at the Outlook Tower in Edinburgh to discuss social problems and solutions.

Geddes achieved a meeting at a time when Lord Aberdeen could and would not. Geddes also met the leaders of the Catholic hierarchy and recognised the role of both the church and their buildings in an enhanced Dublin. He did not approve, however, of the line taken by Dublin Corporation, that there was only a housing problem and that this was a separate issue from town planning. He saw municipal housing schemes as a threat not only to the fabric of the city but also to the people as well.

What he wanted was to preserve the best of the past; the involvement of the people in their own betterment; the rediscovery of the past traditions of city building which deliberately expressed the aesthetic ideals of the community. He urged ordinary people to take up survey work and not to be overwhelmed by the problems of Dublin, where others saw poverty, decay and neglect, Geddes saw a former capital of an independent Ireland, and the elegant centre of eighteenth century culture and a noble city. He passionately wanted his Dublin Exhibition to provide an understanding of place and history in solving the existing problems. His alliance with Lady Aberdeen, in taking a holistic view of addressing Dublin's health and housing problems, must have been refreshing and fruitful for them both and perhaps at odds with those who laid all the problems at the door of the British Government.

Patrick Geddes's impact in Ireland

There were two direct consequences of Geddes's visits to Dublin in 1911. At a local level he initiated a campaign to clean up the estimated 2,000 derelict sites in the city and to turn some of these into children's playgrounds. In conjunction with the WNHA, Geddes's daughter, Norah, therefore spent three years in Dublin, organising gardens for children. Her scheme was incorporated into the national health policy for Ireland, which Lord and Lady Aberdeen were promoting. During this time she worked on the conversion of sites in Cook Street, St Augustine's Street (St Monica's Garden) and the Ormond Market Playground.

In her Presidential report of 1912, to the Housing and Town Planning Association of Ireland, Lady Aberdeen stated that, whenever a garden occupied a vacant site, that site made for the cheerfulness and health of the surrounding houses, instead of accumulating rubbish and encouraging disease. When something pretty was below their windows, people stopped throwing rubbish out of them, and took heart to clean their houses. These gardens served many purposes. In these garden play grounds, adequately staffed, the rough children became gentler, the wild children learned the happiness of active work and play and all benefitted from coming under the benefit of organised games. Lady Aberdeen loved gardens and had benefited from formal gardens all her life, but in espousing the social benefits of gardens she echoes Geddes ideas, as well as those of the American social reform parks.

The other direct consequence of the 1911 exhibition and associated events was the establishment of the Housing and Town Planning Association of Ireland, of which Lady Aberdeen was the first President. The town planning movement had been born in Ireland, but at a time of political turmoil and of intense labour disputes, implementing meaningful planning schemes was practically impossible. Labour disputes lasted throughout 1913 in Dublin and culminated in the 'great lock out' from August until January 1914. Many of the grievances, however, related to housing and poverty and the Local Government Board set up the Dublin Housing Inquiry in 1913. Geddes gave evidence to it on behalf of WNHA, utilising this opportunity to promote planning and his ideas about cities and people.

The general trend of the inquiry was to instigate substantial municipal intervention. Geddes did not approve of the brutality of the proposals, ignoring the survey approach and the benefits of conservative surgery. However, when in Dublin for this purpose he was again a guest of the Aberdeens at the Viceregal Lodge. During the course of his stay with them the Aberdeens encouraged him to return to Dublin once more and this time to organise a large and dramatic Civic Exhibition.

A Civic Exhibition in Dublin 1914

At the meeting of the Housing and Town Planning Association in January 1914, the President (Lady Aberdeen) informed them that they were going to stage a Civic Exhibition in Dublin that summer. An exhibition would clear the minds and concentrate efforts towards the housing of the people and the reconstruction of Irish towns and cities. Lady Aberdeen indicated what had been included in Civic Exhibitions in other countries: housing, roads, sanitation, heating, lighting, water, food and milk supplies, transport – especially facilities for workers who had to travel to their places of employment. Equally important, however, she explained were elegant public buildings, open spaces, playgrounds, recreational and educational facilities, art galleries, libraries and museums, while special attention must be paid to the needs of children, the sick and the aged.

Lady Aberdeen acknowledged that this was a bold project and time was short, but public opinion was on their side. Nothing less than the whole reconstruction of Dublin would do if the city were to thrive in the future. To this end she proposed that a civic survey be undertaken and announced that The Lord Lieutenancy felt so strongly on the subject that he was offering a prize for the best civic plan, 'with the special object of furnishing adequate and convenient housing for the working classes around the city'. The prize committee would consist of experts with an international reputation. This exhibition was for all the people, and therefore, was not to be held in establishment locations of the RDS or Trinity College, this one would be staged in the Linen Hall Barracks, in Henrietta Street, on the north side of the city, in the midst of an area of extreme poverty.

The organisation and implementation of this project was therefore masterminded by Lady Aberdeen and Patrick Geddes. Two forceful personalities, who both regarded a successful exhibition as an essential first stage in implementing changes in a city, a city that nevertheless was a focus for national unrest. Lady Aberdeen, however, put her own particular style on the exhibits and their presentation.

The Exhibition opened on 15 July 1914, with a lavish ceremony. The *Irish Times* reported that:

> The organisers deserved credit for their courage, they have chosen a time when men's minds are grievously troubled about politics and the nations' destinies are in the melting pot, but whatsoever might yet emerge in Ireland would have need of their vision and encouragement.

In spite of the turbulent political and social backdrop of the summer of 1914 or perhaps because of that, the exhibition proved popular with the people of Dublin from the start. A civic pageant from the front of the Mansion House to the Linen Hall Barracks was cheered through the city. Lady Aberdeen was presented with a golden key to perform the opening ceremony and her efforts on behalf of the people of Dublin was praised thus,

> You are not likely to be forgotten in this city for your devotion, unfaltering, resistant, restless, ever-working for the welfare, the health and the prosperity of the Irish people.

Once open, visitors to the exhibition could travel there by tram and the price of entry was sixpence. Inside there was a great deal to see and do. There were pictures representing the beauty and the blackspots of Dublin. Exhibits showed what had been done in England, Scotland and elsewhere, with that of Liverpool regarded as the most impressive. Various government departments including the Land Commission, the Registry Office, the Congested District Boards, and the Department of Agriculture and Technical Instruction all had stands and there were demonstrations of poultry rearing and bee-keeping. A replica of the Ardagh Chalice was on show, plus a magnificent collection of 18th and early 19th century Irish silver, on loan from the National Gallery, as well as examples of Irish printing and bookbinding. In contrast, cookery demonstrations could be watched and boys from the Industrial Schools demonstrated carpentry, tailoring and wire mattress making.

Out of doors agricultural skills were displayed, including manuring techniques, and from Belfast was brought a municipal abattoir. Dublin Corporation showed the latest methods of street lighting and one of the most spectacular exhibits was their electric fountain, illuminated at night. In the child welfare section, there were free medical and dental inspections for school children.

However, as Mary Keane puts it, healthy children were handpicked to give a demonstration of folk dancing and a grand rally was held in Phoenix Park in which 1,200 children took part. Concerts and cinematography programmes were held every half hour in the Hall of the Civic Exhibition and the band of the Old Temple Gardens, played throughout the day. There was a Punch and Judy show, merry-go-rounds, a switchback railway, sailing boats and the 'usual' sideshows. Tea gardens served light meals all afternoon under the direction of the WHNA ladies.

Patrick Geddes of course, presided over the Summer School of Civics. The Aberdeens again provided hospitality and he dined regularly with the 'great and the good' of Ireland. One evening after dinner he was vigorously declaiming:

> I urge not only that the collections in the Linen Hall be preserved permanently, but that the re-planning scheme which wins the Viceroy's prize can be carried out courageously and beginning this very summer.

Later that same evening, Lord Aberdeen, having received a message, broke the news that war had started. It was 4 August 1914.

The exhibition was undoubtedly a success as a summer special, with wonderful attendances, although its popularity was affected by the outbreak of war. There was some criticism, an *Irish Times* editorial observed that:

> There is a very different thing from practice and practice (town planning) must mean a large expenditure of money. The Exhibition will not give us money.

It was particularly hoped by Lady Aberdeen that the exhibition would awaken public opinion. It was therefore unfortunate that at the closing of the exhibition, local residents from the surrounding poor areas invaded and stole what they could including chairs and tables.

Almost inevitably, one by one the projects that would have made Dublin the 'geotechnic capital of the British Empire' were abandoned. John Nelson, the American judge, cancelled his plan to come and judge the competition because of the war. However, the Prize was still awarded, to Patrick Abercrombie for his plan, 'Dublin of the future'. The plan, however, was never implemented. Shortly after the exhibition closed, Lord Aberdeen was recalled to London. Neither wished to leave, they considered their work unfinished. A small consolation was elevation to Marquess and in so doing they took the name Temair in commemoration of their period in Ireland.

Lord and Lady Aberdeen were not without critics and enemies. Indeed, in this most difficult of time in Ireland they seemed remarkably resilient. Keane observes that a charge that Lady Aberdeen was callously unconcerned by the effects of the labour troubles, was no more than a piece of anti-establishment propaganda, as was the implication that she knew nothing of the realties of slum life.

It can be recognised, however, that Lady Aberdeen's barely concealed criticisms of the 'ignorant and feckless poor, who needed guidance from their betters', would inevitably antagonise people, and thus blind them to the practical value of the work of both Lord and Lady Aberdeen. The memory of Lady Aberdeen is not revered officially in Ireland and most historical accounts of the era in which she served, make scant mention of her. They were present, although they did not know it, in the years when Irish identity was vigorously asserting itself, British domination was coming to an end, and the Irish Free State was emerging. In a climate in which the column commemorating Charles Stewart Parnell ('the hero of Home Rule') was toppled by patriots anxious to expunge all trace of Anglo-Irishry there was no place for a couple who, however, well inten-tioned and active in charitable work, were representative of the British crown. From the British government's perspective at this time, the polit-ical turbulence and uncertainty in Ireland, Britain and Europe meant that Lord Aberdeen was no longer an appropriate representative in Ireland at that time. Lady Aberdeen's plans for planning and for Dublin, inspired by Patrick Geddes, were allowed to run into the sand.

Life after Ireland

The Marquis and Marchioness of Aberdeen and Temair left Ireland in February 1915 and almost immediately travelled to America on a fund-raising mission for Irish charitable causes, they hoped to reach their target within six months, but it took them two years. The main beneficiaries were the Women's National Health Association, including the Peamount Sanatorium. At home they moved to Cromar at Glentanar, Aberdeenshire, a beautiful house they had designed and built for their retirement and began work on their reminiscences, published as *We Twa*.[1] Lady Aberdeen continued to work on many charitable and political causes. In 1920 she played a significant role in bringing members of the International Council of Woman together following the war, when she resumed the presidency. She travelled widely, including several trips to Ireland annually.

This Ireland had changed forever. The Easter Rising in 1916 was followed by Civil War, and eventual independence for the Republic of Ireland with partition of the six counties of Northern Ireland. Town planning, even the most holistic of approaches, was no longer a priority for Ireland, or indeed for Lady Aberdeen. She continued, however, in correspondence with Geddes. He was keen to promulgate ideas through her and sent pamphlets for distribution to her organisations. She continued for many years to be a formidable woman of energy and influence. She died in 1939 and is buried at Haddo.

The *Irish Times* in reporting her death considered her as a great friend of Ireland; tribute was paid to her unceasing work on behalf of the poor and her crusade against tuberculosis. The paper regarded the Peamount Sanatorium as a splendid monument of her work. A more glowing assessment of her is as follows:

> Ishbel, Lady Aberdeen – Wife of the Viceroy in the years leading up to the Easter Rising, she worked tirelessly to improve the health and indeed happiness of the people of the Ireland. She campaigned most effectively for greater recognition for Irish industry, especially its arts and crafts and perhaps most important, she was also a major inspiration behind a multi-faceted attack on tuberculosis, the 'White Plague'.

In their lifetime the Aberdeens were accused of many things, including the theft of the Irish Crown Jewels, yet despite both personal tragedy and vilification, Ishbel became one of the most socially influential people in Ireland during the years of the Home Rule crisis. Another assessment was:

> It would hardly be commensurate to say that Lady Aberdeen seconded Lord Aberdeen in the attempt to win the Irish people. It could not be said in truth of so great a personality as that gracious lady that she seconded anyone... She has spent herself in the course of Ireland and the Irish poor. She has swept on her irresistible course, and has fired others with something of her superb energy and courage.

Part III: *Lady Aberdeen and Patrick Geddes: the Relationship and its Legacy*

Was Lady Aberdeen of the Patrick Geddes circle ? She was certainly linked to it, but perhaps they were two concentric circles linked by thinking and influence. It was a mutually beneficial relationship. Like Patrick Geddes, Ishbel Aberdeen was an educator; doing and making a difference by getting people to help themselves; looking at the person as a whole in the context of their own environment. She too knew of the benefit of education through head, hand and heart. This is illustrated from her early days and the Upward and Onward Association and was perhaps why the Aberdeens were keen to have Patrick Geddes and his exhibition in Dublin. Town planning for her was a mechanism to redress the root and branch problems of the cities which manifested themselves in illness. The particular role and responsibilities of women were also fundamental to her work.

Mary Keane observes that Lady Aberdeen's voice was an unusual one, in that it came from the very heart of the establishment and it preached heresy – namely that women were capable of running their own affairs. Child care, home making and the nursing of the sick were traditionally regarded as female concerns, Lady Aberdeen therefore considered it reasonable that women should gain control of their finances and be better educated to carry out what Ishbel regarded as their duties in society. The good sense of her practical proposals made them almost subversive and earned her animosity in official circles. She was certainly not a suffragette, nor in fact could it be claimed that she was a champion of women's rights. She nevertheless contributed to the emancipation of women. A strong personality, she was no diplomat and was impatient with the niceties of negotiation. She saw problems, saw how they could be solved and did not understand why this could not be done immediately. Geddes had many of the same characteristics.

The 'debachal' in Dublin just when success was at hand, was a bitter disappointment to Geddes who clearly foresaw the consequences. He had seen the approach of the war in Europe since 1900 and with others created a ten -point plan for post war reconstruction and renewal, even before the outbreak of war. He considered that the lack of vision and courage of leaders on both sides of the Irish Sea would provide a social and political boomerang. The problems were mounting: the never-ending nemesis of the Sinn Fein Rebellion; continued religious strife and home rule politics in the context of appalling housing, lack of employment and a sickly urban population. Civic survey and town planning schemes could have addressed many of these related issues. Politics won the day and the newly independent Ireland had too many pressing issues to institute town planning. Not least, as it had been promoted by the last but one British Vice Royal. This was perhaps inevitable, but was undoubtedly an opportunity lost.

Geddes's insights are all related to an astute perception of the physical environment and the changes both technological and social which were influencing cities and their regions. Geddes was particularly keen on the historical evolution of the place where they live. In Ireland this at that time was too tied up with the British and the colonial rule.

What would Lady Aberdeen and Patrick Geddes make of the vibrant and exciting Dublin of today, a century after their town planning exhibitions? It is a city with many planning problems, some of them created by the Celtic tiger, but it is a city that is prosperous and peaceful. They would have approved of the buoyant Irish cultural and artistic identity and Dublin's place as a world city. Patrick Geddes and Ishbel Aberdeen were both determined to make a difference. He created the phrase, 'Think Global, Act Local', and she, perhaps without even realising it, thus lived her life. Together they left their mark on the city of Dublin and it is hoped that their influence will increasingly be recognised and celebrated.

Anne-Michelle Slater

Note

1   *We twa hae run aboot the braes,*
    And pou'd the gowans fine;
    But we've wander'd mony a weary fitt,
    Sin auld lang syne.

    (From 'Auld Lang Syne', by Robert Burns)

Chronology

1857	Born Ishbel (Gaelic for Isabel) Maria Marjoribanks, third daughter of the 1st Baron Tweedmouth and Isabella Weir-Hogg in Mayfair, London
1868	First romantic first glimpse by Ishbel of Johnnie (John Gordon, Earl of Aberdeen)
1877	Married John Gordon, 7th Earl of Aberdeen (later the 1st Marquess of Aberdeen and Temair), in St George's Church, Hanover Square, London
1878	First visit to Haddo House, Aberdeenshire, homecoming celebrations lasted for a week
1879	Birth of first son, George, Lord Haddo
1879–80	Extensive renovations and extensions to Haddo House
1880	Birth of first daughter, Marjorie
1883	Birth of second son Dudley Gladstone
1884	Birth of third son Ian Archibald
1886	Appointment of Lord Aberdeen as Viceroy to Ireland
1887–8	Travel in North America partly to promote Irish industry and raise money for Ireland
1893–98	Earl of Aberdeen, Governor-General of Canada and founded the Victorian Order of Nurses and the National Council of Women
1893	Lady Aberdeen elected President of the International Council of Women (which she held until her death in 1939)
1906–1915	Lord and Lady Aberdeen held the Viceroyalty of Ireland
1907	Foundation of Women's National Health Association
1911	Cities and Town Planning Exhibition in Dublin, Director, Patrick Geddes
1914	Dublin Civic Exhibition, organised by Patrick Geddes
1920	Lord Aberdeen retired from public life and moved to Cromar, Tarland, a romantic gothic house built to their design and wrote *We Twa*
1927	Golden Wedding
1934	Lord Aberdeen died. Lady Aberdeen moved to Gordon House, Aberdeen
1928	Awarded the Freedom of the City of Edinburgh
1929	Awarded an Honorary degree by the University of Aberdeen
1931	Awarded the Grand Cross of the British Empire. Led a delegation of six women requesting the ordination of women ministers and appointment of women elders and deacons to the Church of Scotland. This was the first female delegation to appear before the General Assembly

18 April 1939   Died. Buried in the family cemetery at Haddo House,
                Aberdeenshire

Bibliography

Bannon, Michael J (editor), *A Hundred Years of Irish Planning: Volume 1, The Emergence of Irish Planning 1880–1920* (Turoe Press Ltd, Baldoyle, 1985)

Breathnach, Caoimhghin S and Moynihan, John B, 'The Frustration of Lady Aberdeen in her Crusade against Tuberculosis in Ireland' (*Ulster Medical Journal* 2012; 81(1): 37–47)

French, Doris, *Ishbel and the Empire: A Biography of Lady Aberdeen* (Dundurn Press Ltd, Toronto, 1988)

'*We Twa*': *Reminiscences of Lord and Lady Aberdeen* (Collins, Glasgow, 1925)

CHAPTER THIRTEEN

A Suffragette and her Passage to India

Annie Besant, Theosophist (1847–1933)

THE LIFE OF ANNIE BESANT was split in two halves; first in England then India. She and Geddes were linked in each half. Initially she was a pioneering social and educational reformer in England fighting the cause of equal rights for women in general. Best known was her role in the Match Strikes of 1888, when women were being poisoned by their contact with phosphorus used in the manufacture of matches. In Asia she became an ambassador representing the exploited poor, striving to improve education for the young irrespective of gender, dedicating her skills to organising educational centres and opportunities in Varanasi and Chennai.

HM Hyndman said of her work as a social reformer:

> What more could a woman of great ability want in the way of career under existing conditions than that she should be the leading champion not only in the metropolis, but throughout great Britain, and indeed all over the world, of the physical, intellectual and moral development of children...

Her character was portrayed in the following epigram by Cousins the Irish artist/poet and Principal of Madanapalle Theosophical College, India:

> to the individual synthesis of
> intuition & actual
> thought & feeling
> masculine & feminine
> youth & age
> east & west
> past & future

which reminds me in style and content of one of Geddes's Thinking Machines.

Annie Wood was born in London 1847 to middle class parents with Irish origins – which may account for her lifelong dedication to Ireland's struggle for identity and independence. Her father died when she was five and she was brought up by an aunt in Dorset. At 19 Annie met and married the Rev Frank Besant, vicar of Sibsey in Lincolnshire. By the time she was 23 Annie had two children, Digby and Mabel. Shortly before her marriage, as a foretaste of what was to happen in the future, Annie visited Manchester where she was introduced to English political activists and others representing the Manchester Martyrs of the Irish Republican Fenian Brotherhood.

It was not a happy marriage. Annie was deeply unhappy. Her growing political awareness and her tours in Europe as a young woman revealed links between working communities, living conditions, poverty, exploitation and the Industrial Revolution. Her independent spirit clashed with the traditional views of her husband. She was not allowed to keep the earnings from her writing. Whatever faith she had she lost and she refused to attend communion. Frank Besant ordered her to leave the family home. A legal separation was arranged and Digby, the son, stayed with his father, and Mabel went to live with Annie in London. (After the 'Bradlaugh affair' her husband persuaded the court that she was unfit to look after both children, and they were handed over to him permanently).

Annie was able to support herself with a weekly column in the *National Reformer*, the newspaper of the National Secular Society, and occasional journalism. *The Gospel of Atheism* (1877) brought her notoriety, if not wealth. She was in great demand for public lectures. She became a prominent speaker for the National Secular Society (NSS), then the Fabian Society and the (Marxist) Social Democratic Federation (SDF). Tom Mann in 1875 described her skills as an orator:

> Mrs Besant transfixed me; her superb control of voice, her whole-souled devotion to the cause she was advocating, her love of the down trodden, and her appeal on behalf of sound education for all children created such an impression upon me...

The change in her life style from dependent housewife to self-supporting professional woman forced her into a quest to consolidate and broaden her personal social development. Like every other British woman she was excluded from university simply on the grounds of gender. Fortunately there was a not totally unsatisfactory alternative – the Birkbeck Literary and Scientific Institution – which she attended (part-time) from 1874 to 1878. There, her religious and political activities ruffled a few feathers. It is said that, at one point the Institution's governors sought to withhold the publication of her exam results.

In need of a tutor in the 'natural sciences' she (and Charles Bradlaugh's daughter) made use of Patrick Geddes, at that time a protégé of
TH Huxley and senior demonstrator of practical physiology at University
College. As a young man Geddes was probably attracted to both of these
feisty women with a noble cause. What would we give to have an account
of their relationship? The pupil was seven years older than the teacher,
had come through family trauma, was burning with missionary zeal and
had already a public persona. Having recognised the forces of exploitation in Britain and the World she was advocating strong views on over-
population, demanding improved education for all and voluntary birth-
control. The teacher was a provincial with a sketchy academic record, but
who was considered a 'distinguished student' by Huxley and who had had
a paper in the *Transactions of the Zoological Society* correcting an aspect
of Huxley's work.

What correspondence that remains between Besant and Geddes suggests
that they achieved a relationship of mutual respect. On 13 October 1884
A Besant of 19 Avenue Road, London wrote to P Geddes (no address
given), thanking him for lending her lecture notes via a Mr Robertson. I
believe him to have been John Mackinnon Robertson (1856–1933),
Liberal MP from Arran who became a leading secularist and associate of
Charles Bradlaugh (1833–1891). The notes were for her 'course of
lectures on Evolution of Society'. On the previous day, she explained, she
had given a lecture on *The Industrial Period: its products.*

She was encouraged that the responses were strengthening a 'protest
against the destruction of natural beauty now going on in England'.

She must have known Robertson quite well as she mentioned, on his
behalf, that he would write to Geddes soon.

Again, on 29 January 1886, she wrote to Geddes. Her monogram on
the letter-head interlocks gothic letters A and B with the motto *Be Strong*
on a swag below her graphic initials.

Addressed to: 'My Dear Mr Geddes', she congratulates him on his
engagement to Anna Morton. But jokingly tells him to be cautious when
travelling to Greece and not to be 'taken up' by bandits. (Did she know
that he had had a scare in Mexico?) And regarding the Eastern Question[1],
curiously, she suggests that it's best to study books than be on the spot!

> Don't let any leaning to the Hellenes induce you to buckle on sword on
> their behalf when you reach 'the place that was Greece'.
>
> Very cordially always Annie Besant.

Mrs Besant is described as 'a close friend of Charles Bradlaugh, atheist and republican'. Besant lived with him and his daughters, and they worked together on many issues. In 1877 they published a book by the American birth-control campaigner Charles Knowlton, which claimed that working-class families needed to be able to decide how many children they wanted and suggested ways how this could be done. The Knowlton book was dynamite, and was vigorously opposed by the Church.

The pair were arrested and put on trial for publishing the book. They were found guilty, but released pending appeal. Public opinion was polarised, the Liberal press in particular supporting change. While it looked as though the pair would be sent to prison, the case was finally thrown out on a technical point.

Bradlaugh's political prospects were not damaged by the Knowlton scandal and he was elected to Parliament for Northampton in 1881. Because of his atheism, he asked to be allowed to affirm rather than swear the oath of loyalty. Although many Christians were shocked by Bradlaugh, others (like the Liberal leader Gladstone) spoke up for the right to freedom of belief.

Annie also moved into politics, in the limited way now opening up to women. From 1881 women could take part in local elections and Annie put herself forward to represent Tower Hamlets on the London School Board. 'No more hungry children', was her election slogan. Socialist Feminism was the answer:

> I ask the electors to vote for me, and the non-electors to work for me because women are wanted on the Board and there are too few women candidates.

Annie romped home with over 15,000 votes – almost all of whom must have been men. As she wrote in the *National Reformer*:

> Ten years ago, under a cruel law, Christian bigotry robbed me of my little child. Now the care of the 763,680 children of London is placed partly in my hands.

Yet in the prime of her life and vigour she went off into the mystic groves of Hindu philosophy and religion.

The scene in which Besant – and to a lesser extent Geddes – was operating was clearly a facet of the environmental ferment and political dissent which was brewing in the latter part of the 19th century. Emerging from American independence and Thomas Paine's dictum for equality ('My country is the world, and my religion is to do good.') civil rights movements

were driving forward, challenging inequalities and racial abuse; still cont-
inuing to wrestle with moral codes within society, trying to check author-
itarianism and review the form of democracy. Special encouragement for
liberation and emancipation, experienced now, came from actions in North
America with the first Woman's Rights Convention generating publications which examined the role of woman in the American Revolution and
the History of Woman's suffrage in 1881.

Helena Petrova Blavatsky (1831–1891) and Colonel Henry Steel Olcott
(1832–1907) established the Theosophical Society in 1875 in New York
City. Rejecting most western values and embracing Theravada Buddhism
they were drawn to Asia where they established schools in Colombo, Sri
Lanka and eventually set up the headquarters of The Theosophical Society
in Madras (Chennai).

In 1890 Annie met Helena Blavatsky. Gradually her interests in theosophy grew and her life and career started to shift dramatically as she
embraced the theosophical movement. Her introduction to theosophy
was to change her life and lose her many of her original friends but helped
her make so many more across the world.

Annie had become disillusioned by the hypocrisies that she had
exposed in the 'Christian values' of Britain, which were riddled with
inequalities, particularly regarding women. She was equally scathing
about missionary work and is quoted as saying: 'India was a victim of
mischief wrought by Christian missionaries'. Searching for an organisation with shared objectives, as a true politician with charisma Besant
quickly recognised that much of the material world is based on exploitation and she had now found a mission to fight it. In taking on this role she
was vilified and, secretly I suspect, admired for deserting her domineering
husband, whose Christian virtues, as a minister, she considered dubious,
and for taking on her monumental quest.

In her autobiography Mrs Besant calls her changing physical and
mental approach to her humanitarian philosophy 'reaching out'. This is
vividly illustrated by her embarking, almost immediately, on a pattern of
international tours on behalf of the Theosophical Society. Blavatsky
would have recognised that Besant's powerful informed style as an orator
would easily promote the fusion of eastern and western multiculturalism.
At the same time she became the editor of the *Theosophical Monthly*. In
1893 she attended the Chicago World Trade Fair, which had a pavilion
called Parliament of Religions.

The growth in the demand for women's rights and exploring new
religions, such as Hinduism, gave momentum to many forms of spirit-

ualism and the transcendentalist movement of America, reshaping this spirit of internationalism which was engaging such as Emerson, Thoreau and Walt Whitman at the time.

The Chicago World Trade Fair of 1893 also gave profile to world cultures and Theosophy within the 'Parliament of Religions' pavilion, which enabled the full impact and potential of Hinduism to be explored with representatives and spiritual leaders such as Vivekananda and Chakravarti who took America by storm.

A parallel change in Western attitudes to Eastern religion at the *fin de siècle* was going on. Exotic forms of music, art and philosophy were impacting on Western culture. In the arts the Celtic revival, the Secession movement in Vienna and Japanese symbolism influenced many including the French Impressionists and many Scots artists including Charles Rennie Mackintosh. Some followed the great global explorers, as did Mark Twain, who brought his own light-hearted interpretation to these profound matters.

The 1890s were a time of great change in Annie's life. She visited India for the first time in 1893 and in 1895 she established her home in the sacred city of Kanshi (Benares/Varanasi).

Besant's empathy with India was partly spiritual but the decades leading up to her forming a base there revealed the ongoing hardships the communities of India had to withstand. In 1898 she helped establish the Central Hindu College in Varanasi with Dr Alfred Richardson. Within a year the worst famine of a century hit India. The 1890s had brought a Biblical scale of drought. Famine with resulting epidemics claimed many millions of lives in Asia and her awareness of this focussed her compassion. The widespread tragedy engulfed 60 million Indian folk and the resulting calamity may have claimed as many as five million lives.

Serious questions were levelled at the British administration at the time. The causes may have been obscure but the effects were clear enough. How effective was the British Empire's management of agricultural development, horticultural planning, strategy, food storage, emergency distribution, medical care? With a massive rail network and communication links already stretching across India, why was more food not imported and distributed by rail to stem the growing problem and why were there not attempts to try to transport the starving to areas where they could be cared for? What role did the army have in this to try to alleviate the catastrophe?

New agricultural improvement and political solutions were urgently needed. There seemed to be a consensus that improved education, development of rural economies, and applying indigenous alternatives for sustainable living would help.

'Better remain silent, better not even think, if you are not prepared to act' said Mrs Besant and it is understandable that so many missionary groups tried to respond and successive waves of 'Westerners' – like the Geddes family – tried to 'make a difference', in today's jargon.

Besant witnessed the aftermath of this disaster; she may have been reminded of what she had heard of the Irish famine of the 1840s. But this catastrophe in Asia gave extra impetus to the Indian National Congress – ambitions which several Scots had encouraged.

Back in England in 1902 she formed the International Order of Co-Freemasonry and over the next few years she established lodges in many parts of the British Empire. In 1907 she became President of the Theosophical Society. In the same year her Hindu University was supported by Rabindranath Tagore and Mahatma Gandhi. When the latter was interned for challenging the government in Pretoria on issues of racism, she sent him ' a message of hope, of consolation, of friendship'.

'Dr Besant's Tours', mainly representing the Theosophical Society, took her to Scotland, in her own Indian-style outfit, in 1907, 1911, 1914, 1924, 1926 and 1929. She gave 'an extraordinary theosophical address' in 1911 at the Sorbonne. In 1914 she was touring Paris, London, Glasgow and Edinburgh on behalf of the Theosophical Society when war broke out.

The Indian Empire supported the mother country vigorously, to the tune of 74,000 killed in action. At the same time, as in Ireland, there were those who questioned the wisdom of such loyalty and used the war to pursue other aims while attention was focussed on the global conflict. Mrs Besant helped launch the Home Rule League to campaign for democracy in India and dominion status within the Empire.

In 1914, after 20 years of meeting and corresponding with Indian people in Europe, Patrick Geddes arrived for the first of three visits to India, in the course of which he was made Professor of Civics and Sociology at Mumbai and was commissioned to survey and report on 50 cities in the Madras Presidency by Lord Pentland, the Governor. Early in 1915 the tutor from those London days met his former biology pupil Annie Besant – now president of the Theosophical Society, a persistent fighter for Indian independence and soon to be President of the Indian National Congress.

Even within the limited correspondence we have access to, she expresses a growing respect and affection for Patrick Geddes. She wondered whether he would like to 'motor over with CP Ramaswami Aiyar and myself, on

Saturday or Sunday next?' She also wants to show Geddes her 'official house' and arouses our curiosity in writing: 'See how I have been taking your name in vain in enclosed...' (the enclosed material having been lost).

Patrick reported evocatively to Anna, on 9 February 1915:

> Yesterday, Sunday, Mrs Besant and two of her friends took us on a motor-run to the old temple-city of Conjeveram – one of the seven holy cities of India, and the most unspoiled and undegenerated I have seen anywhere... Nowhere have I seen so spacious and well-built an old garden city – for this almost is, and doubtless still more was: so this was an extraordinary object-lesson in that conservatism which I represent here, and confirmed all I had been preaching.

After attending a PG lecture she wrote:

> Dear Professor Geddes,
>
> Your lectures are a joy to me; you are the only second Englishman I have met who sees what India really means to the world... Perhaps the notes on the second page of enclosed may find its way to Mrs Geddes. I am glad you have a more competent assistant in that nice bright lad, with you the last 2 days.
>
> Ever Yours Annie Besant

I wonder what Geddes thought of being 'the only second Englishman'? 'That nice bright lad' was, of course, Alasdair, torn between loyalty to his father and the need to serve his country in its European struggle.

On 14 February 1915 came the recognition that Geddes was a do-er as well as a talker.

> My dear Professor of Beauty,
>
> Some of our people want you to give us a plan for this place – nearly 300 acres; would you, if the case (cost?) is not prohibitive? Are you free Tuesday? If yes, I could call for you at 4 & bring you here.
>
> Yours ever Annie Besant

From 1917 the lives of both parties were to change for ever. Geddes lost his eldest son in the War and shortly after that his wife Anna died in Calcutta during his seminar tour in Darjeeling. These tragic losses can only have compounded Besant's fervour and growing sense of how India was being exploited during the war. Her crusade for independence saw her vigorously campaigning on behalf of the entire Indian population.

In Chapter 3 of *A Case for India* she refers to 'Causes of the NEW SPIRIT in India', stating that:

The awakening of Asia is a part of a world movement, which has been quickened into marvellous rapidity by the world war. The world movement is towards democracy, and for the West dates from the breaking away of the American Colonies from Great Britain, consummated in 1776, and its sequel in the French Revolution in 1789.

Within a six point plan she highlights what must have been seen as 'incendiary' topics; such as Loss of Belief in the Superiority of the White Races, The Awakening of the Masses and, importantly, The Awakening of Indian Womanhood to claim its Ancient Position.

Her mood was quite clear and printed bold in Chapter 3 – *three decades in advance of Partition* – Why India Demands Home Rule / THE VITAL REASON, with the sub-heading: What is a Nation?

Some, clearly, saw her as dangerous, interfering, egocentric and potentially damaging to the financial benefits accrued by individuals and the British Empire (PLATE 5B).

Perhaps because of this, she was elected to be President of the 32nd Indian National Congress. Extensive quotation from her Presidential Address on 26 December 1917 is the best way to illustrate the faith and generosity of this woman.

Fellow Delegates and Friends

Everyone who has preceded me in this Chair has rendered his thanks in fitting terms for the gift which is truly said to be the highest that India has in its power to bestow. It is the sign of her fullest love, trust, and approval, and the one whom she seats in that chair is, for his year of service, her chosen leader. But if my predecessors found fitting words for their gratitude, in what words can I voice mine, whose debt to you is so overwhelmingly greater than theirs?

For the first time in Congress history, you have chosen as your President one who, when your choice was made, was under the heavy ban of government displeasure, and who lay interned as a person dangerous to public safety. While I was humiliated, you crowned me with honour; while I was slandered, you believed in my integrity and good faith; while I was crushed under the heel of bureaucratic power, you acclaimed me as your leader; while I was silenced and unable to defend myself, you defended me, and won for me release. I was proud to serve in lowliest fashion, but you lifted me up and placed me before the world as your chosen representative. I have no words with which to thank you, no eloquence with which to repay my debt. My deeds must speak for me, for words are too poor...

I turn your gift into service to the Motherland; I consecrate my life anew to her in worship by action. All that I have and am, I lay on the Altar of the Mother.

There is perhaps one value in your election of me in this crisis of India's destiny, seeing that I have not the privilege to be Indian born, but from that little island in the northern seas which has been, in the West, the builder-up of free institutions. The Aryan emigrants, who spread over the lands of Europe, carried with them the seeds of liberty sown in their blood in their Asian cradle-land. Western historians trace the self-rule of the Saxon villages to their earliest prototypes in the East, and see the growth of English liberty as up-springing from the Aryan root of the free and self contained village communities.

Its growth was crippled by Norman feudalism there, as its millennia-nourished security here was smothered by the East India Company. But in England it burst its shackles and nurtured a liberty-loving people and a free Commons' House. Here, it similarly bourgeoned out into the Congress activities, and more recently into those of the Muslim League, now together blossoming into Home Rule for India. The England of Milton, Cromwell, Sydney, Burke, Paine, Shelley, Wilberforce, Gladstone; the England that sheltered Mazzini, Kosuth, Kropotkin, Stepniak, and that welcomed Garibaldi; the England that is the enemy of tyranny, the foe of autocracy, the lover of freedom, that is the England that I would fain here represent to you to-day.

To-day when India stands erect, no suppliant people, but a nation self conscious, self respecting, determined to be free; when she stretches out her hand to Britain and offers friendship not subservience; co-operation not obedience; to-day let me: western-born but in spirit eastern, cradled in England but Indian by choice and adoption: let me stand as a symbol of union between Great Britain and India: a union of hearts and free choice, not of compulsion; and therefore of a tie which cannot be broken, a tie of love and mutual helpness, beneficial to both Nations and blessed by God.

India's great leader, Dadabhai Naoroji, has left his mortal body and is now one of the company of the Immortals, who watch over and aid India's progress. Not for me to praise him in feeble words of reverence or of homage. His deeds raise him, and his service to his country is his abiding glory. Our gratitude will be best paid by following in his footsteps, alike in his splendid courage and his unfaltering devotion, so that we may win the Home Rule which he longed to see while with us, and shall see, ere long, from the other world of Life, in which he dwells to-day.

It is easy for us, in our tired and cynical 21st century, to smile a little at Mrs Besant's interpretation of the relationship between her native country and India, but no-one could question her commitment to her adopted country, her tenacity and her optimism for its future.

The Religion of the River

Now, as an artist, I attempt my personal interpretation of the core of Besant's philosophy and modus operandi. And with this introduce my own project work inspired by the international themes as set out in the works of Geddes; namely the ecology of rivers. I have reflected on my own travels and projects in India as a means of giving some context to how things have changed since Besant's death in 1933.

I ask us to consider that the underlying power and passion of Besant's life was partly driven by the central role of interdependence within humanity. A belief in equal opportunity and mutual respect; offering a spiritual renewal within what she recognised in Theosophism and ecological regeneration which lies at the heart of everything.

The metaphor which 'the river' represents is a key symbol for regeneration, something which we have lost in our culture but which lies at the heart of Hinduism and I believe she identified deeply with this. The river echoes the flowing, meandering thread of life – or life echoes the flowing, meandering thread of the river. The strength of Besant's mission equates, I feel, to the majesty of rivers which never fail to stimulate our curiosity and wonder. The power of a river in spate, the devastation of a flood, terrify us, but we find peace by their more tranquil stretches. How many poets have been smitten by, and how many of our ancestors created deities from the spirit of that ever-moving water!

Voltaire (1694–1778), the supreme rationalist, said that:

> I am convinced that everything has come down to us from the banks of the Ganga...

J Krishnamurti a disciple of Besant said of the Ganga:

> It was really a marvellous river, wide, deep, with so many cities on its banks, so carelessly free and yet never abandoning itself. All life was there upon its banks, green fields, forests, solitary houses, death, love and destruction; there were long wide bridges over it, graceful and well used. Other streams and rivers joined it but she was mother (Ganges) of all rivers, the little ones and the big ones. She was always full, ever purifying herself and of an evening it was a blessing to watch her, with deepening

colour in the clouds and her waters golden... Meditation was like that
river, only it had no beginning and no ending; it began and its ending was
in the beginning...

It is the terrifying reality of the forces of nature, their extremes of character, and how humanity engages and copes which ultimately fascinate
us. Annie Besant recognised the essential spirit of India and its rivers as
enabling the renewal of the spirit and irrigation of the soul – a recurring
theme in the poetry of Rabindranath Tagore(1861–1941), another of the
Patrick Geddes circle.

The young Patrick Geddes, scanning the Tay Valley from Kinnoull
Hill, Perth, with panoptic vision experienced a parallel moment of tran-
scendence for him, shaping his global philosophy. The *Valley Section*, his
model (see Fig 15) for examining the interrelationship of Folk, Work and
Place, is synonymous with a diagnostic approach to understanding all
cultures – remembering that the *Valley Section* is really another way of
expressing the course of a river from source to mouth.[2]

By comparison with India, when folk walk along an attractive riverside here, in Scotland, their expectations are very different. But even here
a riverside walk however brief has the capacity to engage us in the most
primeval way with one of the life forces of the planet which seasonally
renews and enriches and at times erodes the route it follows from the
source to the sea. The renewing and revitalising qualities of the river are
inherent in the most ancient of religions and arguably it is locked into our
DNA although we rarely identify with it. We can often feel more relaxed,
energised, thoughtful and joyful – and dare I say inspired – or energised
by the water.

Most of my life has been close to the river Forth where most folk engage
with rivers, shore-lines and the ever more popular coastal walkways.

My own project work inspired by rivers seriously commenced with a
RSA Friends bursary-supported trip to explore the Murray river in Australia
around 2000. This was followed by the *Language of Rivers and Leaves*
project which collaborated with Bengali (PLATE 6A) and Aberdeenshire
river (PLATE 6B) communities in celebrating the 150th anniversary (in 2004)
of the birth of Geddes, in Ballater. In turn, this enabled a collaboration
with Bashabi Fraser in her publication *From the Ganga to the Tay*. The
endless struggle of the river, with rain and snow-melt – driven by gravity
– provides a contemporary metaphor for my particular examination of
what was at the heart of Annie Besant's *raison d'être*. Freedom from
oppression, equal rights for women, the ability to express and renew

constructive humanitarian beliefs depend on rediscovering ourselves as part of the whole eco-system and sharing an overwhelming intensity of intent – to survive and share!

My first expedition to India in 2002 brought my flight into the sultry morning of Kolkata (Calcutta) airport, fringed by tall palm trees. The smell and 'music' of India struck me immediately – one never forgets the first day in India. Hustled past many 'happy' begging children into a 1950s style Ambassador taxi, we sped into an urban dream-world of nearly 15 million people.

Kolkata is a city of extremes; from business folk with privilege and wealth to communities in dire poverty living in cardboard shanty towns along the side of one of the old jute canals – waterways for jute commerce designed by Scots engineers. I also experienced torrential rain and cyclonic storms which would wreak hurricane force damage within an hour and then be spirited away to leave a calm of devastation.

All my senses were electrified by what I witnessed; from flags emblazoned with hammer and sickles of the then communist regional government to a 'blade-runner' drive through the older part of the city, which almost seemed like a village, with all aspects of daily life being performed on the street.

A man gets a wet shave with a cut-throat razor while sitting on an upturned bucket. Cycles and hand-pulled rickshaws manoeuvre expertly, laden with fresh vegetables. Some have lines of white-feathered hens, hanging by their legs from the axles. Moving slowly through a sea of humanity I sensed a meeting between 19th and 21st centuries with scenes which would have been regularly witnessed by Patrick Geddes and Annie Besant – and I'm sure with the same amazed curiosity as my own.

My most traumatic moment in India was not seeing numerous exposed corpses being carried along public roads, exposed cremation ceremonies or even spotting an inflated cadaver happily navigating the Ganges mid stream. It was the realisation of the honest public acceptance of death by most Indian folk. I had travelled by train to Varanasi to witness the epic architectural splendour and some chaos which sees marvellous structures perched on the banks of Mother Ganges. A place which Geddes had surveyed and stressed that it should be preserved.

Shortly after my arrival I walked down to meet a small ferry boat and was alerted to a commotion of feral dogs in the shallow water. Ferry passengers were disembarking normally just 30 metres away. I got close enough to see that the 'dingos' were fighting over the lower torso of some human remains. Some folk simply commit their dead to the fortunes of the massive waterway, without cremation, which for some is seen as the spirit and soul of INDIA.

I wonder how Besant and Geddes felt about the daily public exposure of corpses being immersed in Rivers?

The Besant Legacy

Besant was driven to challenge the religious and political doctrines which had advocated a form of 'divide and rule' within 19th century Britain and the Empire. An ardent social reformer, she fought against inequality, encouraging workers to challenge their exploitative employers and support the emerging trade union movement. Identifying a direct link between poor education, large families, poor housing, unemployment energised her international humanitarian crusade.

The Theosophical Society and its International HQ continue to operate as a powerful and confident organisation in southern India, based at Adyar, Chennai. The current president Radha Bernier is a Sanskrit scholar, educated at the College Besant established at Varanasi. Bernier is part of a dynasty. Her father was the fifth president of TS and she became the eighth president in 1980. She has had a passionate career as an exponent of Indian traditional dance and was given international exposure with a pivotal role in the Jean Renoir film *The River* of 1948, based on the book by Rumer Godden (1907–1998) who lived latterly in Moniaive.

Which returns us to these Indo-Scots connections. Does the *River* provide that common denominator in both east and west which needs to be returned to if we are to have global equilibrium? Were Geddes and Besant both trying to assimilate the spiritual and ecological philosophy of nature? Or are they merely interesting idealists whose quaint paternalistic notions for India have been long superseded?

Narayani Gupta, in *A Letter from India,* sees Annie Besant and Geddes as 'middlemen' who linked two cultures and who talked to Indians as equals, not as subordinates. They came to India at 'an extraordinarily significant moment', just before:

> ... the nationalist movement gained a new vigour under Gandhi's leadership. It was a movement sustained not just by impatience and grievances, but also by the vision of an exhilarating future. It was at this time that Muhammad Iqbal wrote the poem beginning *Saare jahan se achha,* a song familiar to every Indian child. It was a period of increased inter-

action between people and ideas. It was a time of idealism, of preparing blueprints for a future where the best of Indian tradition would be linked to the best of Western institutions. There was a sense of confidence at the potential of Indian music and dance forms and literatures, in the ability of Indians to make a contribution to Western science.

The Indian Empire evolved into the three states of India, Pakistan and Bangladesh and it would be unrealistic to expect them to praise any efforts towards liberalisation but their own. Nevertheless, at a critical point in time, Annie Besant and – to a lesser extent – Patrick Geddes, the incoming Western do-gooders, were able to create more favourable conditions for the advance of the peoples of the sub-continent.

Kenny Munro

Notes

1   The Eastern Question (essentially 'What is to be done about the disintegrating Ottoman Empire?') was a major international – and complex – issue throughout the 19th century. It was famously said that only three men understood the Eastern Question. One was dead, another was in a lunatic asylum, and the third was in Outer Mongolia and could not be found.

It is clear that, even in the 21st century, the Eastern Question remains unanswered.

2   The Valley Section can operate at several levels of sophistication. Kenneth McKellar was a fine Scottish tenor who popularised *The Song of the Clyde,* a picture in 3/4 time of the course of that river from the mines and sheepwalks of the Southern Uplands, through the orchards of Lanarkshire, to the shipyards, where the 'hammer's ding-dong' changes to 6/8 for a round-up of Gaelic place-names. Like the Valley Section, *The Song of the Clyde* is a model which time has transformed.

Bibliography

Besant, Annie, *An Autobiography, 2nd edition* (Gresham Press, London, 1893)

Besant, Annie, *An Autobiography (Adyar Edition)* (The Theosophical Publishing House, Adyar, 1939)

The Case for India – 32 Indian National Congress 1917 (Pelican Press at The Office of the *Herald*, Tudor Street, London, 1918)

Dutt, R Palme, *India To-day* (Left Book Club Edition, Gollancz, London, 1940)

Elmhirst, Leonard, *Rabindranath Tagore – Pioneer in Education* (John Murray, London, 1961)

Fraser, Bashabi, *From the Ganga to the Tay* (Luath Press, Edinburgh, 2009)

Hollyer, Belinda, *Votes for Women: Double Take (series)* (Scholastic Children's Books, London, 2003)

Taylor, Anne, *Annie Besant: A Biography* (Oxford University Press, Oxford, 1992)

Letters quoted from National Library of Scotland Archives, Edinburgh

CHAPTER FOURTEEN

Sister Nivedita, the Dedicated

The Ardent Student

IT WAS A WINTRY morning in New York in March 1900. Professor Patrick Geddes was speaking on the Sociological Method in History. A young woman was listening with rapt attention. Social science was unfolding before her, inviting a deeper probe. That culture and geography could be linked to sociology was a new revelation. She was seeing him for the first time. For long, she had wanted to be his student.

She had come to know of Geddes from her master, Swami Vivekananda who had met him in the World Parliament of Religions at Chicago in September 1893. Patrick Geddes and his family were enamoured by the Swami from whom they started taking lessons in meditation. Later, Geddes wrote the foreword to the French translation of Swami Vivekananda's book *Raja-Yoga*. In the words of Boardman:

> The meeting of the Swami and Geddes had not only interesting consequences, but preliminaries too. Thus in the spring of 1898 a Miss Josephine MacLeod of New York met, near Calcutta, the English woman Margaret Noble who had become the Swami's disciple. The latter said to the American, 'If you ever hear of a man called Patrick Geddes, follow him up. He is the type of man to make disciples.'

How Miss Noble knew about PG is not clear, but in any case two years later, when Miss MacLeod was visiting in California, she chanced to read in the papers that a certain Professor Geddes was lecturing in New York. Thereupon she wrote to her sister, wife of wealthy New York grocer, Francis H Leggett, with the result that both Mr and Mrs Geddes were taken into the Leggetts' mansion as guests in March on their return from Chicago. Miss MacLeod journeyed east in turn and met face to face the Scottish professor she had heard about in India. It was the beginning of a long friendship between her and both PG and Anna.

The disciple – Nivedita – had written in a letter dated 13 March 1900 to Swami Vivekananda:

> Long years ago in England, in the year I first met you, Norman Wyld (the son of that Dr Wyld who had such deep-rooted suspicion of Hindus) told me that if I could only know Prof Geddes, to whom he was proud to be

disciple, my soul would be saved, and my attitude to life determined forever.

Of his first meeting with Nivedita, Geddes said:

> Our acquaintance began in New York early in 1900, and continued into intimacy and collaboration during the following summer, at that meeting of the International Association which became the Summer School of the Paris Exhibition of that in many ways memorable year. Actively occupied as a guide to many of its departments, and carrying on a peripatetic interpretation of them upon lines of regional and occupational evolution, broadly akin to those of Le Play and his disciples, I found no one who so rapidly and ardently seized upon the principle and delighted in every application of it as Sister Nivedita.

Geddes once said of the influence of Nivedita on children:

> With children she was at once a born teacher and a skilled. She would sit with them upon the floor in the firelight and tell them her Cradle Tales of Hinduism, with a power and charm even excelling her written version of them, so touching this or that ardent young soul to dream of following her to the utmost East. Or she might give them a literature lesson – say, on Shelley's Skylark – and here demand, and arouse, their observation and their imagination in touch with the poet's. This union of sense and symbol, which we too easily let slip apart, was ever with her. Thus of our many memory portraits, none comes back more vividly than of her in autumn twilight, now crooning, now chanting, the Hymn to Agni over the glowing, dying embers of a garden-fire. Strange though the words were, we still hear the refrain. It was the tongue, the music, of Orient to Occident, the expression of spirit in nature, a face, a voice, aglow with energy, at peace with night.

Swami Vivekananda opened India's door for Geddes, who went three times to India, stayed there for almost a decade, taught at the University of Bombay, wrote a biography of Jagadishchandra Bose, came in touch with Indian luminaries like Rabindranath Tagore and influenced a host of Indian thinkers, educationists, sociologists, and others. It was to this Geddes that Nivedita came to learn. Let us now have a brief look at the life of Sister Nivedita.

The Dedicated – the Story of a Transformation

Sister Nivedita was born Margaret Elizabeth Noble at Dungannon, County Tyrone, Ireland, on 28 October 1867 to Samuel Richmond Noble and

Mary Esabel Noble. Scots had settled in Ireland for five centuries and the Nobles were imbued with the spirit of nationalism. Margaret lost her father when she was ten and was brought up by her maternal grandfather Hamilton. Hamilton was one of the leaders of the Home Rule movement in Ireland. The rich family tradition inspired her to cultivate a character of truthfulness, religious zeal, patriotism, and a liking for politics.

Margaret got her early education in a strict Church boarding school in London. She earnestly explored literature, music, arts, physics, and botany. Margaret became a teacher when she was only seventeen. Before that she had successfully completed her formal education. Within a short while she opened a school at Wimbledon and started to teach students following her own methods which were influenced by the techniques of Froebel and Pestalozzi. She started contributing articles in various papers and periodicals. In no time she established herself as a powerful writer in the intellectual circles of London.

In spite of fair success in her external life, she was constantly stricken by an unrest within. She had suffered two heartbreaks. In the first relationship, her lover died young and in the other, her lover deserted her. The second heartbreak shattered her and she started searching for solace which she could not find in the formal religious setup. She tried to understand the truth about religion by studying books. But the desired peace ever eluded her and she was feeling dejected. She did not get peace until she met her master, Swami Vivekananda. On a cold afternoon in November 1895, Swami Vivekananda was explaining Vedanta philosophy in the drawing room of an aristocratic family in London. Margaret met Swamiji here for the first time. She was charmed by the philosophical exposition and the personality of the monk.

Thereafter she attended several other lectures and question-answer classes of the Swami in London. She attentively listened to all the lectures, raised questions one after another to resolve her doubts and constantly meditated on them. At

FIG.24
Sister Nivedita. (*Advaita Ashrama*)

last she realised that this Indian monk would be able to lead her to the truth she had been searching for. Margaret accepted him as her guru, spiritual master. And during this period, the Swami also became convinced of Margaret's truthfulness, determination and above all, her heart full of kindness.

Swami Vivekananda felt unbearable pain at the sorrows and sufferings of the common people of a subjugated India. He felt that in order to raise India it was necessary to improve the condition of the masses and that of women. The only way to improve the condition of women was to give them education. With the spread of education, they would become self-confident and would be able to solve their own problems. The swami thought Margaret would be eminently suitable for this task. He invited her for the task of spreading education among the masses of India, women especially. He wrote to her:

> Let me tell you frankly that I am now convinced that you have a great future in the work for India. What was wanted was not a man, but a woman – a real lioness – to work for Indians, women especially. India cannot yet produce great women, she must borrow them from other nations. Your education, sincerity, purity, immense love, determination and above all, the Celtic blood make you just the woman wanted.

Margaret left behind her land, friends, and family and reached India on 28 January 1898 to help her master to rebuild India. But first of all it was necessary to know India. So day after day, patiently and with delicate care, Swami Vivekananda explained to her India's history, philosophy, literature, life of the masses, social traditions, and also the lives of great personalities, both ancient and modern. He held before Margaret the matchless image of the eternal India, rich in her spiritual heritage, great in renunciation and austerity – the eternal India that lay behind the poverty-stricken, superstition-riddled, subjugated India. She began to love India and developed an irresistible urge to accept the Indian life. Gradually India and she were merged together, as it were, to become one.

Within a few days of her arrival she got the audience of Holy Mother Sarada Devi. The Holy Mother accepted Margaret spontaneously as her daughter. Margaret realised Sri Sarada Devi was an incomparable personality of love, purity, sweetness, simplicity, and knowledge, a marvellous creation of Providence. Margaret felt sanctified by being the loving baby of the Mother.

After a short while Swami Vivekananda formally initiated Margaret in the vow of *brahmacharya* and gave her the name Nivedita or 'the dedicated'.

He advised her to maintain strict continence and to dedicate her life for the good of others, like Buddha. Henceforth, the sole purpose of her life was to serve India. She realised the truth of his words that the world's good was dependent on the good of India and that India's spirituality would show the path of beneficence to the entire world. So she deemed her service to India to be the service to the entire mankind indeed. As desired by him and supported at first by the Ramakrishna Sarada Mission she set up a girls' school (PLATE 7A) and started the work of women's education following the national ideal of India.[1]

FIG.25

A European Margaret Noble with Sri Sarada Devi (1898). (*Advaita Ashrama*)

In 1902 Swami Vivekananda passed away. But Nivedita did not take the time even to mourn. Many unfinished tasks of Swami remained to be attended to. India, the ever-adored deity of her Guru, was to be awakened in all directions. Since her arrival in India, Nivedita had personally witnessed the nature of British torture in the name of administration. She was sad and angry to see Indians suffering indignities and oppression at the hands of the British. It appeared to her that the main obstacle of India's development lay in her dependence. She realised in the core of her heart that foreign rule was responsible for the moral degradation and weakness of the Indians.

In her forceful desire to free India from the British rule she actively associated herself with politics. Swamiji's direction was unequivocal – the Ramakrishna Math and Mission could not have any relation with politics. But in Nivedita's perception the topmost priority for India was to gain national freedom, so she could not disassociate herself from politics. Therefore the only way left was to sever her formal relationship with the Ramakrishna Mission. It was the most painful of all decisions, but she had to take it. However, her inner relationship was never cut off. She always maintained a respectful and loving relationship with Sri Sarada Devi, the spiritual Mother of the Order, the Math's president, Swami Brahmananda, and other brother disciples of Swami Vivekananda. And she always identified herself as 'Nivedita of Ramakrishna-Vivekananda'.

From now on Nivedita became restless to give a concrete shape to the great India that Swami Vivekananda had dreamt of. She tried her utmost to enthuse the entire nation with nationalist ideas. Nivedita's conception of nationalism was to awaken a nationalistic consciousness in all the areas of national life – education, literature, science, history, arts, and folk culture. Carrying afloat the banner of the Swami's ideals, Nivedita now set out on lecture tours throughout India. She appealed to the countrymen to forget all differences of caste, creed, and culture and come forward united to serve the motherland. Herself the image of selflessness, renunciation and austerity, Nivedita's sincere appeal touched the hearts of the people and enkindled patriotism in many a heart. She especially associated herself with the youth and student community. She urged them to become honest, hard-working, and brave.

The Bengal Partition Act 1905 of Curzon triggered the Swadeshi Movement in India, more specifically in Bengal. For the first time the people started to oppose the British rule in India. Nivedita helped the leaders and the workers of the movement through all possible means. The British tried to crush the movement ruthlessly by resorting to police torture, repression, arrest, deportation, and stringent censures against the newspapers holding nationalist ideals. When the British repression crossed all limits, people's wrath took to secret revolutionary paths. Many patriotic Indian youths were involved in secret murders and terrorist activities.

Nivedita maintained very close relations with Sri Aurobindo, the chief of the then revolutionary movement and other revolutionary leaders and workers. She was almost imprisoned on many occasions. She was ever alert to save these selfless people, dedicated to the cause of their motherland, from the imperial wrath. She would secure secret news from the Government sources through her friends, and cautioned the revolutionaries well in advance. She also helped them through her counselling and made sure that the anti-people activities of the British Government were publicised in England, and that a strong public opinion was built against such activities. She was in touch with most of the front-ranking political leaders throughout India. Her foremost effort was that the Indians should unitedly fight against the foreign rule without creating divisions amongst themselves. But she never had the least intention of assuming the leader's role in political movement; rather she thought, as Vivekananda felt, that such a role was reserved for those who were Indians by birth and tradition. Nivedita's active role in politics evoked the suspicion of the British and to elude the eyes of the police she sometimes had to move about in disguise.

Nivedita accepted India, the motherland of Ramakrishna and Swami Vivekananda, as her own country. She served the people of India in their days of sufferings and distress, caring the least for her own life. In 1899, when plague broke out in Calcutta she plunged into relief work with the band of monks of the Ramakrisha Mission – according to Swami Vivekananda's desire. Under her leadership, nursing of the ailing patients began, and side by side – as a remedial measure to fight the disease – the cleaning operation of rubbish and refuse of the localities continued. Nivedita herself took in her hand broomstick and basket to clean the rubbish and also nursed the patients. The thought never occurred to her that she herself might contract plague for such personal involvement, and that plague was as good as death. Following her example many local youths joined the relief work.

Nivedita always stood by the side of her neighbours in their hours of pleasures and pain. Her sincerity made the neighbours feel that she was one of them. Still she never crossed the social barriers regarding touch and food. Gopaler Ma holds a unique position among the women devotees of Sri Ramakrishna. Hailing from a Brahmin family, she was a widow with very orthodox habits. Throughout her life she worshipped baby Krishna very sincerely; and in a vision, she saw baby Krishna in Sri Ramakrishna. Both Sri Ramakrishna and Sri Sarada Devi considered her as their mother. When in her old age she became ill and infirm, Nivedita brought Gopaler Ma to her own residence and nursed her. Gopaler Ma who was so strict in her orthodox habits, did not hesitate to accept Nivedita's nursing.

Nivedita's love for the Indian masses was matchless. When East Bengal was ravaged by a terrible flood, followed by a famine, she rushed there with her people for relief work. Wading through water and mud she reached the doorsteps of the common people and began to serve them.

According to Swami Vivekananda, the development of science was very important for India. He used to feel that the ideal India would grow with a proper synthesis of Vedanta and scientific knowledge. Vedanta would purify man's inmost being while science would beautify man's external life. Jagadish Chandra Bose – the Bengali polymath, physicist, biologist, botanist, archaeologist, and early writer of science fiction – created a sensation in the world by his original scientific work. Swamiji used to feel very proud about Jagadish Chandra Bose. But in a dependent India, Bose had to carry on his work under extremely unfavourable conditions. The contemporary scientists of the world were unwilling to offer him the honour he richly deserved. He had to carry on his work amidst scores of anxieties, depressing conditions and financial stringency. The foreign government was in no mood to help him. Nivedita knew Bose's worth. With a mother's heart she came forward to help him. By exerting her influence, she secured for him many facilities and assistance from the Government. She relentlessly carried on propaganda work through newspapers and periodicals so that his scientific inventions were credited with due honour. As his research work entailed substantial expenses, Nivedita helped him financially also, and when Jagadish Chandra Bose fell ill in a foreign land, she even nursed him.

Nivedita regarded Jagadish Chandra as a national asset and loved him as her child. Without Nivedita's inspiration and active help, Jagadish Chandra could hardly have continued his scientific research. She also made a unique contribution in developing an art movement on national lines. This movement, that grew with Havell and Abanindranath and culminated in Nandalal Bose, owes much to Nivedita. In the same way she greatly encouraged eminent personalities like Romesh Chandra Dutt and Jadunath Sarkar in writing history conforming to nationalist ideals.

Nivedita was an extraordinary orator and a powerful writer. Even before she came to India at the age of 30, she had established herself as a writer in English intellectual circles. When she arrived in India and dedicated herself to the awakening of India's nationalist consciousness, she came to realise that her pen would be her main source of power. She started contributing articles on religion, literature, sociology, arts, and various relevant issues in both Indian and foreign journals, *The Statesman, Amrita Bazar Patrika, Dawn, Prabuddha Bharata* and *Bal-Bharati* being some of them among the Indian newspapers and periodicals. She also wrote several books, the most remarkable of which are: *Kali the Mother, The Web of Indian Life, Cradle Tales of Hinduism, The Master As I Saw Him.* Many distinguished personalities of the day used to visit her residence regularly. Her versatile genius and knowledge in various subjects would charm everybody. She even designed a national flag for India long before Independence.[2] (PLATE 7B)

About her small school that was founded according to Swamiji's ideals and consecrated by the Holy Mother, she had the conviction that their blessings were ever with it. She believed that in future prophets would emerge from amongst the students of this school. Nivedita had to work in an extremely conservative society. Not all parents were willing to educate their daughters. So Nivedita had to walk from door to door to enlist her students. She used to teach the girl students history, geography, natural sciences, and a little bit of English. She would also teach them sewing, drawing, and handicrafts. She also encouraged them to take up physical exercise. Above all, she helped them increase their innate sense of religion and introduced them to the Indian culture. She also made arrangements so that elderly married ladies and widows might have a little learning and know the art of sewing and other handicrafts. She gave special instruction to a few educated ladies in order to make them good teachers.

She had to earn money from her writings and lectures. But she spent all her income to meet the expenses of the school. She was ever unmindful of keeping even the barest for herself. Many a day she had to go without food. All this hardship and the tremendous heat of the summer told heavily upon her health. She began to fall ill repeatedly. She went to Darjeeling in 1911 to recover but became more ill there and finally passed away on 13 October 1911 at the young age of 44. Her last words were: 'The frail boat is sinking but I shall yet see the sun rise.' (PLATE 8A)

Assisting Geddes

Having met Geddes, Nivedita could not wait to work with him. She found an opportunity to work with him and learn from him by becoming his secretary for the Congress of the History of Religions at Paris in 1900. She was fascinated with many of his theories regarding the evolution of society in relation to environment. Wanting to study them more deeply, and seeing in them an application to India's problems, she committed herself to working for him, for a time as secretary. She arranged to meet him in Paris in early July. She wanted to equip herself well for the Indian work.

> She spent week after week trying to assimilate Prof. Geddes's philosophy and to learn his method of interpreting social life. She followed him on his visits to the Exposition and the city, listening to every word of his, taking down notes and rewriting them afterwards.

In order to work with Geddes in a better way Nivedita started following him closely. In Geddes's own words:

> Retreating at times from the intricacies of the great city and its galleries of arts and industries, we would set out to seek for simpler correlations, such, for instance, as unified the admirable simplicity of the Swiss Village... Returning refreshed to the study of Paris we carried our readings of simple rural and suburban fairs on into World's Fair itself, and even into that strangely mingled medley of deteriorated rustic life with ever-renewing synergy of evolving arts, whose action and interaction so much make up the chequered life and history of the great city. Eager to master these evolutionary methods, and to apply them to her own

studies, to Indian problems therefore above all, yet also generously insistent towards my own even then too long deferred publication of examples of them, she settled above our home into an attic cell which suited at once her love of wide and lofty outlooks and her ascetic care of material simplicity; and there she worked, for strenuous weeks, at first on the elaboration of my too informal and colloquial presentments, then at definite essays of joint authorship and towards a projected volume.

She spent her time in doing all the clerical work involved – cataloguing, indexing, reporting, and so on. She was simply swept off her feet by the sheer expanse of Geddes's knowledge. While doing so, she realised that she was not suited to this kind of work. To be an able assistant she had to abstain from expressing her own creativity and had to align fully to the thoughts of the person she was assisting, more so if that person was a great luminary as Professor Patrick Geddes. Nivedita was trying to assimilate and organise the thoughts of a person who:

> … was undoubtedly a rare genius with vision far ahead of his time, and, like all such, not widely appreciated in his own day – nor, for that matter, in ours.

In a moving confession in a letter of 1 July 1900 to Josephine MacLeod, Nivedita wrote:

> I feel torn to pieces. He wants a voice that will utter his thought as he would have done. I try then to make a mosaic in which the bright bits are his words, and I provide only grey cement of mere grammatical context. You can imagine how feeble this is… One has to possess the idea, and to be free in the possession in order to do work of the quality he needs. Even then I doubt that I could do it. I have even less education, and less ability intellectually than we have supposed. But supposing that I had the ability and could do the thing as well as he needs it, it would be so different that he would not see himself in it anywhere. And this is a renunciation for which this exquisite soul is not yet prepared. I am at bottom totally divergent, and you know this appalling sincerity of mine. I cannot be a reporter – it is not that I will not! It is that I cannot. When I try, I disappoint him so much, because I am not even a good stenographer…What would money or fame be to Mr Geddes? What to any of us? It is all very well to think oneself a miserable sinner. One is, but not in the form of the pickpocket or the glutton. It is mischievous to go on in fear of these things, surely. It is certainly mischievous to take credit for being quit of them… So I believe that Mr. Geddes is asking the impossible of the world. And I am fool enough to feel that I would die to give it him, with the utmost joy, as I cannot die, and could not help if I did, I shall go on

struggling with my expression and adding to the disappointment in his heart till the moment of Swami's signal comes. But I wish he had not had more exquisite hopes at the beginning of my discipleship. Each one is a thorn now.

Unable to grasp Geddes and yet charmed by his intellect, Nivedita was at a loss. Swami Vivekananda had advised her to be not too much involved in the work of Geddes. This did not go well with Nivedita and she became cross with the Swami and she took some time to recover from her dissatisfaction with him.

Her otherwise cordial friendship with Prof Geddes suffered on account of this conflict which was emerging to the surface. Finally unable to bear the strain of the work, she gave it up since it affected both her health and mental vigour. She wrote to Mrs Ole Bull who invited her to spend some time with her in the village Perros Guirec, near Lannion in Brittany. Nivedita accepted her invitation and forthwith left Paris.

Applying Geddes's Thought in India

Going back to India, she corresponded with Geddes to get as much as possible. She wrote from Calcutta,

> I want some of your big thoughts brought before the Indian people. I wish it might do for them as a whole what it seems to have done for me – make them able to think of the synthesis of the national life! The sequence of Place – Ideals – Place, I want *badly*. The sequence or web of Education as School – University – Research – Society, I want. The nature of the historical process, I want *badly*.

She wanted his help to understand the cause of famines in India and trace them to ecological problems. She asked for his help to setup an institute for advanced research in science with the patronage of Jamsetji Tata. She called this project the 'Tata Scheme'. She wanted to start a university suited to Indian needs:

> If you were an Indian prince, with immense revenues at your disposal, if you wanted to make an Indian University possible, two generations hence, what preparations would you make in this matter? What books would you put into your scheme? And what books would you order to be translated? If you had no time to write a book, would you at least be prepared to make a syllabus of the study of which I speak which dint of questions and authorities would enable me to help someone or other to struggle into the necessary knowledge?

Nivedita wanted Geddes's thought to be a reality in India. It was as though she represented the 'synergy' Geddes was so fond of, particularly in the Indian context. Though she could not work closely with Geddes, she was greatly indebted to him. She wrote:

> I cannot tell you how Mr Geddes's work has helped me – nor of how much use I hope to make it before I am finally silenced.

She wanted to use his techniques properly:

> Prof. Geddes gave me a tool beyond all price. He may be disturbed by my use of it, but it can never be taken away from me now.

She applied this tool whenever opportunity arose. She has been acknowledged as a good disciple of Geddes:

> According to a famous Austrian economist and sociologist, the two scholars who have contributed most to a real understanding of the Indian economic life in its proper social and cultural setting, are Sister Nivedita and Dr Radhakamal Mukherjee, both students of Geddes and indebted to him for their new approach and methods.

Nivedita's sociological thought was Geddes all over. Writing on *The Relation* between Famine and Population she said:

> As in honour bound, I have reported the teachings which I heard in Paris in the year 1900 from a group of sociologists of European reputation, as I conceive that they intended them.

A sociologist remarked in 1968:

> Although the social ideas of Sister Nivedita grew gradually as and when she met the problems, they have not been left just so many incoherent and haphazard ideas. They got a rational, scientific and systematic mould before they came out from this rare intellect. Few in this country know today that Nivedita had always been a keen and ardent student of sociology and was the pioneer in introducing the modern Sociological Method of Studying History in India.

Geddes's Appreciation of Nivedita

Sir Patrick Geddes held Nivedita in high esteem. Introducing her to an European audience before her talk on *Indian Thought* he said:

> I have much pleasure in introducing Sister Nivedita of Ramakrishna-Vivekananda, who has been a student of social matters, first in Europe and now in India. In India she has found that the great problems of

Indian life turn on nature and occupations and natural conditions of all kinds; turn on the family, and largely on Indian thought, primarily on Indian religion; and steeped as she has been in this great world of idealism, she is peculiarly welcome to us in bringing an interpretation of the East which is still uncommon among us. We have heard vague and mysterious presentments of Indian thought, and it is something to have a reverent and sympathetic student who still keeps grip of science and the relations of the world.

Nivedita herself was very happy with this appreciation, and wrote to Josephine MacLeod:

Mr Geddes has just given me two stunning literary introductions, in which he says that my range extends from Sir William Wedderburn to Lafcadio Hearn.[3]

Nivedita was friends also with Anna Geddes and felt as one of the family. Again to Josephine MacLeod she wrote:

I have to go through and fight the missionaries – for which Mr Geddes gives me an introduction to the Contemporary. By the way I wish you had heard poor Mr Geddes. What do you think – he spoke so warmly of my work for him, and begged me to come and do more! I told him that from the time Mr Mavor came he had worked no more with me, and Mrs Geddes sat by and confirmed this – and he was so astonished.

On 13 June 1905, she wrote to Anna a long tortured letter explaining her difficulties with Geddes:

I wish I could give him someone who would bring patience and imagination to bear upon the task of writing a history of India at his feet! He has helped me so much! Yet always in some unsuspected way he is like a man talking in hieroglyphics (a bull!) and when you are far away, and not thinking of him, some cryptic utterance flashes suddenly into meaning, or you find that as you stood looking, a curtain has been silently drawn away, and a landscape is revealed without your noticing the change. But why oh why, won't he put any 'oughts' and 'shoulds' into his teachings? I am lost, in a world which knows only classification and contemplates, and can find no place for the ethical imperatives! And besides, I cannot tell whether it was by patience or by imagination (that is to say, by having a reserve of foreign experiences) that I was best served in dealing with him. I still feel that if I could only have sat down and written from his dictation for hours and days, I could afterwards have served him well by arranging and altering and preparing a book for the press, and could have at the same time have assimilated perhaps his whole idea, myself. In such a task, patience would be more than imagination. And as it is, since he was never able to use anything I did, I can only feel that he gave what I could in his sense repay... Ah, were he only a wandering *sannyasin*, teaching his disciples under a tree, in this tropical land, he could inspire both the love and the work that that task would need! Dear Mr Geddes! How I love and admire you, for the courage that made you tackle Edinburgh! I fully believe that your unselfish faith and daring will bring that matter through in the long run... Still more, I wish you were here with me and could refresh your soul for an hour in the simplicity of the East, that you might go back to the stern struggle and fret, knowing that it will work out into victory for all who see that the outer is the unreal, and the unseen the true reality. One gains so much from short withdrawals!

Conclusion

The coming together of Sir Patrick Geddes and Sister Nivedita was the coming together of vision and passion. The vision of Geddes was too broad and too ahead of his times to be understood by many. Sister Nivedita was one of the few who could grasp his thought. She had the passion, the feeling for the masses and also the sensibility to protect the culture of the privileged. But her passion took its toll on her health.

Had she lived longer she could have worked with Geddes when he came to India, their combined power would have brought some differences in the state policies in World War I. She did not live to carry out her dream project of creating an Indian university where the curriculum would be based on indigenous wisdom rather than being a mere transplantation of alien thought. She could not witness the growth of Sociology in India, which could have been enriched with her application of Geddes's thought.

One can recall her vividly through Geddes:

The whole personality of Nivedita – her face, her voice, her changing moods and daily life, were ever expressing the alternating reaction of outward environment and inward spirit which goes on throughout the individual and social life. She was open at once to the concrete and the abstract, to the scientific and the philosophic, and her many moods were in perpetual interplay – sparkling with keen observation, with humorous or poetic interpretation, or opal-like, suffused with mystic light, aflame with moral fire. All came out in her talks, her occasional lectures – each a striking improvisation – now in gentlest persuasiveness leading her audience into sympathetic understanding, or even approval, or some aspect or feature of Indian life, unknown or perhaps repellent before; or again, bursting into indignant flash and veritable thunder upon our complacent and supercilious British philistinism.

Swami Narasimhananda

Notes

1   Sister Nivedita prepared a booklet asking for funds and collected funds from abroad, mainly from the USA. The administration of the Sister Nivedita's Girls' School was transferred in 1959 to Ramakrishna Sarada Mission, an independent all-woman monastic organisation. Today it runs on donations from India and abroad and has excellent standards of education.

2   The Indian National Congress wanted to celebrate India's *Swarajya* or self-rule and was looking for a good design for a national flag. Sister Nivedita designed this *Vagra* or thunderbolt and presented it to the Indian National Congress in 1906. Sister Nivedita's flag had the Vajra in the middle, sur-rounded by 108 oil lamps. (Not present in PLATE 7B). *Vajra* is the weapon of the Hindu king of gods, Indra, and is the symbol of power. The upper Sanskrit line reads 'I salute the motherland' and the lower: 'Wherever there is right-eousness, there is victory'.

In the event Mahatma Gandhi in 1921 presented another flag just like the present Indian flag, but with a spinning wheel in the middle instead of the Ashoka Chakra. India achieved independence on 15 August 1947, and the national flag is flown every year on 26 January.

3   Sir William Wedderburn (1838–1918) resigned from the Indian Civil Service when proposed reforms were blocked. Supported aspirations of Indians, co-founder of Indian National Congress (President, 1889 and 1901). Tried to reconcile Hindu/Muslim rift and constitutional/militant Congress factions.

Lafcadio Hearn (1850–1904) was an American writer, with an especial interest in Japan.

Chronology

28 October 1867	Born in the small town of Dungannon, Co Tyrone, Northern Ireland
1884	University graduation; took up teaching at Keswick
1888	PG Professor of Botany, University College, Dundee
1895	First meeting with Swami Vivekananda
1898	Landed on the soil of India (Calcutta). First visit to Dakshineshwar and attended Belur Math for the birth anniversary of Sri Ramakrishna. First public speech in India at the Star Theatre. First meeting with the Holy Mother Sri Sarada Devi. Margaret Noble formally initiated in the vow of Brahmacharya by Swami Vivekananda and named 'Nivedita'. Went to North India with Swami Vivekananda and others. Visited Amarnath with Swami Vivekananda
	Opening of Nivedita's school by the Holy Mother Sri Sarada Devi
1899	Nivedita fighting plague epidemic in Calcutta (Under advice of Swami Vivekananda)
	With Swami Vivekananda and others left for the West.
1900	PG's First visit to United States
	SN Meets Professor Patrick Geddes in New York
	International Assembly at Exposition Universelle, Paris
1902	Return to India. Last meeting (and death) of Swami Vivekananda (at Belur Math). Started touring India, giving lectures on theme of 'Nation Making'
1903	The book, *The Web of Indian Life*, was published
1904	Journey to Bodh Gaya
1905	In Bengal, Swadeshi Movement started. Participated in Kashi Congress
1906	Death of 'Gopaler Ma'. Went to East Bengal ravaged by flood and famine for relief work. Became seriously ill on account of brain-fever
1907–1909	Revisited the West
1910	Her famous book on Swami Vivekananda, *The Master as I saw Him*, was published
	Pilgrimage to Kedar Badri and other shrines with the JC Bose family
13 October 1911	Passed away at Darjeeling

Bibliography

Atmaprana, Pravrajika, *Sister Nivedita of Ramakrishna-Vivekananda* (Sister Nivedita Girls's School, Calcutta 1961)

Atmaprana, Pravrajika, *The Story of Sister Nivedita* (Kolkata: Ramakrishna Sarada Mission Sister Nivedita Girls' School, 2012)

Basu, Sankari Prasad, *Nivedita Lokamata* (Bengali) (Kolkata: Ananda Publishers, 2007), 5 vols

Burke, Marie Louise, *Swami Vivekananda in the West: New Discoveries*, 6 vols (Advaita Ashrama, Calcutta 1985)

Ekatmananda, Swami, *Sir Patrick Geddes*, Prabuddha Bharata, 91/3 (March 1986)

Geddes, Patrick and Vivekananda, Swami, *Prabuddha Bharata*, 53/5 (May 1948)

Prabuddhaprana, Pravrajika, *Tantine: The Life of Josephine MacLeod* (Sri Sarada Math, Calcutta 1990)

Prugh, Linda, *Josephine MacLeod and Vivekananda's Mission* (Chennai: Sri Ramakrishna Math, 2001)

Ratcliffe SK, *Margaret Noble* (London: Herratt and Hughes, 1913)

Reymond, Lizelle, *The Dedicated: A Biography of Nivedita* (New York: John Day, 1953)

Nivedita Commemoration Volume, ed. Amiya Kumar Mazumdar (Vivekananda Janmotsava Samiti, Calcutta 1968)

Nivedita of India (Kolkata: Ramakrishna Mission Institute of Culture, 2007).

Nivedita, Sister, *Studies from an Eastern Home* (London: Longmans, Green and Co., 1921)

The Complete Works of Sister Nivedita, 5 vols (Advaita Ashrama, Calcutta 1999)

The Complete Works of Swami Vivekananda, 9 vols (Advaita Ashrama, 1–8, 1989; 9, Calcutta 1997)

The Letters of Sister Nivedita, ed. Sankari Prasad Basu (Kolkata: Advaita Ashrama, 2013), 2 vols, (In press)

CHAPTER FIFTEEN

Professor Mary Jacqueline Tyrwhitt
1905–1983

FIG.26
Jacky Tyrwhitt (1905–1983).
(Sofia Leonard)

MORE COMMONLY KNOWN as 'Jacky', Tyrwhitt is the link between Sir Patrick Geddes, and the Architectural and Planning professions. Geddes was an important formative influence on her career and she was instrumental in bringing his town planning theories to a wider audience after his death in 1932.

Mary Jacqueline Tyrwhitt was born in Pretoria, South Africa on 25 May 1905 where her father Thomas Tyrwhitt was working as an architect. According to Gwen Bell, her close friend and colleague:

Jacky was born into an upper class English family. She was one of four children. She had always wanted a career, but in that class and at that time women did not pursue careers.

When she was two years old, her mother brought her and her infant sister back to England where they spent their childhood in London. During this period they often visited their grandmother and great aunts in the country. They had large and beautiful gardens, and this could have started her lifelong interest in gardens and gardening.

In London from 1918–1923, Tyrwhitt was a Janyon Scholar at St Paul's Girls' School at Hammersmith, and took matriculation on the classical side, with intention to work for a History Scholarship to Oxford, but her father recommended her to study instead at the Royal Horticultural School. She entered that school in 1923 and obtained a General Horticultural Diploma.

There followed a lengthy period of further studies, including taking the First Medical Examination which required a thorough grounding in Botany, Zoology, Anatomy and Organic Chemistry. In 1924, she enrolled on a course at the Architectural Association in Bedford Square, London. It was at this time that she first encountered Patrick Geddes, a meeting that changed her life. She was greatly taken by Geddes's view of Town Planning as the cultivation of organic growth in response to the needs of society rather than a pattern to be imposed on society.

After graduation from the AA in 1925, Tyrwhitt studied Town Planning at the Technische Hochschule, Berlin University. Back in London, she went on to study as an evening student at the London School of Economics. Later on, also as an evening student, she attended the School of Planning and Regional Development in 1937–39 and obtained an Honours Diploma.

Meanwhile she took up various jobs and further study periods in gardening, agriculture, architecture, town planning and industry, as well as a spell as Parliamentary Secretary to the MP Sir Richard Bull. In 1939 as a resident at 3 Blackmere Road, Welwyn Garden City, she wrote the Report of the 1939 Survey of the Garden City which included historical and socio-economic factors such as the living conditions of the population. Her report became a model for subsequent Planning reports.

At the outbreak of World War II in 1939, the War Office asked the School for Planning and Regional Development to deliver a correspondence course on town planning for members of the armed forces. This, the first planning school in Britain, had grown out of the Architectural Association. Tyrwhitt was appointed to organise and run the course practically single-handed. A very intensive and successful programme, it continued throughout the War and after 1945 was available to demobilised architects, engineers and surveyors.

In 1941 she was invited to be Principal of the School, replacing EA Ambrose Rowse who had been called up for military service. Rowse, following Geddes's vision for interdisciplinary education, had invited students from the social sciences and administration as well as architecture, engineering and surveying, a policy that Tyrwhitt enthusiastically continued.

She was also director of studies at the School, and became director of research when, near the end of the War, it was renamed the School of Planning and Regional Reconstruction. These were positions that saw her much involved, following as always the vision and guidelines of Patrick Geddes, in the reconstruction of a devastated post-war Britain. She also conducted a number of research projects and wrote or edited 12 books dealing with planning subjects. The last of these was *The Heart of the City*, published in Canada in 1953.

Many of Tyrwhitt's students at this time went on to become leading international planners, amongst them Max Lock, John Turner, Colin

Buchanan, William Holford, AE Smailes, Frank and Mary Tindall, George Franklin, Kenneth Watts, JE Vulliamy and Percy Johnson-Marshall. Johnson-Marshall, founding Professor of the postgraduate department of Urban Design and Regional Planning at the University of Edinburgh, was to attract in excess of 600 students from 80 different countries, offering them an education in planning based in a substantial measure on Geddes's ideas and principles. He founded, also at Edinburgh, the Planning Research Unit and later the Patrick Geddes Centre for Planning Studies (1985–1998).

In 1947, Tyrwhitt met the Swiss art historian Siegfried Giedion and became translator and editor of his books. Giedion was the second major influence in her professional life. Her links with international thinkers grew stronger through Giedion's network of contacts and she left England for Canada in 1951.

The next 14 years were spent mainly in North America, at the School of Graduate Studies in Toronto, the United Nations, and later at Harvard University where she was instrumental in helping Dean José Luis Sert establish the Urban Design Program. She joined the faculty there in 1955 as Associate Professor of Urban Design (1958–1969).

In between her teaching assignments at Harvard, and also at Yale, Tyrwhitt returned to England as a partner to Wells Coates working on the Town Planning Exhibition for the 1951 Festival of Britain, her last significant work in Britain.

When working for the UN in India 1953–4, she met the Greek architect and visionary Constantin Doxiadis. He became the third major influence on her thinking after Geddes and Giedion.

Doxiadis had developed a science of human settlements, named 'Ekistics', which in its application aimed at achieving harmony between the inhabitants of a settlement and their physical and socio-cultural environments. In 1955 he launched, a highly regarded planning journal, *Ekistics*, with Tyrwhitt as editor, a task she was to carry out, apart from a two year break, until 1972, after which she continued as consultant editor until 1983. She was much involved from the start in Doxiadis' work and began to spend all her summers in Greece.

She participated actively, with Hassan Fathy and Richard Meier amongst others, in the first major research project launched by Doxiadis in 1960 and developed for more than ten years at the Athens Centre of Ekistics (ACE). Under the title *The City of the Future* (CoF), the research addressed the largest scale of human settlements and was concerned with long range future projections of urban development. Its goal was to provide a road map for understanding the mega-cities of the future, a phenomenon for which the term 'Ecumenopolis' was coined in the first *CoF* internal report in 1961. The study envisaged the coming era of world-wide urbanisation and portrayed a possible pattern of human settlements to be reached by mid 21st century.

The last, posthumous, issue of *Ekistics* on which Tyrwhitt worked was that of May/June 1983. She died in February of that year and a double issue, Sep/Oct-Nov/Dec 1985, edited by her successor P Psomopoulos, was published in her memory. It carried a selection from her own writings and also contributions on her life and work by friends and colleagues. Doxiadis wrote that she was:

> An exacting collaborator and the most suitable he could have selected to be the first editor of *EKISTICS*.

In 1976 she had taken part in the UN Habitat Conference in Vancouver as representative of ACE, and as editor of *EKISTICS* at the Non-Governmental Organization's Forum. The Vancouver Conference is significant as it was the first of a series of UN conferences focusing on environment and ecology at a global level and drawing on the principles of Patrick Geddes. Other followers of Geddes attending and shaping this Conference included Philip Boardman, Arthur Geddes and Percy Johnson-Marshall.

In 1969 Tyrwhitt retired from her professorship at Harvard and went to live permanently in Greece, settling at Sparoza, an Attic hillside near the village of Peania. The Greek climate suited her because of increasing problems with asthma which had afflicted her for a long time.

At last she could dedicate herself to her dream of making her own garden. The one she created on the Attic hillside was different from any other in Greece at that time, or indeed, the great gardens established on the French and Italian Rivieras. Being at the forefront of ecologically responsible thinking, she was very aware of the damage to the delicate balance between flora and fauna which could result from the introduction of non-native plants. She wanted, in addition to having cultivated garden plants, to introduce and sustain as much native Greek flora as she could. She made a book about her experiment, a labour of love that she entitled *Making a Garden on a Greek Hillside*. She wrote:

> The hillsides of Attica are stony and arid. Overgrazed in the past by goats and sheep, they have few trees and are covered in dense, prickly scrub. Relentless sun and often strong winds prevail for five months of the year, but in the autumn and spring months the miracle of the extraordinary variety and beauty of the Greek flora is revealed to the discerning eye.

She describes month by month the plants that grew, thrived or merely survived there. Her vivid description of those plants, reveal a great sensitivity to the delicate beauty of the natural world. With equal sensitivity and an observant eye she also describes the events and activities – the agricultural life, the feasts and festivals – of her neighbours and in the nearby village, following Geddes's great 'triad', Place-Work-Folk.

While working in her garden she continued to receive hospitably a constant stream of family, friends, students and colleagues from all over the world. At the same time too she continued her work as an editor, teacher and consultant.

She died on the 21 February 1983, aged 77, while she was working in the final chapter of her *Making a Garden on a Greek Hillside*.

She bequeathed her house and garden to the Goulandris Natural History Museum. In 1944, with the permission of the Museum, a group of gardeners conceived the idea of a Mediterranean Garden Society (MGS), to be headquartered at Sparoza, Tyrwhitt's garden being the very embodiment of the MGS principles. The Society, which has become a model for other international garden groups, welcomes students anxious to increase their knowledge of Mediterranean plants and gardening to reside at Sparoza and work under their supervision.

Tyrwhitt's legacy for Planning is equally great. A landscape architect and town planner of international renown, and inspired by Geddes's vision, she emphasised throughout her teaching the need for an interdisciplinary and holistic approach to planning, and the importance of the region as a planning unit and also of the analysis of social and economic factors. Her work, in Britain's first school of Planning, at Harvard and elsewhere, carried great influence internationally, and through it she played a key role in launching the new profession of town and regional planning.

As a person Tyrwhitt is remembered for her many very special attributes. After her death many tributes and messages poured in to and were published at the 1985 special issue of *Ekistics*. Her colleague Diana Ladas wrote:

> The most outstanding characteristic was her generosity with her time – the most precious commodity of all. Though she was extraordinarily disciplined and devoted to her work, she always had a moment to lend a sympathetic ear and enjoy a good laugh at work. Despite having lived alone most of her life, she was a social being in the broadest sense. The Jacky we most remember and miss is not the quintessential editor, the brilliant teacher, the efficient organiser or the concerned Planner, but the warm, compassionate human being who cared about us and whom we loved.

A post war planning course student wrote:

> She was the ultimate cosmopolitan, fostering friendship between the multiple races and nationalities of the people that knew her. We always felt that through her we belong to an enlightened international brotherhood.

Max Lock, who went to the AA School a few years after Jacky, remembered asking her why she had never set up in practice:

> She replied that she had come to think of herself as 'catalyst' rather than as a practising architect or town planner, one who, while not herself changing, makes vital changes in others.

The British architect E Maxwell Fry, director of the MARS group and colleague of Gropius in England and Le Corbusier at Chandigardh, wrote:

> Jacky Tyrwhitt was born of a family distinguished by its service to its country and will be remembered by many for her devotion to the arts of Architecture and Town Planning which she saw very much through the eyes of the planner-philosopher Patrick Geddes whose work *Cities in Evolution* she was later to re-edit.

Professor Percy Johnson-Marshall, always spoke to me very highly of Jacky. He valued greatly the collection of the APRR papers, mostly her work, which were sent from London to join the papers of Sir Patrick Geddes in the archives of the Patrick Geddes Centre for Planning Studies, now housed in the Edinburgh University Library Special Collections. Percy remembered Jacky for her 'courage, determination, unquestioned integrity, efficiency and infinite capacity for hard work'.

Tyrwhitt is sometimes said to have been one of the last 'Moderns' who worked willingly as 'the woman behind the man'. Disciple of Patrick Geddes, translator and editor of Siegfried Geidion and collaborator of Constantin Doxiadis, she extended greatly the influence of all three and thus shaped the professional work of several generations.

Sofia Leonard

CHAPTER SIXTEEN

The Patrick Geddes Memorial Panel

I WAS DELIGHTED to be commissioned to make the commemorative stained glass panel, seen on the cover of this book, and to be able to contribute to the lasting memory of Sir Patrick Geddes. I confess I knew very little about Geddes before I was given this opportunity, and as I began my research I realised just how relevant his concerns were to our lives today. Particularly the environment issues, which I used as one of the main themes in the panel.

Background

The panel was organised by four separate bodies, the Scottish Arts Club, the Sir Patrick Geddes Memorial Trust, the Cockburn Association and the Edinburgh City Council and it was decided to gift the panel to the new City of Edinburgh Council headquarters on Market Street. The aim was to commemorate Geddes and celebrate his achievements 150 years after his birth. Much of the panel costs were covered by fundraising and generous donations from business and private funders.

I became involved in the project towards the end of 2004 when I was one of ten stained glass artists invited to prepare a proposal for the creation of a glass panel about Patrick Geddes. These proposals were then exhibited in the Museum of Edinburgh and the Scottish Arts Club, and during the following year I was approached by a committee made up from representatives from the four separate bodies to develop my ideas further.

Ideas Behind the Panel

I used the phrase 'Think Global, Act Local' from *Cities in Evolution* as the central focus in the panel. I felt that it was appropriate as it reflected the environmental issues that we all face today. To make small changes to the way we deal with our routines, can make a difference on a larger scale. This situation concerns everyone and everyone can help.

I have used Geddes's actual handwriting throughout the panel, taking

parts from a letter he wrote to John Nolen, an American landscape architect. I liked his spidery writing. Often I couldn't make out every word, but
I liked the flow of the writing and used extracts to create a pattern on the
glass front and back. The main phrase is not Geddes's actual handwriting
but stylised to give the impression of it. To create the text I sandblasted
onto the surface of the glass and highlighted it with glass paint giving a
texture and depth to the glass. (Sandblasting is a technique using an abra-
sive grit fired at pressure through a pistol and creates a frosted opaque
effect on the glass.)

The panel incorporates a range of traditional materials and techniques, from glass painting to leading and soldering, to construct the glass
together and reflects Geddes's belief in nurturing and sharing traditional
skills. The palette contains various shades of blue and green glass with a
little orange. Within the orange glass I have painted an interpretation of
Edinburgh Castle sitting on its rock base, and placed Geddes handwriting
behind the castle. I thought that this was an appropriate landmark to
reflect his passion for Scotland. (PLATE 8B)

The green and blue colours symbolise growth in nature and in people
through access to education and learning. Geddes was committed to
exchange and creating partnerships. He was one of the founder members
of the Scottish Arts Club, and was active in establishing summer schools
and the first halls of residence in Edinburgh. He believed that art, nature
and music were important issues to help enrich and develop communities.

Most of the glass used in the panel is mouth blown. It is traditionally
made, by creating large cylinders of glass which are scored, then flattened
in a kiln to form the sheets of glass. Through this process, the glass
contains beautiful individual characteristics, from small seeds (air bubbles
trapped in the glass) to rich variations of colour within one sheet. I used
mainly French glass as I thought this was appropriate to tie in with his
connection to Montpellier.

The overall frame for the panel is made from steel and contains 12
spaces for the various shaped leaded panels to fit into. On the left hand
side are the names of the nine twinned cities and the three partner cities
with Edinburgh, each name placed in a simplified seed shape. I wanted to
represent the current links with different communities and cultures and I
thought that a 'seed' was a good image to use, as it could reflect growth,
development and the possibilities for future exchange with these countries. The seed pods are housed in a framework of grid lines which refer
to Geddes's thinking machine *Place, Work and Folk*.

'By leaves we live' is another phrase coined by Geddes and is written in my handwriting in the lower right hand side of the panel. I wanted to reflect Geddes's origin as a Botanist and I decided to do this by using leaves.

I selected several leaves from my garden and was interested in the overall shape and texture of each leaf. I then printed with them directly onto the glass using traditional glass paint (which was fired onto the glass with a kiln) to create a layer of textures. In some parts of the panel I have enlarged some of these leaves and used their structures to create patterns onto the glass, creating a depth to the glass. In one section, I layered the leaf details onto a street map of Edinburgh. I wanted to compare the similarities of the natural flowing lines of the leaf veins, to the main mean-dering artery roads of the city, which run in the centre. I was also aware of the green belt sites within the city and the similar shapes echoed in the leaf. I sandblasted these shapes onto the base of the glass and then layered the outlines of the local roads on top and used blue glass to represent the local boundary of the Firth of Forth.

Within the central globe shape, the unravelling fern shape is a positive symbol to suggest future growth, and I have intersected this image with the word 'global' from the main phrase as a reminder of the task ahead.

By creating the stained glass panel my aim was to reflect the energy, enthusiasm and the richness of the life of Patrick Geddes. This panel is intended to serve as a strong reminder of our responsibilities for our envi-ronment and the future and the growing recognition of Patrick Geddes.

The panel is located on the left hand side of the entrance to Waverley Court, the City of Edinburgh Council offices on Market Street. It is a few metres inside the door and is accessible to view by the public.

Kate Henderson

Geddes Chronology

1854	Born 2 October, in Ballater, youngest of five children
1857	Family moved to Mount Tabor, Perth
1871	Left Perth Academy for work in bank and 'free home studies'
1874	Biology at Edinburgh (one week) and London (under Huxley)
1878	Roscoff (Brittany) and the Sorbonne
1879	Set up Scottish Zoological Station at Cowie, Stonehaven
	The Mexican Adventure
1880	Demonstrator in Botany, Edinburgh University
1882	Letter from Charles Darwin (quoted by Aubrey Manning)
1883	PG developed Order Garden for Grange House Boarding
	School, read paper to Royal Botanical Society of Edinburgh
1886	Marriage to Anna Morton
1887	Norah Geddes born
	University Hall, first self-governing hostel
1887–1900	Summer schools set up and run every August
1888	Professor of Botany, University College, Dundee
1891	Alasdair Geddes born
1892	Outlook Tower started
1893	Ramsay Garden created as co-operative flats
1895	Arthur Geddes born
1897	Cyprus – survey and planning
1900	Held International Assembly at Exposition Universelle, Paris
	First visit to United States
	Return visit to United States
1903	Dunfermline development plan and publication of City Development
1908	Crosby Hall (Chelsea) relocated and restored as residence for university women
1910	Cities Exhibition at Chelsea (then toured till lost at sea 1914)
1913	Cities Exhibition awarded Grand Prix in Ghent
1914–15	First visit to India (with Alasdair)
1915	*Cities in Evolution* published
1915–17	Second visit to India (with Anna)
1917	Deaths of Alasdair and Anna
1919	Retirement and Farewell Lecture (Dundee)
	Planning in Jerusalem and Tel Aviv
	Professor of Civics and Sociology at Bombay
1919–23	Third visit to India (with Arthur)
1923	Third visit to USA

1924	Left Bombay for Montpellier (health reasons)
	Collège des Écossais founded
1925	Civil List pension of £80 awarded
1926	Compensation of £2,054 paid for loss of Cities Exhibition
	Geddes's plan for city of Tel Aviv accepted
1928	Marriage to Lilian Brown
1932	Offer of knighthood accepted – accolade 25 February
	Death at Montpellier – 17 April
1956	Frank Fraser Darling published *Pelican in the Wilderness: A Naturalist's Odyssey in North America*
1962	*Silent Spring* – Rachel Carson
1969	Reith Lectures – Wilderness and Plenty (Frank Fraser Darling)
1972	'Blueprint for Survival' (*The Economist*)
1973	Establishment of Sir Patrick Geddes Memorial Trust
	'Geddes-awareness' campaign started by Bulletin of Environmental Education
1974	*Small is Beautiful: Economics as if People Mattered* – EF Schumacher
1975	*A Most Unsettling Person* – Paddy Kitchen
1978	*The Worlds of Patrick Geddes* – Patrick Boardman
1982	Commemorative events in several locations, home and abroad
1985	Patrick Geddes Centre for Planning Studies set up (in the Outlook Tower)
1990	*Patrick Geddes: Social Evolutionist and City Planner* – Helen Meller
1991–92	International Summer Meetings run by Patrick Geddes Centre
1992	Rio Earth Summit and Local Agenda 21
2004	Geddes Garden at Scots College, Montpellier, restored
	Ideas in Evolution – Geddes 150th Anniversary Symposium, Edinburgh
	Patrick Geddes: The Regeneration of Edinburgh – Anniversary Exhibition at the Matthew Gallery, University of Edinburgh
	Think Global, Act Local: The Life and Legacy of Patrick Geddes –Walter Stephen (ed)

Select Bibliography

Philip Boardman, *The Worlds of Patrick Geddes*, (Routledge and Kegan Paul, London, 1978)

Amelia Defries, *The Interpreter Geddes: The Man and His Gospel* (Routledge, London, 1927)

Bashabi Fraser (ed), *A Meeting of Two Minds: the Geddes-Tagore Letters* (Wordpower Books, Edinburgh, 2005)

Gifford, MacWilliam and Walker, *The Buildings of Scotland: Edinburgh*, (Penguin Books Ltd, 1984)

Jim Johnson and Lou Rosenburg, *Renewing Old Edinburgh: The enduring Legacy of Patrick Geddes* (Scottish Centre for Conservation Studies, Edinburgh College of Art, Argyll Publishing, Edinburgh, 2010)

Paddy Kitchen, *A Most Unsettling Person* (Victor Gollancz, London 1975)

Sofia Leonard, 'The Regeneration of the Old Town of Edinburgh by Patrick Geddes', (*Planning History* Vol 21 No 2, February 1999)

Murdo Macdonald (ed), 'Patrick Geddes: Ecologist, Educator, Visual Thinker' (*Edinburgh Review*, Issue 88, Summer 1992)

Kenneth MacLean and Walter Stephen, *Exploration: Get to know your own Place and Work and Folk* (Hills of Home, Edinburgh, 2007)

Philip Mairet, *The Life and Letters of Patrick Geddes* (Lund Humphries, London, 1957)

Helen Meller, *Patrick Geddes, Social Evolutionist and City Planner*, (Routledge, London, 1990)

Walter Stephen (ed), *Think Global, Act Local: The Life and Legacy of Patrick Geddes* (Luath Press, Edinburgh, 2004)

Walter Stephen (ed), *A Vigorous Institution: The Living Legacy of Patrick Geddes* (Luath Press, Edinburgh, 2007)

Walter Stephen, *Where was Patrick Geddes born? The Last Word?* (Hills of Home, Edinburgh, 2008)

Primary sources:

The Papers of Professor Sir Patrick Geddes from the Outlook Tower (National Library of Scotland)

The Papers of Sir Patrick Geddes (Strathclyde University Archives)

Geddes Family Correspondence

Memoir (Norah Mears)

Patrick Geddes

Extract from Who's Who – *1930*

GEDDES, PATRICK, late Professor of Sociology and Civics, University of Bombay; Professor of Botany (retired), Univ. College, Dundee (St Andrews Univ); Senior Resident of Univ Hall, Edinburgh; Director of the Cities and Town Planning Exhibition; b 1854; y s of late Capt. Alex. Geddes; m 1st, 1886, Anna (d. 1917), e d of Frazer Morton, merchant, Liverpool; two s, one d; 2nd, 1928, Lilian, 2nd d. of late John Armour Brown, Moredun, Paisley. Educ: Perth Academy, Royal School of Mines, University Coll, London; Sorbonne: Univs of Edinburgh, Montpellier etc. Successively Demonstrator of Physiology at Univ Coll., London; of Zoology at Univ at Aberdeen; of Botany at Edinburgh; Lecturer on Natural History in School of Medicine, Edinburgh; with intervals of travel, e.g. exploration in Mexico, visits to Continental universities, zoological stations, and botanic gardens, as also to Cyprus and the East, to USA etc. *Studies:* geography, biology, history, art, social economy and civics. Educational work (besides teaching) mainly in organisation of University Halls, Edinburgh and Chelsea, each as a beginning of collegiate life, eg at Edinburgh, with its Summer Meeting and Outlook Tower. This is a regional, geographic, and synthetic type-museum, with associated undertakings of geotechnic and social purpose e.g. city improvement (Old Edinburgh, etc.), gardens, parks etc. Publishing house (Geddes and Colleagues) associated with Celtic and general literature and art, with geography, education and synthetics. Actively occupied in city improvement, town-planning, and educational initiatives at home, on continent and in India, etc. and with University designs (India, Jerusalem, etc), and development of Cité Universitaire Mediterraneanne at Montpellier. *Publications: Evolution of Sex, Evolution, Sex, Biology and Life in Evolution* (jointly with Prof. J. Arthur Thomson); *Chapters in Modern Botany; City Development; Cities in Evolution; The Life and Work of Sir Jagadish C Bose,* FRS, *1920; The Coming Polity* (with VV Branford); *Ideas at War* (with Prof. Gilbert Slater); *Our Social Inheritance* (with VV Branford), etc. *Recreations:* gardening, rambling. *Address:* Outlook Tower, Univ Hall, Edinburgh; c/o Sociological Society, Leplay House, 65 Belgrave Road, SW1; *Collège des Écossais*, Montpellier, France.

Think Global, Act Local

'Think global, act local' was the mantra made famous by Patrick Geddes (1854–1932) Peace Warrior, Biologist, Sociologist, Town Planner – and much more. In his time his revolutionary ideas appealed to women and he was surrounded by more than a generation of clever and forceful women.

One who could say that 'life is not really a gladiator's show; it is rather – a vast mothers' meeting!' could not fail to attract followers.

Women like Annie Besant who in the prime of her life and vigour went off into the mystic groves of Hindu philosophy and religion. Or the meddling Marchioness who was changing Ireland through planning and public health campaigns till the Easter Rising and World War I changed that nation's priorities. Or 'the horrible Dick May'. Or the ladies of the Edinburgh Social Union who were so busy making a difference in the city that they had no time to fight for the vote.

Supported by the Patrick Geddes Memorial Trust a team of Modern Geddesians – all experts in the field – have produced a gallery of portraits of women who found Geddes liberating and inspiring – but also frustrating and demanding. They certainly learned from Geddes, but he, in turn, was all the better for learning from them.

Underlying it all is the creative tension between the brilliant Geddes ('I am the little boy who rings the bell and runs away') and the bevy of serious, industrious, and above all, organised women, dedicated to changing society – locally.

Think Global, Act Local: Life and Legacy of Patrick Geddes

Edited by Walter Stephen
ISBN 978 1842820 79 7 PBK £12.99

Town planning. Interest-led, open-minded education. Preservation of buildings with historical worth. Community gardens. All are so central to modern society that our age tends to claim these notions as its own. In fact they were first visualised by Sir Patrick Geddes, a largely forgotten Victorian Scot and one of the greatest forward thinkers in history.

Gardener, biologist, conservationist, social evolutionist, peace warrior, and town planner, Geddes spent many years conserving and restoring Edinburgh's historic Royal Mile at a time when most decaying buildings were simply torn down. With renovation came educational ideas such as the development of the Outlook Tower, numerous summer schools and his Collège des Écossais in Montpellier. In India much of Geddes's belief in people planning can be seen, taking the form of pedestrian zones, student accommodation for women, and urban diversification projects.

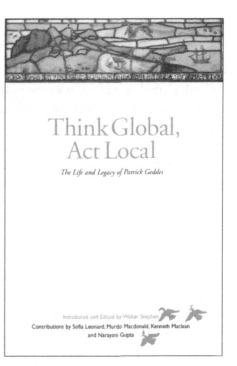

Think Global,
Act Local

The Life and Legacy of Patrick Geddes

Introduced and Edited by Walter Stephen
Contributions by Sofia Leonard, Murdo Macdonald, Kenneth Maclean
and Narayani Gupta

A Vigorous Institution: The Living Legacy of Patrick Geddes

Edited by Walter Stephen
ISBN 978 1905222 88 9 PBK £12.99

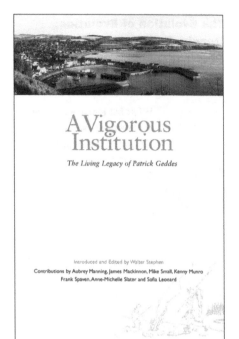

Patrick Geddes was an original thinker and innovator, an internationalist steeped in Scottishness. His achievements included conservation projects in the Old Town of Edinburgh and in London; community development through greening the urban environment; and town plans for Dunfermline, Cyprus, Tel Aviv and over 50 Indian cities. He pioneered summer schools and self-governing student hostels, used public art to stimulate social change, and established his own College of Art in Edinburgh and a Collège des Écossais in Montpellier.

Aspects of his life are re-examined in an attempt to further understand his thinking. How much of an anarchist was he? How influential were his home and childhood experiences? Why did he change his name and why – till the publication of this book – was his birthhouse shrouded in mystery?

The Evolution of Evolution: Darwin, Enlightenment and Scotland

Walter Stephen

ISBN 978-1-906817-23-7 PBK £12.99

What led Darwin to form his theory of evolution? To what extent did the Enlightenment influence Darwin's work? How did Scots help Darwin to publish the most successful and controversial book of his time?

In 1825 Darwin began to study medicine at Edinburgh University, the seat of the Enlightenment. The Enlightenment had created a thirst for science, and in his two years at Edinburgh, Darwin became involved with the people and ideas that were to shape the world's understanding of the natural sciences, including Darwin's concept of evolution and natural selection.

The Evolution of Evolution is a well researched and thoughtfully written book that recognises the importance of Scotland in the formation of evolutionary thinking and the role of Scots in both mentoring and influencing Charles Darwin throughout his life.

SCOTTISH REVIEW OF BOOKS

Walter's Wiggles

Walter Stephen

ISBN 978-1906817-68-8 PBK £12.99

Come with me round some of my 'random' places and see why I think they are important. What do they tell us about ourselves? Most of them are off the beaten track – although not very far. I think I can guarantee an interesting journey.

WALTER STEPHEN

Spurred on by *Fernweh* – a longing for faraway places – Walter Stephen shares thoughts sparked off by destinations which have intrigued and attracted him. Using these places as inspiration for musings on subjects such as history, culture and science, Walter builds up a unique picture of the world that you won't find in any guidebook.

But are these ramblings really as random as they seem? Soon his personal reasons for choosing each location become clear, with an awareness of the duality of man's relationship with the world coming into view. Facing his own mortality, Walter contemplates both the powerful beauty of the world and man's capacity for destruction in a book that is poignant, entertaining, informative and thought-provoking.

And just what are Walter's Wiggles? A unique escarpment path leading to Angels Landing in Zion National Park, Utah; one of the many fascinating places on Walter's travels, and part of a journey that is not as random as it first seems.

Bodysnatchers to Lifesavers: Three Centuries of Medicine in Edinburgh

Dorothy Crawford and Tara Womersley
ISBN 978-1-906817-58-9 HBK £16.99

 From dissecting bodies 'donated' by murderers to developing lifesaving treatments, the Edinburgh medical community has always been innovative and challenged entrenched medical ideas. This has ranged from setting up an inspirational public health system to discovering chloroform as an anaesthetic, which was fiercely opposed as pain relief for women during labour.

Bodysnatchers to Lifesavers gives a fascinating insight into the development of modern medicine and the leading role that Edinburgh played on the medical stage.

The tale of Edinburgh's medical past is told through the stories of colourful characters including the bodysnatchers Burke and Hare, the evolutionist Charles Darwin, surgeons Joseph Lister and James Syme as well as Sophia Jex-Blake, who headed the campaign for women's right to study medicine, and 'James Barry', Britain's first female doctor.

From the Ganga to the Tay: A poetic conversation between the Ganges and the Tay

Bashabi Fraser
ISBN 978-1906307-95-0 PBK £8.99

 *The mythical qualities of Indian rivers is profound with daily rituals imprinted in community consciousness. Scotland's rivers were also recognised as the life blood of mother earth, and considered sacred, but cultural evolution seems to have clouded our ancestors' respect for Scotland's most powerful river, the Tay.*
KENNY MUNRO

From the Ganga to the Tay is an epic poem in which the Indian River Ganges and the Scottish River Tay, the largest waterways in their countries, relate the historical importance of the ties between India and Scotland. The rivers are potent natural symbols of continuity and peace. With stunning photographs, the conversation between the rivers explores centuries of shared history between Scotland and India as well as each river's personal journey through time.

In the art of Bashabi Fraser the cultures of India and Scotland richly blend, and in this magnificent poem the two living traditions speak to each other through the riverine oracles of the Ganges and the Tay.
RICHARD HOLLOWAY

Women of Scotland

David R Ross

ISBN 978-1906817-57-2 PBK £9.99

 In a mix of historical fact and folklore, 'biker-historian' David R Ross journeys across Scotland to tell the stories of some of Scotland's finest women. From the legend of Scota over 3,000 years ago to the Bruce women, Black Agnes and the real Lady Macbeth, through to Kay Matheson – who helped liberate the Stone of Destiny from Westminster Abbey – and Wendy Wood in the 20th century, these proud and passionate women shaped the Scotland of today.

Leading his readers to the sites where the past meets the present, this is a captivating insight into some remarkable tales of the Scottish people that have previously been neglected, a celebration of and tribute to the Women of Scotland.

Women of Scotland, it is you who will bear and nurture our future generations. Instil in them a pride in their blood that will inspire the generations yet to come, so that our land will regain its place, and remain strong and free, defiant and proud, for the Scots yet unborn.

DAVID R ROSS

Women of the Highlands

Katharine Stewart

ISBN 978-1-906817-92-3 HBK £14.99

 The Highlands of Scotland are an evocative and mysterious land, cut off from the rest of Scotland by mountains and developing as a separate country for hundreds of years. Epitomising the 'sublime' in philosophical thought of the eighteenth century, the Highlands have been a source of inspiration for poets and writers of all descriptions.

Katharine Stewart takes us to the heart of the Highlands with this history of the women who shaped this land. From the women of the shielings to the Duchess of Gordon, from bards to conservationists, authors to folk-singers, Women of the Highlands examines how the culture of the Highlands was created and passed down through the centuries, and what is being done to preserve it today.

Women of Moray

Edited by: Susan Bennett, Mary Byatt,
Jenny Main, Anne Oliver, Janet Trythall
with contributions by the editors and
Richard Bennett, Janet Carolan,
Lorna Glendinning, Sheila McColl,
William Smith and Eleanor Thom
ISBN 978-1-908373-16-8 HBK £16.99

Women have been sidelined throughout history in the rush to tell the stories of great wars, great battles and the achievements of great men. But in Moray – an area of Scotland encompassing both Highland and Lowland areas between Inverness and Aberdeen – a group of people have begun a project to uncover the stories of the women who lived in Moray from medieval to modern times.

Discover Flaming Janet, James IV's mistress; Elsie Watson who rode solo across South Africa on a motorcycle in 1912; the Queen's Nurse in Foula and Fair Isle in the 1920s; the spymaster of Albanian agents during the Second World War; the Traveller born in the bow-tent, and more.

This book captures the tales of over 70 women whose lives have made an impact on history both in Scotland and abroad. It sheds light on their misfortunes, prejudice and abuse, and shows how these challenges have been overcome.

Women of Moray is a unique glimpse into the history of the region, looking at women marginalised, forgotten and usually uncelebrated across the centuries. For the historian, the genealogist and the general reader, this is a book that will change your view of history.

Napier's History of Herbal Healing, Ancient and Modern

Tom Atkinson
ISBN 978-1-905222-01-8 PBK £8.99

Herbalism is the practice and study of herbal medicine as carried out for thousands of years and is the oldest form of medicine. It is also the most widely used form of medicine, world-wide. Over hundreds and thousands of years the breadth and depth of knowledge about herbs has increased as the generations passed, improving the lives of the sick and injured.

The author explores the history and early development of herbalism throughout the world, before delving into the history of herbalism in Scotland where the hereditary doctors to Scotland's medieval kings used herbs to complement the teachings of Hippocrates and other classical physicians. This herbalist tradition carried on into the 19th century when Duncan Napier first opened his dispensary in Edinburgh's Old Town.

The story of Napier's Herbalists is told in the words of two of those who have contributed to the history and success of the business. Duncan Napier's story is told in his own words in the form of his autobiography and a current herbalist tells the story of a career as a herbalist in the modern world.

Luath Press Limited

committed to publishing well written books worth reading

LUATH PRESS takes its name from Robert Burns, whose little collie Luath (*Gael.*, swift or nimble) tripped up Jean Armour at a wedding and gave him the chance to speak to the woman who was to be his wife and the abiding love of his life. Burns called one of 'The Twa Dogs' Luath after Cuchullin's hunting dog in Ossian's *Fingal*. Luath Press was established in 1981 in the heart of Burns country, and now resides a few steps up the road from Burns' first lodgings on Edinburgh's Royal Mile.

Luath offers you distinctive writing with a hint of unexpected pleasures.

Most bookshops in the UK, the US, Canada, Australia, New Zealand and parts of Europe either carry our books in stock or can order them for you. To order direct from us, please send a £sterling cheque, postal order, international money order or your credit card details (number, address of cardholder and expiry date) to us at the address below. Please add post and packing as follows: UK – £1.00 per delivery address; overseas surface mail – £2.50 per delivery address; overseas airmail – £3.50 for the first book to each delivery address, plus £1.00 for each additional book by airmail to the same address. If your order is a gift, we will happily enclose your card or message at no extra charge.

Luath Press Limited
543/2 Castlehill
The Royal Mile
Edinburgh EH1 2ND
Scotland
Telephone: 0131 225 4326 (24 hours)
Fax: 0131 225 4324
email: sales@luath.co.uk
Website: www.luath.co.uk